The Civilization of the American Indian Series

(COMPLETE LIST ON PAGE 355)

GEORGE CATLIN

Episodes from *Life Among the Indians*
and *Last Rambles*

Crow Indians

George Catlin

EPISODES FROM *Life Among the Indians*
and *Last Rambles*

With 152 Scenes and Portraits by the Artist

EDITED BY Marvin C. Ross

Norman
University of Oklahoma Press

~~~~~~

Frontispiece: *Crow Indians*

[Ba-da-ah-chón-du (He Who Outjumps Every One), second chief of the tribe (center), in a rich costume, his headdress of eagle's quills, and he carries his shield, quiver, and lance; Eeh-hée-a-duhks-chee-a (He Who Ties His Hair Before), chief of a band (left), in full costume, his natural hair reaching to the ground; Bi-éets-e-cure (The Very Sweet Man), a warrior of distinction. 1832 (Cart. No. 25.)]

The publication of this book has been assisted by a grant from the Alumni Development Fund of the University of Oklahoma

Library of Congress Catalog Card Number 59–7959

To ROBERT WOODS BLISS
whose enthusiasm for the early arts of the American Indians
has contributed so much to our understanding,
not only of their arts,
but of the Indians themselves.

EDITOR'S ACKNOWLEDGMENTS

THIS BOOK HAS only been possible through the assistance of several institutions and people. Of first importance is the American Museum of Natural History, present owners of the Catlin cartoons used for all illustrations except the frontispiece. Especial thanks are due to the president of the Museum, Alexander M. White, and to H. L. Shapiro, curator of physical anthropology, and Miss Bella Weitzner, associate curator of ethnology. The Frick Art Reference Library through the courtesy of Miss Helen Clay Frick, the director, and Mrs. Henry W. Howell, Jr., the librarian, photographed all but four of the cartoons, making the photographs available to me so that the book could be properly illustrated.

The Catlin painting used for the frontispiece and the jacket of this book is No. 32 in the collection of Catlin paintings and drawings at the Henry E. Huntington Library and Art Gallery, San Marino, California, and is here reproduced through the courtesy of that institution. It depicts the Crow Indians identified by Catlin as Eeh-hee-a-duhks-chee-a, Ba-da-ah-chon-du, and Bi-eets-e-cure, reading from left to right, and was originally intended by the painter to accompany his unpublished manuscript, "The North Americans in the Middle of the Nineteenth Century, a numerous and noble Race of Human Beings fast passing to oblivion and leaving no monuments of their own behind them." This painting is a reconstruction by Catlin of three separate portraits painted by him in 1832 and acquired by Joseph Harrison, Jr., of Philadelphia. It is a replica of No. 25 in the *Cartoon Catalogue* of 1871 and illustrates how Catlin in later life, when replacing the earlier portraits lost to him, painted them in the technique that he had developed in South America rather than that used by him in his younger days in the then "Far West." (See pages 149–50 below for accounts of these Indians.)

Last, but most important of all in many ways, has been the assistance, help, and advice of my wife, Lotus Robb Ross, without whom the book would never have been finished.

MARVIN C. ROSS

LIST OF PLATES

Frontispiece: Crow Indians

(after page 183)

List of Plates

GEORGE CATLIN WAS trained to follow the profession of his father—law —but after practicing for four years, he abandoned it for the study of art. His talent afforded him considerable success as a portrait and miniature painter but did not mark him for fame until it was fired by his ambition to record pictorially the vanishing American Indians.

Catlin's long career of devotion and sacrifice to this end may be truly said to have been determined by his meeting with an Oneida Indian when he was a small and terrified boy of nine venturing to hunt in a forest of Broome County, New York. The kindness and generosity of the red man and the understanding with which he encouraged the young hunter struck a deep note of friendship. This Catlin never forgot, and the memory was doubtless quickened years later when he saw a group of Indians passing through Philadelphia on a visit to Washington. It was at this point that his ambition, moved by the noble bearing of the Indians, took definite form and set his life on its true course.

Catlin studied the paintings in the Peale Museum of Philadelphia and probably had some instruction from Thomas Sully. Then during the 1830's he proceeded to make the most remarkable portraiture record of North American Indians known to us. After exhibiting this collection of portraits, scenes of Indian life, and some accompanying artifacts in New York and other cities, he sailed in 1839 for England. There, both in London and in the provinces, the collection met with great success. Equal good fortune awaited Catlin in Paris, where for four years he enjoyed general acclaim and to some extent the patronage of Louis Philippe. At the outbreak of the revolution of 1848 he escaped to England, taking his collection, which, however, did not meet there with its original success, and Catlin became involved in financial difficulties. In 1852 his obligations were taken over by Joseph Harrison, Jr., of Philadelphia, who got possession of the collection and shipped it home to be stored in a factory building of the Harrison Boiler Works, where it remained until 1879, when Harrison's widow presented it to the Smithsonian Institution in Washington, where it is still housed.

Eventually Catlin returned to Paris. There, while reading in the *Bibliothèque Impériale,* he chanced upon a stranger who told him a story of lost gold mines in the Crystal Mountains of South America. These he actually set sail to seek in 1852. After the disappointment of this tangent, he resumed his course and again painted Indians and scenes of their life wherever he went. During 1852–55 he worked in South America and along the coast of North America west of the Rocky Mountains, seeing and painting Indian tribes and places unknown to him on his earlier travels, and in 1855 went again to South America. In this period he created a second corpus of important documentation, which with few exceptions, has been heretofore unpublished. Until now Catlin's fame has been based chiefly on the group of pictures painted in the 1830's. His later on-the-spot work is now illustrated as a whole in this present book for the first time.

The paintings known as the Cartoon Collection, so called by Catlin to distinguish them from the original collection made in the 1830's, were in part painted in Brussels during a period of practical seclusion. From his early notebooks, sketches, and memory he made duplicates in a new technique of the pictures in his first collection then lost to him. To these he added his more recent on-the-spot pictures from South America and the West Coast of North America. On his return to America in 1871 he exhibited the whole Cartoon Collection in New York, but with little success. He was allowed, however, to hang it temporarily in the Smithsonian Institution in Washington.

There had been a prospect of selling the first collection of the 1830's to the government, a project strongly favored by Daniel Webster and others. Negotiations were again under way for the purchase of the Cartoon Collection, but the government failed to buy in this instance also. The collection was finally bought by the American Museum of Natural History in New York from the surviving daughter, Elizabeth Catlin, through a gift from Ogden Mills.

Catlin found, while painting in the jungle, that he must devise a different method of working. In the 1830's, when he first recorded the

Indians in paint, he used canvas, which had to be rolled up and packed while traveling. This was not successful in the humid climate of the South American jungles where paint on the canvas dried slowly, and so he switched to Bristol board, which was more easily packed and carried and on which paint dried more quickly. In addition, less of the precious paint materials were necessary, and the pictures kept much better in the jungles. In assessing Catlin as an artist, these two methods of working which were so very different and achieved an entirely different effect, must be taken into consideration and the paintings of his two main periods judged separately. Hitherto, this procedure has not always been observed, and the oversight has caused some confusion among art critics writing on Catlin as an artist.

Of the paintings from South America and the West Coast of North America listed in Catlin's own exhibition catalog of 1871, fifty-five South American and seven West Coast pictures from the Cartoon Collection are now missing. These may well be the ones reported to have been destroyed by the family because of their poor condition when the Cartoon Collection was moved from Washington in 1893. Many of the destroyed South American paintings were landscapes, but some were of Indian activities and would be of interest today. The West Coast paintings included both Indian portraits and scenes of Indian occupations, and they are a decided loss to persons interested in our Northwest of the early days. Three paintings of the Cartoon Collection are omitted from the illustrations in this book—two because they can no longer be identified in Catlin's catalog and the third, entitled *Ignus Fatuus,* partly because it is in poor condition but principally because the subject is more clearly depicted in another illustration already included. Otherwise, all the existing on-the-spot paintings known to me that were made by Catlin during his last travels in North and South America are included among the plates in this book. Included also is one painting of Esquimaux in Labrador dated 1855 which must have been made on one of Catlin's voyages to or from Europe in that year.

The on-the-spot paintings reproduced here and made by Catlin in the 1850's are unique, as are also the on-the-spot paintings in the Smithsonian Institution made on the Plains in the 1830's. These pictures are unlike the other pictures in the Cartoon Collection at the American Museum of Natural History that were made from notes, sketches, and memory, in Brussels, to replace the on-the-spot pictures of the original collection acquired by Joseph Harrison and removed by him to Philadelphia. Hence the Cartoon Collection, important as it is, falls into two groups in regard to significance of the pictures.

Catlin did paint a number of studio duplicates of his South American and West Coast paintings for various patrons. Among these copies are four South American scenes of Catlin illustrating the use of his Colt revolver, "Sam," as he called it. These were made for the Colt Firearms Company to reproduce for advertising, along with several others now dispersed, one of them being in the Rochester Museum of Art. The Royal Museum of Archaeology in Toronto owns thirty-three Catlin paintings, several of them replicas of pictures made on his travels in the 1850's. These were exhibited in London in 1859 and bought by the King of the Belgians, later going into the collection of Richard Smithill of Rockbeare, Hants, before being acquired by the museum in Toronto. In the collection of the late Archibald Rogers, of Hyde, New York, was Catlin's material for a proposed book on Indians of the Americas, announced by a Baltimore publisher. Among the paintings and drawings intended for this proposed book are a number of portraits and scenes of Indian life—replicas of pictures made by Catlin on his last travels. There may be a few other copies scattered here and there, but none of them could have the value of his on-the-spot paintings in the American Museum of Natural History, unless they should prove to be copies of those pictures lost from the Cartoon Collection, such as those supposed to have been destroyed by the family in 1893.

Every effort has been made by the staff of the Museum of Natural History, the Frick Art Reference Library, and myself to identify correctly the portraits, scenes, and landscapes as listed by Catlin in his 1871 *Catalogue*. Catlin had great difficulty in obtaining the names of the Indians in South America, as he, himself, explains. Consequently his identification of some of the tribes may not be accurate or the designation given them today. However, his identifications, so far as he was able to make them, have been retained for whatever value they may have. Anthropologists, having learned much during the intervening century, will make their own adjustments.

While I was studying the paintings of South American Indians in the Museum of Natural History, a large number of artifacts and photographs, collected about 1900 among some of the same tribes painted by Catlin, were spread out for classification quite near where I was working. It was, therefore, a simple matter for me to check Catlin's paintings with this more recent evidence. This proved to my satisfaction that

Catlin not only correctly rendered the Indians themselves, but had observed and painted faithfully their manner of dress and the ornaments they wore. And so Catlin was as accurate in picturing the Indians during his later years as he was in the 1830's, as has been confirmed in recent years.

The illustrations here of Catlin paintings not generally available to anyone short of a visit to the American Museum of Natural History form an important addition to our knowledge of South American Indians and Indians west of the Rocky Mountains. Few painters of the Indians of the Northwest—George Gibbs was one of the few—have left early records, which gives to Catlin's work added value. He showed wisdom in not occupying himself with Indians in the area around San Francisco and in concentrating on those who were still fairly primitive and farther away from civilization.

Aside from a few landscapes of the Crystal Mountains and the Amazon River at the beginning of the group of plates, the paintings of Indians reproduced in this volume are loosely grouped by areas. The portraits and scenes of activities are combined, as far as possible, with landscapes of the places where the particular tribes lived. This arrangement is quite different from Catlin's customary way of separating the portraits from the scenes of occupations and the landscapes, but it seems more logical because it allows the reader to see the portraits of a particular group of Indians in association with their native landscape and representations of their activities. Also, it is more varied and interesting for the nonspecialized reader.

For the titles of the plates, extracts have been made from the now almost unobtainable catalog of Catlin's exhibition in New York in 1871. Catlin's identifying captions have the following form (Plate 11):

(————); a secondary chief, leading his little son.
O-ho-kó-ra-u-ta (————); a medicine man and orator of the tribe.
(————); a young warrior, armed with his lance.
   A small remnant of a numerous tribe, on the coast of Venezuela, decimated by dissipation and small-pox.

The awkwardness of this treatment for modern-day readers has suggested minor revisions, as shown below for the same plate:

A secondary chief (center), leading his little son; O-ho-kó-ra-u-ta, a medicine man and orator of the tribe (right); a young warrior, armed

xxiii

with his lance (left). A small remnant of a numerous tribe, on the coast of Venezuela, decimated by dissipation and smallpox.

In this way we have at a glance all the information that Catlin himself had, or did not have, about the Indians he painted. The pictures and the text have never before been brought together. Catlin's exhibition catalog was not illustrated, nor was his proposed book on North and South American Indians, in which he intended to use most of this material, ever published. This may account for the fact that occasionally (though only rarely) there seems to be an error in the caption, as will be readily evident to the reader. However, specific attention should be called to discrepancies between catalog description and painting for four of the cartoons: While Nos. 144, 124, and 120 in this book (Cartoon Nos. 85, 99, and 102) still have the corresponding numbers in Catlin's own handwriting, each has had a figure painted out and another put in. Apparently Catlin made the changes in the paintings and did not change the catalog. Number 149 in this volume (Cartoon No. 115) has the number in Catlin's own hand, but there was once a sticker pasted over this number which has fallen off and been lost, although the outline is still visible. This painting is reproduced with the catalog description for No. 115, even though it may be conjectural whether this is exact.

The main text of this book is taken from two volumes that were written by Catlin for young people, *Life Amongst the Indians: A Book for Youth,* first published in 1861, and *Last Rambles Amongst the Indians of the Rocky Mountains and of the Andes,* printed first in 1866. All of the chapters dealing with his actual travels are included here except two, which were quoted from the letters of a young Englishman, called Smythe, who voyaged with Catlin for a time. These two chapters are merely anecdotal and add nothing to what can be found in Catlin's own chapters or his captions for the illustrations. Two appendices from the 1871 exhibition catalog are also included: one because it gives details of Catlin's methods of painting as well as the difficulty he had in inducing the Indians he portrayed to tell their names; the other because in it Catlin gives a detailed account of his itineraries of the 1850's, which are difficult to follow in his narrative, partly because the chapters are from two books and, also because, as Catlin said of himself, he paid little attention to such matters as dates and where he was at definite times. We have here all of Catlin's published writing of any importance dealing with his last travels in the Americas. Only slight references to omitted woodcuts have been deleted from Catlin's text and the few changes made are of minor importance.

It is only by the publication of all Catlin's significant work and the evaluation of it by anthropologists and art historians that we can arrive at a true estimate of this remarkable man, whose charm and seriousness of purpose can be felt through all his work.

It seems appropriate to quote here Catlin's creed about the Indians which tells us much of the man himself!

I love the people who have always made me welcome to the best they had.

I love a people who are honest without laws, who have no jails and no poorhouses.

I love a people who keep the commandments without ever having read them or heard them preached from the pulpit.

I love a people who never swear, who never take the name of God in vain.

I love a people "who love their neighbors as they love themselves."

I love a people who worship God without a Bible, for I believe that God loves them also.

I love the people whose religion is all the same, and who are free from religious animosities.

I love the people who have never raised a hand against me, or stolen my property, where there was no law to punish for either.

I love the people who have never fought a battle with white men, except on their own ground.

I love and don't fear mankind where God has made and left them, for there they are children.

I love a people who live and keep what is their own without locks and keys.

I love all people who do the best they can. And oh, how I love a people who don't live for the love of money!

GEORGE CATLIN

Episodes from *Life Among the Indians*
and *Last Rambles*

PART I

South American Indians

~~~~~~

CHAPTER I

Gold Hunting in the Crystal Mountains

(CHAPTER II FROM *Last Rambles*)

. . . IN [ANOTHER] BOOK the reader learned that I had travelled eight years amongst the tribes of North America, east of the Rocky Mountains, and made a collection of more than 600 portraits of Indians and paintings illustrating their modes of life; and that I made an Exhibition of the same in New York, in Paris, and in London.

That Exhibition was very popular, and gained me great applause, and money, also; but, like too many fast men, I was led into unfortunate speculations, and, like them, suffered injurious consequences.

At this time, however, the Senate of the United States was considering a Bill for the purchase of my collection, for the sum of $65,000. A committee had reported a bill in favor of the purchase, and in their report had stated that they considered the price of $65,000 to be a moderate compensation for it; and I had encouraging assurances of its success.

Messrs. Webster, Seward, Foote, and other Federal members were in favor of the appropriation, and voted for it; and the Democratic members voted against it. Mr. Webster advocated the purchase, in a long and eloquent speech, of which the following is a brief extract:—

Extract from the Speech of the Hon. Daniel Webster, on a Motion in the Senate of the United States for the Purchase of "Catlin's Indian Collection," in 1849.

Mr. President—The question is, Whether it does not become us, as a useful thing, to possess in the United States this collection of paintings, &c., made amongst the Indian tribes? Whether it is not a case for the exercise of *large liberality*—I will not say *bounty,* but *policy?* These tribes, sir, that have preceded us, to whose lands we have succeeded and who have no written memorials of their laws, their habits, and their manners,

5

are all passing away to the world of forgetfulness. Their likeness, manners, and customs are portrayed with more accuracy and truth in this collection by Catlin than in all the other drawings and representations on the face of the earth. Somebody in this country ought to possess this collection—that is my opinion; and I do not know how there is, or where there is to be found any society, or any individual, who or which can with so much propriety possess himself or itself of it, as the Government of the United States. For my part, then, I do think that the preservation of *"Catlin's Indian Collection"* in this country is an *important public act.* I think it properly belongs to those accumulations of historical matters respecting our predecessors on this continent, which is very proper for the Government of the United States to maintain. As I have said, this race is going into forgetfulness. They track the continuation of mankind in the present age, and call recollection back to them. And here they are better exhibited, in my judgment, better set forth and presented to the mind and the taste and the curiosity of mankind, than in all other collections in the world. I go for this as an *American* subject—as a thing belonging to us—to our history—to the history of a race whose lands we till, and over whose obscure graves and bones we tread, every day. I look upon it as a thing more appropriate for us than the ascertaining of the South Pole or anything that can be discovered in the Dead Sea or the River Jordan. These are the grounds, sir, upon which I propose to proceed, and I shall vote for the appropriation with great pleasure.

The following letter also, which I received at that time, I have a right to introduce in this place:—

Letter from General Cass, Secretary of State of the United States of America.

Dear Sir—No man can appreciate better than myself the admirable fidelity of your *Indian Collection* and Indian book, which I have lately examined. They are equally spirited and accurate: they are true to nature. Things that are not sacrificed, as they too often are by the painter, to things as (in his judgment) they should be.

During eighteen years of my life I was superintendent of Indian affairs in the north-western territory of the United States; and during more than five I was Secretary of War, to which department belong the general control of Indian concerns. I know the Indians thoroughly. I have spent many a month in their camps, council-houses, villages, and hunting-grounds; I have fought with them and against them; and I have negotiated seventeen treaties of peace or of cession with them. I mention these circumstances to show you that I have a good right to speak confidently upon the subject of your drawings. Among them I recognise many of my old acquaintances, and everywhere I am struck with the vivid representations of them and their customs, of their peculiar features, and of their costumes. Unfortunately, they are receding before the advancing tide of our population, and are probably destined, at no distant day, wholly to disappear; but your collection will preserve them, as far as human art can do, and will form the most perfect monument of an extinguished race that the world has ever seen.

Lewis Cass

To Geo. Catlin.

Mr. "Jefferson Davis," at that time a member of the Senate, before giving his vote, made, in a speech of two newspaper columns in length and now matter of record, the most complimentary eulogy that has ever been passed on my works, stating that I was "the only artist who ever had painted, or could paint, an American Indian; that he had been a campaigner with me for several months amongst the Osages, the Comanches, Pawnee Picts, &c., whilst he was an officer in the 1st Regiment of Mounted Dragoons; that he had sat by me and seen me paint many of my portraits from the life, and knew their accuracy, that the collection was one of great interest and value to our country, and that it would be a shame if it were sold in a foreign land." And yet, when the stage of the voting showed that his vote was to turn the scale, stated that, "from *principle,* he was bound to vote against the appropriation," which he did, and defeated the bill.

This unexplained *"principle"* I construed to be clearly the principle adopted and proclaimed by President Jackson many years before, of removing all the southern tribes of Indians west of the Mississippi River, that their 250,000,000 acres of rich cotton lands might be covered with slave laborers; which principle, with an accompanying hostility to everything Indian, had been and was being carried out by the successive administrations, convincing me that I had nothing further to expect or claim from my country for the labors I had expended and the collections I had made in the Indian countries.

This discouragement and the explosion of my pecuniary affairs in London came upon me together, and both contributed to impede my return to my native country (which I had contemplated at that time), as will be seen, till after my subsequent wanderings, to be briefly narrated in the following pages. In this dilemma I was lost; but *my collec-*

7

tion was saved to my country by an American gentleman—an act so noble and so patriotic that I cannot believe my country will forget it.

My "occupation gone," and with no other means on earth than my hands and my brush, and less than half of a life, at best, before me, my thoughts, as with all that is human and mortal, tended towards Dame Fortune, to know if there was there anything yet in store for me. The thought was an extremely unpromising and visionary one, and yet, without a superstition, seemed worthy of a trial.

In this state of mind, therefore, into one of the eccentric adventures of my chequered life I was easily led at that time, by the information got by a friend of mine, a reader in the *Bibliothèque Impériale* of Paris, from an ancient Spanish work, relative to gold miners some 300 years since, in the Tumucamache (or Crystal) Mountains, in the northern part of Brazil.

According to this tradition the Spanish miners, after having accumulated great riches, were attacked by the Indians and massacred in their houses, or driven out of the country, leaving their gold behind them. This wonderful relation, with other corroborating legends I had received, had enough probability (with the additional circumstances already narrated) to excite my cupidity, and what follows is a brief account of my singular enterprise entered upon at that time.

In my wandering contemplations, ten years, at least, of solitudes in voluntary exile, with my pencils and sketch-books, were before me as agreeable realities; nuggets of gold of all sizes appeared in my dreams, and in my waking hours I had allowed a half superstition to intimate to me that Dame Fortune might have something precious in store for me, which she could not bestow without the suitable opportunity. As traditions had said that the gold miners of the Crystal Mountains had accumulated vast amounts in gold dust and nuggets, imagination naturally and easily depicted these riches left behind, buried within the walls of their adobe houses when the miners were destroyed or obliged to flee from their villages.

The wealth of London was to be at my command if I succeeded; a company, with unbounded capital, was to be formed, and a concession was to be obtained from the Government of Brazil for the right of working the mines and *carting* the gold away; and I had yet the stimulus of an unexplored country before me.

With such reflections and anticipations I started, in 1852, for the Crystal Mountains in Brazil. I sailed to Havannah; from thence I went

8

to Carraccas, Venezuela, to see the wonderful "Scylla," described by Baron de Humboldt. From Carraccas to the Orinoko and Demerara, designing to ascend the Essequibo to the base of the Crystal Mountains.

Learning from friends in Demerara the jealousy with which the unsettled boundary between British Guiana and Brazil was at that time guarded, and the consequent difficulty, if not impossibility, of passing the frontier post at the Grand Rapids of the Essequibo, I obtained a British passport for Brazil, and an incognito cognomen, as kings and emperors sometimes do, resolved to leave the river below the "Sabo" or great cataract, and approach the mountains by a land route, taking a guide and escort from some of the Arowak or Taruma villages I should have to pass through.

Having previously met my old acquaintance, Sir Robert Shombergk, returning from his second exploring expedition to the sources of the Essequibo, he had explained to me the uncertainty of getting permission from the post-holder to pass the Grand Rapids, and also the extreme difficulty of ascending the Essequibo and from that to the mountains, owing to the numerous rapids, requiring a strong force of men. He approved my plan of taking the eastern route; and having learned from me the object I had in view, stated that he had long since heard legends of the Spanish gold mines in these mountains, and that were it not that he was at that time executing a special command of Her Majesty the Queen, he would have accompanied me in the enterprise.

Joined in Georgetown by an enterprising young man by the name of Smyth, an Englishman, a good shot, and carrying a first-rate Minié rifle, and armed myself with Colt's revolving carabine, we left the Essequibo below the grand cataract, and, after a desperate encounter with rivers and swamps, reached an Arowak village. Received in this village with great kindness . . . we procured hired horses and mules, on which, with an Indian guide, passing several Indian villages, and a country of three or four hundred miles, we reached the base of the mountains, and then with a half-caste interpreter and guide, who knew the route, and a mule to carry our packs, we trusted to our legs for a passage across the mountains into the valley of the Amazon, which we accomplished, but with great fatigue and some distress, to the forks of the Trombutas, from which we descended in an Indian pirogue to the Amazon, to Santarem, and to Pará . . . .

Instead of finding the Tumucamache (or Acarai) a single mountain ridge, which I had contemplated, we found ourselves in the midst of a *series* of mountains of palaeozoic rocks of the most frowning and defying aspect for a breadth of fifty or sixty miles. In the midst of these our poor mule gave out, and we were obliged to leave it and most of our packs, and trust to our weapons for subsistence. Food and life and progress now became subjects of more importance than gold; and in our jaded and exhausted condition we were but miserable nugget hunters. We *hunted,* however, passing over extensive beds of auriferous quartz, in some instances distinctly exhibiting to the naked eye the precious metal.

In a beautiful valley amongst the mountain ranges we struck upon an ancient waggon-road, which we followed for several miles, showing intelligible proofs of mining operations. This, however, we lost, from the thick overgrowth of a sort of thorn, not unlike a compact hedge, extending in some places for miles together and entirely impenetrable to man or horse until cut away.

From such causes all my nugget fever for the time passed away, and I was happy to be again at my old vocation, and safe and sound in the valley of the Amazon. . . .

In my boarding-house in Pará I made the agreeable acquaintance of Señor L——, to whom I gave a description of my long voyage and the object I had had in crossing the Crystal Mountains. He told me he had long heard traditions of those gold mines and the massacre of the miners by the Indians; and he added that he had no doubt of the facts, nor any doubt but that great wealth had been left concealed in or about the miners' adobe houses.

He informed me that he lived on an island in the Amazon, some hundreds of miles above Santarem, which he had stocked with several thousand head of cattle and horses; that he was returning by steamer in a few days; and that if I would accompany him, he would fit out another expedition at his own house, and at his expense, approaching the mountains from a different direction and in a different place; and, he thought, with a better chance of success.

I accepted this gentleman's kind offer, and in three days we were prepared for our coming campaign. At Para we obtained each a tunic and leggings of strong buckskin, and other articles necessary for our tour, and various trinkets and other presents for the Indians.

I had at the time in my employment a first-rate Negro man (a maroon), six feet and two inches in height, *"Caesar Bolla,"* who had freed himself from bondage by leaving his master, Señor Bolla, in Havannah, and had proved to me his value in a tour of five or six weeks which we had just made together amongst the Xingu Indians, on the river by that name.

My former companion, Smyth, having left me in Pará, I purchased of him his Minié rifle, which I put into Caesar's hands, and of which he was very proud.

Señor L—— proposed to take two of his own Negroes and employ a couple of friendly Indians living in the vicinity of his residence as guides and interpreters, making in all a party of seven.

This hospitable gentleman had on his island ten thousand cattle and horses and fifteen Negroes. He told me before starting that, as we were going into a section of country known to be rich in minerals and guarded with great jealousy by the Government, we should be more or less liable to fall into the hands of one or three garrisons of bare-footed soldiers, stationed at the Barra and at the base of the mountains; and that in such event he should much rather answer to the name of Señor Novello than that of Señor L——.

His motive for this he knew I could correctly appreciate when I showed him my passport and at the same time told him my real name, with which (when he heard it) he said he had been for some years familiar. He spoke the Portuguese, the Spanish, and the *"Lingua-geral"* (the language of the country), and Caesar spoke the Spanish and the English, and our two Indian guides spoke the *"geral,"* and the Indian language of the tribes where we were going; so that on the score of languages we had nothing to fear.

The route proposed was to descend the Amazon some fifteen or twenty miles in a huge and unwieldy pirogue; then ascend a small and sluggish stream some twenty or thirty miles, leave the pirogue, and traverse the vast and gloomy forest until we reached the *llanos* (prairies), where we would hire mules of the Indians to take us to the mountains.

We were several days making the necessary preparations; laying in salt and dried meats, coffee, sugar, biscuits, tea, salt, &c., and a few culinary articles; and amongst them a large tin pan from his wife's pantry, for washing gold, and a heavy hammer for breaking the rocks, and a cold chisel for cutting the nuggets which we might find too large to be transported entire!

Embarked in our heavy pirogue, with all our stores and equipment laid in, we were venturing on a tour (which probably no white man had ever made before, and of which we had no knowledge except that obtained from our two Indians, who had traversed several times before) of wading, of creeping and crawling, through the vast and sunless and pathless solitudes which lie between the Amazon and the *llanos* that spread out at the foot of the Tumucamache, or Crystal Mountains. And those who would appreciate the grandeur, the vastness, the intricacy, and the mysteries of the Amazon forests without seeing them, now listen!

Gently and easily we floated down the northern shore of the river for the distance of fifteen or twenty miles; most of the way the banks, the shore, and the trunks of the lofty trees were entirely hidden by the outrolling and outstretching masses of foliage of various hues and various patterns which seemed to be tumbling over our heads into the river.

Without discovering the least appearance of a landing-place, or mouth of a river or stream, *"Ya-ka, ya-ka"* ("There it is, there it is"), cried out one of our Indians, and pointing to it, when our pirogue was steered about, and plunged by force of paddles amidst the hanging boughs that were dipping in the water. In a moment we were out of sight of the mighty Amazon, and ascending a deep and sluggish stream of unknown width, for the hanging foliage was everywhere bathing in the stream, and hiding the muddy shores and the trunks of the trees from our view.

A sort of *"Lingua-geral"* boat-song was now raised as the Negroes were plying the paddles; and the two Indians, in the bow, with their paddles were dividing and lifting the drooping boughs out of the water and passing them over our heads as the boat moved on. When raised, they were struck with the paddle, and most of their water discharged, but enough still filled the air, like a mist or a gentle shower of rain.

The little Indians, with their entirely naked bodies, who were thus nicely and comfortably cooled, were laughing at our buckskins, in which we were completely drenched.

The song progressed, the paddles were plied, and we still went on, whilst the artificial rain was falling and the sun was shining. Night approached; and we found a comfortable landing-shore, where our hammocks were slung, and between two tremendous fires we passed the night, amidst the howling of monkeys and hooting and screaming of nocturnal birds.

The third day of this perpetual shower-bath brought us to the head of navigation of this little river without a name, where there were lying three other pirogues belonging to Indians, each one fastened to the shore with a thong of rawhide, and claimed by the owner's totem and the figure of a knife drawn on a piece of bark with blood-red paint, and fastened to the rawhide thong.

Here was a little spot of open timber, comfortable for an encampment and we remained two days, arranging our packs and preparing for our march through the forest, leaving our canoe for our return, labelled and claimed in the manner of those of the Indians; and our Indian guides assured us that no Indians would ever remove it.

Now our mighty task began. So far the pirogue had carried our "bags and baggage," but now we had to divide them amongst ourselves, each one carrying his load upon his back as he squeezed and crept through the mazy network of shrubbery and twisted vines. Our Indian guides professed to be "following a road"; but what a road! A road here is where the Indians have, with their knives, cut away the vines and made an opening large enough for a man's body, as he stoops, to pass through; and this, in a few months or weeks, requires the same process repeated to make it passable again.

Strapped upon Caesar's back was always my large portfolio, containing a large number of cartoon portraits of North American Indians, and blank cartoons for other portraits to be made, protected by a waterproof covering. Over that was fastened the tin pan for gold washing. On his left shoulder his Minié rifle, and in his right hand the sledge-hammer for getting at large nuggets, for which my cupidity was now for a second time becoming roused.

Señor N—— and myself carried our rifles, and each his knapsack of provisions, &c.; and the other articles were divided amongst the two Negroes and the two Indians, the two last of whom were armed with their *sarbacanes* (or blow-guns), with poisoned arrows.

Thus freighted and thus equipped, we started on our long and painful campaign, little knowing of, and little caring for, the toils and difficulties ahead of us—those of an *Amazon Forest,* and yet to be described. The ground was shrouded with an endless impenetrable mass of green leaves, of twisting vines, and wild flowers of various hues, which were penetrated, where we walk, or stand, or creep, by the trunks of the stately moras, hackeas, and palms, and fifty other sorts of trees, whose tops, and even branches, are lost in the chaotic mass of foliage that embraces them.

Man wanders under and through these vast canopies without finding a log or a stone, or even the roots of a tree, to rest his wearied limbs upon. No tree, even in its natural decline, falls to the ground, but, like the masts of vessels with their cordage, they are held and braced up by twisting vines, whilst their decaying trunks are wasting away in the moist alluvion, and they gradually settle down (as they arose) to the earth from which they came.

No stone has been dropped here from a drifting ice-berg, or tumbled along in a mountain torrent; the roots of trees, to be seen, must be dug for; and so rapid is the accumulation of soil around them, that the trunks of trees have the shape of piles driven into the ground.

Owing to the shade and perpetual dampness of those solitudes, fire never makes any progress, and the heaviest showers of rain generally fail to reach the ground, otherwise than in a light mist, or by creeping down the branches, trunks, and twisting vines by which it is broken and conducted.

In the fresh air and sunshine at the tops of the trees, which we can never see, there is a busy and chattering neighborhood of parrots and monkeys, but all below is a dark and silent matted solitude, in which a falling leaf, from want of wind, may be a month in reaching the ground, and where a man may be tracked by the broken cobwebs he leaves behind him.

On, on we go, from day to day, in "Indian file," cutting our way, without the slightest change, encamping at night between our fires, always serenaded by the frightful *ariguatoes* (howling monkeys), whilst we are beating off the mosquitoes, or shaving our legs to the knees with our knives to destroy the thousands of red ticks that fasten their heads in the skin.

Our progress is slow, perhaps some ten or twelve miles per day. If man were but knee high, or, like a serpent, could crawl upon his belly, he might travel farther. Not only are we impeded by the vines that are twisting about our necks and our legs, but the ground we walk on is painful and fatiguing owing to the vast quantity of leaves that fall, which have neither winds nor heavy rains to flatten them down, or fire to burn them.

Nuts, and shells of nuts, are dropping on our heads, disengaged by monkeys and birds engaged in the tops of the trees, the chattering of which we constantly hear, though we don't see them. The falling nuts are lost to the eye when they reach the ground, owing to the depth and looseness of the leaves amongst which they are hidden; the peccaries, in search of these, throw up the leaves around their sides until they are often nearly lost sight of, but the troupe thus engaged always keep sentinels on the look-out, to give the alarm when an enemy is approaching.

On the fifth day of our march, getting into a region a little elevated and with more open timber, we passed a large gang of these little fellows busy in their furrows; and a short time after, our little Indian *"Bok-ar"* announced that they had taken up the line of march, and were following us, and that we were in great danger unless we could reach a small stream that was a few miles ahead of us. At his request we relieved him of as much of his load as we could, and he went back to meet them, and keep them at bay by some sort of charm that he was master of, and which I did not learn; the same, he told us, that the jaguar uses to decoy them up to a leaning tree or other place where he can pounce upon the fattest of the herd, and, with it, leap to a nook above their reach.

About three or four o'clock in the afternoon we reached the anticipated stream, and forded it, the mud and water reaching to our waistbands. All hands safe over, we came to a halt and laid our packs upon the ground, the Indians assuring us that our enemies would not enter the water for us.

Our daring little *Bok-ar* was in full view, dancing backwards towards us, singing, and now and then squeaking like a young peccary, but staring at them as they were advancing in a solid phalanx upon him, chafing their tusks and preparing for battle.

Bok-ar waded the stream, and joined the party, whilst the band of nut-gatherers advanced to the edge of the stream, in a body as thick as they could stand, little else being seen than their heads, with their noses pointed towards us.

Thus they stood, chafing their ivory, the sound of which was like that in a marble-yard when stone-cutters are chipping marble; their eyes were blood-red with rage, and a white froth was dropping from their jowls.

As near as I could judge, there were from five to six hundred of these bristly little warriors in the group, and the reader will easily imagine that so wild and savage a spectacle could not escape a place in my sketch-book.

This done, we were resolving to give them a broadside with our rifles, when I saw the little *Bok-ar* slipping a poisoned arrow into his blowgun. We lowered our rifles, and gave the two Indians a chance to exhibit the powers of their insignificant-looking weapons. They seemed very proud of the compliment thus paid them, and smiled as they slipped the fatal knitting-needles into the slender reeds.

The distance across the stream was some twelve or fifteen yards. The little *Bok-ar* asked me which one he should hit, and I pointed to one of the largest, standing with its feet at the water's edge, and with its head elevated, exposing its breast and the veins of its neck. A sudden whiff! and the deadly missiles were off.

Bok-ar's pig pitched forward into the mud, and never moved, the arrow having struck the jugular vein; the other victim, shot in the side, wheeled about, and after reeling and staggering for two or three seconds, gave a squeak or two and fell, when a scene commenced that baffled all description. The sagacious group around the falling animal seemed to know that it was dying, when they pitched upon it, ripped and tore it, and tossed it in all directions.

I ordered Caesar to fire his Minié rifle over their heads, when the whole group took fright and disappeared in an instant, and we saw no more of them.

The Indians waded the stream, and both recovered their arrows, and returned them to their quivers, and (as they told me) as ready and efficient for battle as if they had not been fired! How wonderful this poison, and what can it be? Some have thought it extracted from the rattlesnake's tooth, but that can't be, for the poison of a serpent's tooth produces immense swelling—the poisoned arrow's victim never swells at all.

[Elsewhere in this book] I have given a fuller account of this wonderful weapon and its effects, from experiments I witnessed and made while amongst the Connibo Indians. When the Indian requires for such deadly effects but an almost imperceptible quantity of the poison on the point of his needle-arrow, I would ask what awful havoc would be produced in war if an army or regiment of men were armed with the ancient bell-muzzled arquebuses charged with duck-shot that had been rolled in this liquid and dried, and driven by powder instead of the Indian's feeble breath?—or if small field-pieces were charged with such missiles? No surgeons would need to follow, no wounded would be left upon the field of battle, for where one drop of blood is drawn, death *must* ensue.

A conic rifle-ball, charged at its point with this poison, entering the body of an ox, a tiger, or an elephant, would, in my opinion, produce death as instantaneous as the flash of a gun.[1]

[1] Six or seven years after my adventures in that country, a correspondent in Pará states in one of his letters:—"Since your visit to the Upper Amazon, several agents have been traversing the whole country, both on the Amazon and in Guiana, and buying up all the Indian poison at any price, but for what purpose no person

To proceed on our voyage. The surface of the country over which we were now passing was beginning evidently to rise, and after some five or six days' farther march the forest became more open, its twisting vines and other impediments in a measure disappeared, and its true grandeur and beauty, more fully developed, showed us that we were on the divide between water-sheds, and that we were consequently approaching the *llanos* (prairies), which we should soon meet, pointing into the forest.

Encouraged, we marched easier and farther each day, and on the eleventh day from our start we beheld the opening to the prairie—the sun shining upon it, the smoke from a Zurumati village and the blue Acarai (or Crystal) Mountains in the distance. Our Indians soon found their acquaintances; our views were made known to them, and we were received with hospitality and kindness. Caesar soon got my portfolio open in a suitable place, and began his usual lectures on the portraits of their *"Red bredren"* in North America, as he held them up one by one to their view. Great excitement and amusement were produced by the pictures, but all were afraid to be painted when it was proposed, and no one would consent to the operation.

The women had not yet come forward, and one of the chiefs very respectfully inquired if the women could be allowed to look at the portraits the next day; they should be dressed properly for the occasion.

The next day about noon, some fifteen or twenty of them came, mostly young and unmarried girls.

On this occasion, to be, as they had proposed, in full dress, they had very curiously (and, indeed, in some cases very beautifully) painted their round and pretty limbs with vermilion and other bright colors, and ornamented their bodies and limbs with long and sweet-scented grass, parts of it plaited in beautiful braids, forming kilts, that extended from the waist to the knee. Braids of this grass also ornamented their ankles, their wrists, and their necks; and wreaths of evergreen boughs, tastefully arranged, encircled their heads and waists, enlivened with orchids and other wild blossoms of the richest hues and odors, whilst their long and glossy black hair, which is generally kept in braids, was loosened and spread in beautiful waves over their breasts and shoulders.

Gaiety, modesty, and pride were imprinted on every one of their

has been able to ascertain, God forbid that it should be used for the advancement of civilization, for the Indians themselves have long since ceased to use it in Indian warfare."

faces, and evinced in all their movements, which were natural and exceedingly graceful. And oh, that a photographic impression could have been taken of this singular and pretty group, which would have vanished like a flock of antelopes had I attempted to have made a sketch of it. Caesar was embarrassed, but with his *Lingua-geral,* which these Indians partially understood, he got along tolerably well in showing them the pictures.

With a dozen or two of knitting-needles for arrows to their blow-guns, and some other little presents, we easily engaged men with mules to convey us with out packs to the base of the mountains, a distance of forty or fifty miles; and if anything on the face of the earth could properly be called a paradise, it was the beautifully rolling prairies, with their copses and bunches of graceful leaning palms and palmettoes, encircled with flowers of all colors, spotted here and there with herds of wild cattle and horses, and hedged in a hundred directions with the beautiful foliage bordering the rivulets and rivers wending their serpentine course through them.

We had no time or disposition for the chase, and the only gun fired in our course was fired by myself, and much to my regret. A wild cow, lying directly before me shook her head, and seemed to dispute the right of way with me. I raised my rifle and shot her dead; and, on approaching, found the poor creature had been watching over the body of her calf, which had been some days dead, and, from its swollen condition, we supposed from the bite of a snake.

In this ride we forded several streams, and, amongst them, the west fork of the Trombutas; and, if the Indians informed us rightly, something like one hundred miles from its junction with the eastern branch . . . .

After two days' ride, the blue of the mountains became grey and green, as we were at their base. In some places, for many miles together, they were in perpendicular palisades, like shore cliffs of ancient seas, with higher mountains rising above and behind them; and, at their base, sloping descents of clay, with gullies of great depth, and a thousand curious forms winding down and blending with the prairies.

With no instruments to determine our meridian or latitude, we supposed we were here directly under the equator, and something like two hundred miles northeast of the Barra, at the mouth of the Rio Negro.

The "nugget fever" was now raging on us. Our Indian *employés,* with their mules and with our hammocks and other packs which we should not want, went back, as they were afraid of the Woyaway Indians in the mountains, and their mules were of no further service to us amongst the rocks, which we were obliged to scale on our own bones and muscles.

A sad occurrence here embarrassed us very much. One of the mules, on the night before they left, had, by accident, stepped its foot into our "tin pan," our only gold-washer, and completely broke its bottom through, rendering it irreparably useless, and narrowing our "golden" prospects to the chances there might be of *nuggets* alone.

Gates were here and there opening into these mountain escarpments, into one of which we entered, and found ourselves in one of the most beautiful valleys in the world, surrounded by high ridges on the north, the east, and the west, the slopes of which were beautifully ornamented with vines and with natural orchards of orange and fig trees, bending down with their fruit.

Here we established our headquarters, building a sort of cabin with rocks, and covering it with palm leaves. This valley, of some six or eight miles in length, and varying from two to three in breadth, was filled with boulders of granite, and gneiss, and quartz, not transported by ice-bergs from foreign sources, but descended from the mountain slopes around it, and which were consequently an unerring index to the minerals of the beds from which they came.

Several days were spent amongst these by Señor N—— and myself, but with no success. A few days' rest, and our next expedition was to strike for the ancient road which I had before discovered and crossed, or to meet the Woyaway or other Indians of the mountains, from whom we might obtain some information of the ancient mines and the remains of the adobe houses to which I have before alluded.

For this, leaving in *cache* a part of our provisions to fall back upon in case of emergency, we started, with our knapsacks on our backs, in a northeasterly direction. We scaled the rugged mountain behind us to get a glance at the country beyond it, but then a deep and desolate ravine succeeded, and beyond that another mountain range of greater height than the one we had ascended. We gained the summit of this, and then beheld the field for all our labors spread out before us.

Not a "crystal mountain," but a succession of mountains—hills peeping o'er "hills—Alps on Alps arising," until they were blue and lost in the distance. Their summits were capped, not with snow, but some with naked granite, and others with grass and rhododendrons, their sloping sides and deep ravines, seeming to sink down, down, far below the earth's surface, were covered with evergreen thickets that tried the nerves of the boldest and bravest who undertook to penetrate them.

In this pictured landscape, long and broad valleys were seen, and lakes reflecting the white equatorial sky that was over them; and glistening waterfalls and cascades were seen in various directions; but not the smoke of an Indian's wigwam could be discovered with the most patient telescopic examination. How desolate and yet how beautiful!

We kept on our course for several days, crossing ravine and ravine, and mountain and mountain, having nothing but a pocket-compass and mountain landmarks to guide us. As the naked rocks were chiefly granite and gneiss, and the others covered with impenetrable vegetation, and our means of washing in the earthy deposits were gone, our only remaining chances for discoveries were in the beds of the deep ravines, where the rocks, descended from the mountain sides, were exposed and washed by the running streams.

Many of these streams we traced for long distances with various success. One of these, a large and dashing stream—its course, where we struck it, from east to west, and probably one of the sources of the Essequibo—presented us many huge blocks of a greyish rose-colored quartz, containing frequent speculae of gold, easily apparent to the naked eye.

These blocks were undoubtedly from a vein of quartz in the slope of the mountain above, but which we were too feeble to uncover, or even to get sight of.

In one of these blocks of several hundred tons weight, lying in the bed of the stream, I discovered a cluster of nuggets, from the size of a pin's head to the size of a pea, washed bare and polished by the action of the water. We now believed we had arrived at or near our "El Dorado": all hands were gathered around it, until these, by chisels, screw-driver, &c., we extracted, when Caesar set to work with the sledge-hammer, in hopes to make an opening into further and richer discoveries.

In one of his tremendous swings, when all hopes were high (as if Dame Fortune was set against us), the hammer slipped from its handle and plunged into the foaming stream, dashing among the rocks below us! Every possible search was made for its recovery, but from the depth and maddening force of the water amongst the rocks, our efforts were in vain. Various smaller nuggets were afterwards secured with our lighter tools, and others were picked up in the sands and gravel of the stream.

The beds of several other streams presented us similar quartz rocks, and in some instances lesser evidences of their auriferous character.

Nuggets having been our only chance for the last few days, and that chance now reduced to a failure and our supplies running low, we swung around for two or three days in desperate marches, in hopes still to rediscover the "ancient road," or to strike upon some Indian villages or Indian paths, but none of which could we discover, when we turned our faces again towards the valley of the Amazon, which we entered some forty or fifty miles from where we had left it.

We reached our hidden stores in a few days in a starving condition; after that, the friendly Zurumati village, our pirogue, and at last the mighty Amazon, more ragged than Falstaff's men, and actually richer in gold than when we started, two months before, by *just two ounces!*

MORAL.—In this wise Dame Fortune's kind favors were solicited; and if she bestowed not upon me the visioned mines of gold, should I complain? She has given me what is better—life, and health, and wisdom, and greatly added to my only wealth, my portfolios, to which she has long been a liberal and kind contributor.

CHAPTER 2

~~~~~~

Venezuela and the Orinoko

(CHAPTER XIV FROM *Life Among the Indians*)

Now FOR THE fields and forests of everlasting and never ending green—
of all Nature's uninterrupted joy—of bloom, of gaiety, and song! where
dreary winter's blasts are not known, and leaves are dropping, and buds
and flowers are growing at the same time! I have said that I knew such
a place as this. Who has breathed the delicious air, seen the gaudy colors,
and heard the sweet notes of this flower-garden, this music-hall, this
aviary of the world—the grand and boundless valley of the Amazon—
and who will not, if his life and his purse be long enough, go there
and see it?

But we are not quite in it yet—*Carraccas* is not in the valley of the
Amazon, nor is it the beginning, exactly, of South America, but it is
not a great way from it. It is in Venezuela, on a sandy, scorching coast.
It was there that I [landed on my first trip].

From some unknown accident in the giant furnace that is burning
underneath that region of country, a terrible shock and a shake were
given some sixty years since, destroying ten thousand inhabitants; and
back of the town, and for a long distance on the coast, you may still
see the frightful chasms which were opened at that time.

Natural things are on a large scale in the country now ahead of us.
What is forged in the mighty furnace underneath us, and how long it
has been worked, nobody knows. It formerly threw out its smoke and
its cinders at the top of Chimborazo, only 19,000 feet high. Chimborazo
(Tchimboratho) is "laid up"—the chimney now at work is Cotopaxi
(Cotopassi), of equal height; its groanings and bellowings can only be
heard 600 miles, at the utmost! and a block of granite of 327 cubic feet
it was only able to project a distance of nine miles!

The Orinoko is a large river, not far from us; the Amazon is much larger—larger than the Missouri, but not quite so long; at the head of tidewater it is but thirty miles wide; it has but about 1,500 islands, and the largest of them, occupied by individual nabobs, only contain 50,000 head of horses and cattle! Naval engineers who have surveyed the bed of the Amazon at the expense of the United States Government report that the "Pennsylvania," a 140-foot gun-ship, built in Philadelphia, could only go as high as Tabatinga in low water; that is, only 1,800 miles from its mouth! and ordinary passenger steamers could only go 1,000 miles higher without being liable to get aground if the water was low! These distances are not very great. The valley of the Amazon is rather large; but it could not possibly hold with comfort more than the populations of England, France, Belgium, and the United States put together, for putting more than that number in might make some men's farms rather too small.

The precipitous wall of rock just back of the town of Carraccas is only 6,000 feet in height! and in the "shakes" it "shook and shuddered so that the stones and trees were tumbling down from its reeling sides in all directions." Can one rise it? No. But by a hard day's work you may get to its summit by going a great way round. And then, where is the town? and where the ocean? If the day is perfectly clear and sunny, you can see neither. If the weather is thick and overcast, you may see a little strip of white sand and some little red patches at your feet, if you can venture near enough to the brink; but the sky and the ocean are one, and you can't divorce them; and on the top—the cloud-capped summit—what's here? Here is a pebble! a seashore pebble! worn round by the waves on the seashore, not in the bottom of the ocean, for there are no waves there—the waters lie still in that place. What bird could have brought this here?—but stop, here's another, and another and then, thousands of others!

These pebbles are flint—they contain silicified zoophytes! Everything has a life and a death; these have lived—zoophytes live and grow only in the sea; their beds have been cretaceous. We are only 6,000 feet above the sea, and looking into it at our feet. When were these pebbles rolled by the waves of the sea? Where—for thousands of years to be rounded as they are? In what cretaceous bed lay they for thousands of years, and perhaps for thousands of centuries, to be changed from the living animal, with all their curious and intricate tentaculae, into silex before they were rolled? and how long have they lain here? and then, how came they *here*? or where has *here* been? But don't let us go mad;

let us get down from this place, we are too high. No; it's too much trouble to get back again; we are now on the top of the "Scylla," the grand plateau that sweeps off to the Orinoko. There are Indians on these plains, and I, of course, must cross them. Have any Indian tribes ever escaped me? Yes. Shall I ever see them all? I don't believe so.

How easily the reader travels! how soon he is across the Atlantic! how quick upon the summit of the Scylla and the plains of Venezuela! His sea voyage don't cost him fifty pounds—his knees don't ache like ours. He sits at home and smokes his nice little cigar perhaps, and sips his glass of wine, while he reads and smiles at our tugging and groaning; but he loses much that we see—he carries no knapsack, and the escape from one rattlesnake, from one tiger, or from one drowning produces, perhaps, in one minute, more pleasure than he enjoys in a month. This *may* be so—who can contradict it?

My knapsack is heavy, but I have resolved to carry it. Dr. Hentz, a German botanist, and his man, are with me. We have no horses, but we resolve to cross these beautiful plains on our legs; may be the *Gautchos,* with their mules, will help us. Angosturo is on the Orinoko, it is but 150 miles—that's nothing.

The prairies in this country are *pampas;* in shape and distant appearance they are much like those which "Charley" and I passed over between Fort Gibson and St. Louis, rolling and sloping about in all directions, with beautiful clear streams winding through them, and copses and bunches of timber and bushes on their sides and along the banks of the streams.

But those bunches and copses, when we came near to them, oh, how lovely! There are the beautiful bananas, the pennated, lofty, and dwarf palms, and, at their feet, palmettoes; acres on acres of geraniums in flowers of all colors and of various odors; of wild roses, and fifty kinds of flowering plants. The meadows are filled with lilies of various hues; the hedges are bending with wild plums and wild grapes. The orange and fig trees are on every little hillock, and yellow with fruit, and still white with sweet blossoms. Pinks of a hundred colors and patterns, and violets of all hues are under our feet, and now and then a huge rattlesnake!

The busy little humming-birds are buzzing about us, and ten thousands of beetles and other clumsy flyers, that no one stops to inquire about, are knocking and butting against us. Spathes of palm-flowers are opening, and these swarm in myriads about them.

The sun looks as it does at home, though perhaps a little smaller, and more over our heads; we have to bend our necks more to look at it. Man begins here to feel less than he does in England—his shadow is shorter—it don't follow him so exactly, and so far behind him.

The Indians—are there any? Yes, but not many. Smallpox and rum and whiskey have destroyed the most of them. Here are the *Chaymas* and the *Goo-a-gives,* semi-civilized, mostly mixed with Spaniards. Some full-bloods; color and character much like the Ojibbeways in North America. Rather small and slight in stature, but quick and powerful men, beautifully formed, and no deformities amongst them.

Who is the happiest man in the world just at this time? Why Dr. Hentz, while he is gathering these beautiful plants and lovely flowers and packing them in his large books, which a Chayma is employed to help carry to Angosturo; and who the next happiest? Why I, of course, who am putting these beautiful scenes into my portfolio—and yesterday, that beautiful dance! What dance? Why, the *mach-ee-o-a* (handsome or glad dance)—glad, or thankful, because the Indians are pleased with us, and perhaps have received some valued present, and also because the *medicine* man has told them that I am *great medicine.* What! medicine men here too? in South America? Yes, exactly the same as in North America. The chief's portrait was held up by the corners in the same way, and the medicine men had a grand dance around it. And then the warriors danced the war-dance, and gave the war-whoop. What! the war-whoop here, too? Precisely the same—and then—and then what? Why then came the *handsome dance.* The young women dance in this country, but not often. Three young and beautiful women were selected by the chief to give this dance; it was an extraordinary compliment paid to my *medicine;* for many years it had not been seen. Was it beautiful? The most beautiful thing I ever saw. How were these girls dressed? Each one had a beautiful tiger-skin spread under her feet, upon which she danced; their hair, fastened by a silver band passing around the head, was falling down in shining tresses on their backs and their pretty breasts; long pins of silver were run through their under lips, and strings of blue and white beads were dangling from them, large and small beads hung in great profusion around their necks, and polished brass bands were worn, with strings of blue and white beads on their slender wrists and ankles; their cheeks were painted red, and their bodies and limbs from their throats downwards were colored white with white clay.

Had these girls no other dress on? Not a particle.—Did they raise their feet from the ground when they danced? No, not quite, their

25

toes were always on the tiger-skins.—Did they separate their big toes? Not an inch.—Did they dance to music? In perfect time to the beat of the drum and a chaunt of the chief's.—Were they graceful? Yes, and as thoughtless and innocent, and as white and as beautiful, and as modest as the marble of Venus on its pedestal.

Nothing can be more beautiful of their kind than the rolling plains between Carraccas and the Orinoko. They are abundantly stocked with wild horses and wild (not buffaloes, but) cattle, which answer all the same purposes for food to the Indians as well as to white men. These are taken both by the Indians and the Spaniards, not with the bow and arrows or lance, but with the deadly *bolas*.

The bolas is a cord of rawhide, branching three ways from the center, each branch being some eight or ten feet in length, with a leaden ball of half a pound or so in weight at its end. One of these balls the rider holds in his right hand, while his horse is at full speed, and the other two are swinging around and over his head until he is in the right position, when he lets go his ball, giving them a sling at the same time. The three balls keep their respective opposite positions as they are whirling about in the air, till one of the cords strikes the neck of the animal, around which and its legs the cords instantly wrap themselves, and the animal falls upon its head and becomes an easy and certain prey to its assailant, who, with a long lance, from his horse's back, or with his knife, by dismounting, does the rest.

This mode is used only for "killing." The wild horses are killed in this manner for their skins and their hair, and the wild cattle for their flesh, their skins, and their horns.

In taking wild horses for their *use,* this mode would not answer; for in nine cases out of ten the fall of the horse while at full speed, and entangled in the folds of the bolas, would break the animal's neck, or disable it for life.

For *catching* the wild horse, therefore, the *lasso* is used by these people much in the same way as it is used by the Indians in North America, which has been described; with the only difference that when the horse is arrested by the lasso and its speed is stopped, they strike it with a short baton (loo-tank), loaded with lead (something like a "life-preserver"), on the back part of the head, which stuns the animal, and it falls to the ground. The captor then places a bandage around its eyes and gets upon its back. The horse, recovering from the blow and rising, soon yields to the wishes of his cruel master, not daring to run with its eyes blinded.

By the effects of this mode of breaking, which I have seen and closely studied, I believe the natural spirit of the animal is irretrievably lost, to such a degree as greatly to diminish its value.

At the small town of Chaparro, about sixty miles from the Orinoko, we learned that a large armed force of insurgents in the civil war at Venezuela, which had suddenly broken out, was marching on Angosturo; and by the aid of mules which we employed of the Gautchos, we got posted on to San Diego, and from that to a point thirty miles below Angosturo, to the banks of the Orinoko; a canoe took us to Barrancas, and from that we got a steamer to Georgetown, Demerara, in British Guiana.

But stop—we did not come to Demerara in a moment—we *could not,* and why *should* we? what did we see, and what did we do? Why, we saw from our little "dug-out" the stately and dark forests overhanging the shores of the Orinoko. Is there anything like them on earth? I don't believe it.

"Stately," did I say? Yes, and lofty. The towering *mora*—the *miriti,* with its tall and elegant shaft—the tough *hackea*—the *green-heart*—the *ebony*—the *copal locust*—the beautiful *hayawa,* and the *olow,* with their sweet gushing resin, and the graceful *banana,* the queen of the forest, and twenty others, mingled and intermingled with cordage and ropes of creeping, and climbing, and hanging vines; with clumps and bouquets of beautiful flowers of all colors and at all heights; and chattering monkeys leaping from branch to branch with their little ones on their backs, cunningly ogling us as we passed.

The solitary *tocanos* bowing to us from the withered tops of the lofty moras, and saluting us—"Tso-cano-tso-cano! no—no—no! go on there, go on there!" The beautiful white swans by the hundreds, and pelicans also, as white as snow, were flapping their long wings, and on the air before I could get "Sam" to bear upon them. "Sam! who's Sam?" Why *Sam Colt,* a six-shot little rifle, always lying *before* me during the day and *in my arms* during the night, by which a tiger's or alligator's eye, at a hundred yards, was sure to drop a red tear—but don't interrupt me. The last of these were everywhere basking in the sun and plunging off from their slimy logs as we approached. The timid turtles were shoving down from the banks of sand, and the tortoises, with their elevated heads, came pacing out of the forest where they roam, taking shelter under the waves whilst their enemies passed.

It is easier to fly over the water and between these hundreds of islands, with their matted and twisted and almost wedged foliage, than through them; and these crooked avenues, for birds and wild fowl, are what the Strand and London Bridge are to the Londoners.

There are all sorts and all sizes and all colors on the wing; some slow and some fast—some actually loungers, and some evidently expresses, as they dart through the crowds like a shot. Many are gossippers, for they chatter as they travel. So there is din as well as motion; and in the midst of this, once in a while, a flock of wild geese must pass (an omnibus!); the crowd must give way! they fly in a triangle—their leader is a "conductor" and distinctly cries, "Get in, John! Get in, John! Paddington! Paddington!" while the beautiful tocano turns his head sideways, and rolls his piercing eye down from the top of the mora, as he echoes—"Go on, John! Go on, John! go on! go on!"

"Here's a swarm of bees ahead of us," said Dr. Hentz; "we shall be stung to death!" "No, Doctor, it's only the opening of a spathe; and you know what a spathe is better than I—that's in your line, Doctor." "Well," said the Doctor, "that's true, and I'll tell you.

"There are over two hundred different varieties of palm trees in this country, and each sort has its blossoms and its fruits in some shape or other. The fruit of all palms grows just where the leaves and branches start out from the trunk; and before the fruit, immense large sacks or spathes, containing the flowers, are visible for weeks, and sometimes for months, before they are sufficiently perfected to open. These spathes on some palms are large enough for the back-loads of three or four men, and, when opened, present from ten to one hundred thousand fragrant and honey-bearing flowers of purple, of pink, and other colors, perfuming the atmosphere for a great distance around them.

"The honey-sucking birds and insects generally get a few days' previous knowledge of these important approaching events, and gather in myriads around them, ready for the onslaught, when a bright and clear morning shows them their feast opened and spread before them. That is the scene now before us. You see in the midst of that whirling cloud of insects the spadix of a palm in full bloom, and here is now just going on the *"set-to,"* and *pêle mêle* for honey. There's no danger of being stung now, I admit. These busy little creatures, though most of them with their stings, are all at work—they have their little ones to feed, and no time now to sting. Let's stop and look at them a while." Thank you, Doctor. This was a short lecture in botany—the Doctor has given us many.

We stopped our canoe and looked at the busy group. Through my opera-glass the scene was indescribably curious. Whilst thousands of honey-bees, of bumble-bees, of beetles, and humming-birds, and other honey-sucking insects were whirling around it, like all other riches and luxuries of the world, it was easily seen that they were divided amongst the lucky few. The surface of these clusters of flowers seemed chiefly engrossed by the swift-darting and glistening little humming-birds, of all sizes and all hues, whose long and slender bills entered every approachable cell, as they balanced on their trembling wings, and ready to dart away when danger comes. These seemed masters of the feast. But there were others apparently even more successful; the busy, fearless little bees and bumble-bees and others, that crept between and through the winding maze of flowers, and culled their choicest, freshest sweets, where others could not enter—but then, where were they? Like too many of the world who enjoy the sweetest things, the nearest to eternity.

The sharp claws of the bright-eyed little bee-hawk suspended him from these mats of flowers; he loves honey, but sucks it not; he gets it in a shorter way—he picks up these little laborers as they come out with their rich loads and puts them in his crop. His feast finished, he flies but heavily with his plundered prey, and knows the gauntlet he, too, has to run: *his* enemies are of his own kin, but stronger and fleeter on the wing. *They* sit like silent sentinels on the dry limbs of overhanging trees, and swoop upon him and snatch him up as he passes through the open air. Amidst these incongruous masses of contending and jealous insects, with their deadly weapons, many conflicts and many deaths ensue; and many such, with their accumulated treasure, drop to the ground beneath, in the grass, and there—(Let's go ashore," said the Doctor, "and I'll show you"), and he did show me.—"There, do you see that little green snake, and that white one too? they are both of one species, though their colors are different; they both are honey-eaters, though the world don't believe it. They know just as well as these insects when a spathe of flowers is opened, and here they are, as seen to be. They take the honey-loaded carcasses of the unlucky combatants that fall." How did you learn this curious fact, Doctor? "From the Indians."

"Doctor," said I, "next to the Indians, the thing I wish most to see is a cocoa-nut tree, and to hear your description of it." "I don't think there are any near here," said the Doctor; "the cocoa-nut is not a native of America, but it has been introduced, and we shall probably see many of them before long; but I have not met one yet."

29

George Catlin

Well, we were jogging along on the Orinoko, were we not? Look, next time you go to the Museum, for the beautiful *cotingas;* there are several sorts of them, a size larger than the humming-birds, and equally beautiful in plumage. They are all here, and in great numbers are darting about amongst us.

And the *campañero* (strange bird!), their notes like the tinkling or tolling of a bell, exactly. They give the forest the most singular character. They are a solitary bird, I take it, for we never see them. We hear their strange notes, and then, from some mystery in sound not yet explained, we can't tell which way they are; if we go one way or the other to look for them, it's all the same; the sound is equally near, and all around us— it seems a mile distant, but it may be within a few yards—it tolls only just at night, when it is too late to see it, or just at daybreak, when the difficulty is the same. There's *medicine in this?* it's like the thunder-bird of the "thunder's nest." I never could see one, though I am a *"medicine man."* Is it a bird? or is it some sort of *mirage of sound?* Is it not a distant cow-bell? It's not a *phantom*—phantoms "fly before us"; this does not fly—it's all around, before and behind us, and travels with us— but we'll drop it, and perhaps hunt for it again.

Though these forests and these lovely river-shores are constantly ringing with song, still one-half of animal nature seems to sleep during the day; for when one set of songsters are done, another begins: but how different! The songs of the day are all joyous and cheering, if we could understand them—characteristic of the glow and warmth of sun-shine; but in the dark, how emblematic of the gloom and loneliness about us, and characteristic of that stealth with which the animals of the dark steal upon their sleeping, unprotected prey! The frequent roar we often hear of the hungry jaguar—the doleful howlings of the red mon-keys—the hooting of owls—and *every* night, the inquisitive *goat-sucker,* who lights upon a limb as nearly over us as he can in safety, and shocks our nerves, in his coarse and perfectly masculine and human voice— "Who are you? go away! go away!"

Well, we'll *go* away—we'll jog on—we are stopping too long in this place—but then, one word more before we start. What great ugly beast is that I see yonder, hanging under a branch of that hayama tree? That? that's a *sloth,* sir—the laziest animal of all the world, and perfectly harmless; it hasn't the energy to stand upon its legs, but hangs all day without moving, and fast asleep under the limb of a tree—hangs by his long toe-nails. What! hangs and sleeps all day? well, that's easier than to *stand* and sleep—it's like sleeping in a hammock. What a gentleman! —sleeps all day? but he is a fat-looking fellow. I believe he is up all night; and if you have a henroost I advise you to beware of him—he seems well fed—the world is full of such gentlemen. He can't move, ha? hand me "Sam"—I'll prick him up a little and see what he's made of. Bang!—he falls into the river! but he swims! and now upon the bank! and at one leap upon the side of a tree! and at another of forty feet, upon another tree! and the next, out of sight! That's your lazy gentleman, ha! Why no alligator could catch that fellow in the water —no dog could catch him on the land—and amongst the trees, few monkeys would be a match for him. I believe he is a great rascal.

We are at Barrancas now; Barrancas is a large town; but what are large towns to us? London is considerably larger. This steamer goes to Demerara—just where our little canoe can't go, and where we *must* go. "A good chance to overhaul and air your plants, Dr. Hentz."

"First-rate, Mynheer."

This is a strange-looking place, Captain. What a vast number of islands there are ahead of us! We are at the mouth of the Orinoko?

"Not quite."

It has a hundred mouths, I am told?

"No; only fifty."

How grand and magnificent the forests around us! those thousands and tens of thousands of lofty palms, their trunks standing in the water, actually!—why they seem like a grand colonnade or portico of some mighty edifice!

"Yes, they are truly so; but they don't look exactly so in low water. The tide is getting well nigh up now. I see you are an Englishman, sir?"

No, Captain, not exactly; I am an American; that's not far from it.

"Give us your hand, stranger; you know who I am; we'll have a long talk after a while."

But, Captain, before you go below, what sort of birds' nests are those in those trees on the shore, and on that island ahead of us? they are too large for rooks, I think.

"Well—*don't* now! you'll make me smile, sir, if you don't take care. They are a large sort of bird, sir, and you'll see them hovering about us in a little time. These birds fly upon the water, sir; not in the air; they live upon fish and oysters; and I expect some fresh supplies from them by-and-by.

31

"These birds, sir, are called *Guaroanes* (Carribbees); they build their houses in the trees, and go up to them by a ladder from their canoes, and never venture out except when the tide is up—and that always in their canoes, when the tide is out, all is deep mud and slime about them, which nothing can walk through."

Captain, I would give almost anything if we could stop near some of these for a little time.

"That's quite easy, sir, for I've got to lie-to a little, till the tide gets high enough to take us over the bar, and you may have a first-rate opportunity to see them, and visit them too, if you wish; for I am going to send the yawl to one of them with that Spanish gentleman and his two daughters sitting in the bow yonder, who are going to them."

Splendid! Captain, splendid!

CHAPTER 3

Brazil

(CHAPTER XVII FROM *Life Among the Indians*)

. . . BEFORE LEAVING Demarara with my little outfit, I visited the neighboring tribes in that vicinity; the *Carribbees* and *Macouchis,* the *Accoways* and the *Warrows,* in Dutch Guiana, in the neighborhood of Paramaribo and New Amsterdam; and the *Arowaks,* on the Rio Corontyn; and on our way, on the headwaters of the Essequibo, the *Tarumas* and *Oyaways,* which, with those on the plains of Venezuela, are, in fact, but the names of different bands or sections of the great *Carribbee* family, which occupy one-fifth at least of the southern hemisphere.

This numerous tribe also occupied all the lesser Antilles at the time of the discovery of those islands by Columbus, and since have been destroyed, or fled from the islands, to evade the slavery endeavored to be fixed upon them by the Spaniards, to the coast of South and Central America, where they are living.

These people are generally rather small in stature, and inferior to the North American races, but not inferior to some that may be found there; and enough like them in features and color, as well as in customs, to stamp them, without a doubt, as a part of the great and national American family.

These tribes in this vicinity, which show a strong resemblance to one another in complexion and customs, also speak a language much resembling, showing them to be a family group. Their skin is a shade darker than that of the North American races, and their modes of dress very different; the latter of which is undoubtedly the result of the difference of climate. The weather in the tropics admits of but little clothing, and these tribes are chiefly naked, both women and men, seldom wearing anything more than sandals under their feet, and mere "fig-leaves," or bandages, about their loins; yet they have and support a

33

strict sense of decency and modesty at the same time, for which these poor creatures deserve great credit.

Their naked limbs and bodies are rubbed over with some soft and limpid grease every day, and though often reputed filthy, they are nevertheless far more cleanly and free from filth and vermin than any class of people equally poor in any part of the civilized world, where they are, from necessity, loaded with a burthen of rags that don't have a daily (and oftentimes not a weekly, nor a monthly, and sometimes not an annual) ablution.

We are now in the great and verdant valley of the Amazon! What shall I say first? The *Acarai* (or Tumucamache, or Crystal) Mountains which we have passed over, forming the boundary line between British and Dutch Guiana and Brazil, are truly sublime; not unlike the Rocky Mountains in North America in some respects, and very much unlike them in some others.

The descent from these mountains, and their graceful slopes off into the valley of everlasting green, were . . . truly grand and magnificent.

Let us sit down a few moments; we are weary—our mule died ten days ago, and our packs are now heavy. We have come out from that gorge! that awful ravine! It is frightful to look back, or to think back! Why should we, when here is a blue sky, and the sun and the ocean again before us? How warm and how cheering!

And what a curious cloud! what a straight line it makes across the sky! Yes, it must be. And what a boundless ocean of green and blue we are looking over, and not a vessel to be seen! But stop! that can't be. That can't be the ocean! we are on our course? Give me the pocket-compass. There! that's south—there's no ocean there. We are steering into the valley of the Amazon; and here it lies before us—we are right! And what's at our feet? green grass and beautiful flowers? Not at all—yellow and blue clay, and nothing else. And what beyond, beneath us? Clay. And what those thousand winding, twisting channels, that seem to soften into blue in the distance, down, down, so far below us? Clay, clay, and nothing else. Yes, *something* else; they glisten in the sun; they have specks that sparkle like the Bude light; they may be diamonds? No, they are crystals of quartz, but they are very beautiful— let's fill our pockets. But here are some that are quite yellow, and others purple; oh, how beautiful!—let's throw away those we have got. These are topaz and amethyst, and far more beautiful; and now and then there is one of carmine. And still more lovely! these are smaller and more scarce—

they are rubellites. These are washed down from the mountains? Undoubtedly. And it just now occurs to me that some of the Spanish writers call these the "Crystal Mountains." Gold mines were worked in these mountains two hundred years ago. There is gold, then, under our feet? Not a doubt of it; but we can't wash; there is no water within some miles, and our tin kettle is of no use.

But we begin to see more clearly—we see streaks of light green running down between these crevices and ravines, stretching off into the ocean, as it were—they become a solid mass of green, and then of black, at last.

The first of these are the rolling prairies, and then the level valley, with its dark and boundless forests of palms. But where's the end of it? It has no end; it is infinite. Take the glass and look—it's all the same— it rises up, up, and up, until it forms that blue line we see in the clouds! It *can't* be so! It must be so! And the black streak we see on the left beneath us is the timber skirting the *Rio Trombutas,* to which we have got to wend our way. Shall we reach the timber today. I don't think so.

We feel like boys here, don't we? Exactly so. Our shadows are all under our feet—how awkward to step on one's own head! we are now exactly under the equator. At noon, where is the south?—which is the north? No one but our little compass can tell. How droll! but this clay is not so hot? No, the rays of the sun are straight down, and there is little refraction.

Like ants, we wandered and crept along over the winding gullies of clay; and, at length, met tufts of grass and sage, and afterwards patches and fields, and at last, an ocean of grass, speckled and spotted and spangled with all the beautiful colors of the floral world. Clumps and bunches of palms and palmettoes and geraniums, each little group like a peep into the glass-house at Kew—though more beautiful, and filled with gay and chattering birds and insects.

And on and over these beautiful plains immense herds of wild cattle and horses of various colors were grazing and flying before us as we approached.

A fine fat cow was here felled by the "old Minié," and we were again happy. We had a plenty of good beef, and rawhide for soling our moccasins, and a clear and running brook for bathing and for washing our shirts; what could we want more? Some three or four days' rest put us on our legs and on our route again.

The Indian trails, and at last the feeble smoke of their distant wigwams showed us we were again in the land of the living, though we were worn almost out of it. We were kindly received and treated by all the tribes on the Trombutas, which we were now to descend. These Indians—*War-kas, Xurumatis, Zumas, Tupis,* and several others—are very different from the Carribbee races living on the other side of the mountains. They are a taller and heavier-built race, and somewhat lighter in color. They belong to the great family of Guarani, which may be said to occupy the whole of eastern and northern Brazil, and often called *Tupi,* but for what reason I cannot tell. *Tupi* is the name of a band (or section) only, of the Guarani, speaking the same language, with very little variation, and no doubt from the same root. It is a matter of little consequence, however, whether they are all called Guarani or all called Tupi, for whichever they are, there never has been, and never will be, any boundary fixed between them.

From the early Spanish history of South America we learn that there was somewhere in the valley of the Amazon a nation of Amazons; and the river and the valley seem to have taken their names from this tradition. The Spaniards and Portuguese have pushed their conquests and subjugations of the Indian tribes as far as they have been able to do; and not as yet having found the Amazons, their more modern historians have attributed them to the banks of the Trombutas, where the Indians have been successful in keeping their invaders at a distance, and where it was natural to infer that the Amazons resided, as they certainly were nowhere else.

At the same time it was easy to suppose, as they reported, that these people were cannibals, and ate foreigners who ventured amongst them. I had all these *frightful* reports to contend against, and it will easily be imagined how my nerves were excited. This required a stronger nerving up, if possible, than the approach to the "Thunder's Nest!" But see, how many marvellous things vanish when we come close to them!

I soon found that there were no *Amazons* on this river, nor *Dianas,* nor *Bacchantes,* but hosts of *Gladiators,* of *Apollos,* and *Fauns.* Their young men and boys are all *Fauns. Castor* and *Pollux,* and old *Silenus,* with his infant *Bacchus* in his arms, may be often seen amongst them.

The nearest thing I could discover or hear of to the Amazons were the women, in some of the tribes, who were famous for mounting their horses, and, with the deadly bolas, to bring down the wild ox or the wild horse as easily as their husbands could. And on inquiring amongst the various villages for the cannibals, I was laughed at even by the women and children for asking so ridiculous a question; a thing, apparently, that they never had heard of before.

One said they had not got to be quite so poor as to have to eat each other yet, but they might perhaps be reduced some time or other to the necessity of doing it. And in the midst of this conversation, diffident young men stepped forward and said, "Yes, tell the white man there are some such persons further down on the river. He will find some white men, living in two or three wigwams on the left bank of the river, who eat the flesh of their own relations, and, what was worse, they sell their skins!" This created a great laugh amongst the Indians; and on descending the river, some distance above Obidos, at its mouth, we found these cannibals—several Frenchmen and Americans—killing monkeys and sending their skins to Paris for the manufacture of ladies' gloves; and living, as they told us, entirely on the flesh of those poor brutes!

This was the nearest approach to cannibalism that I have discovered in my travels amongst North or South American Indians. Books are full of it, but the wilderness is without it! I have traveled and lived fifteen years amongst Indians, and I have not yet found it; and I don't believe that any man has seen anything nearer to it in these countries than what I have above described.

Cannibalism may have been practiced, and still may be, under certain circumstances, in some of the South Sea islands, and in some parts of Africa. We have frequent reports of such practices from travellers, and those very respectable men; but these reports don't *prove* the fact. None of these travellers tell us they have seen it. No doubt, they tell us what they have heard and what they believe. But how do they get their information? Not from the savages; they can't speak with them. Every savage race on earth has its foreign traders amongst them. These are generally the interpreters for travellers who come, and jealous of all persons entering these tribes, to overlook their nefarious system of trade and abuse.

These traders have an object in representing the savage as ten times more cruel and murderous than he is; and amongst other things, as a cannibal, who is sure to kill and eat travellers if they penetrate further into their country.

It is the custom with most savage tribes (and this in America as well as in Africa) to apply the term "cannibal" to their enemies around them as a term of reproach; but when we enter these tribes, the cannibals are not there, they are in the next tribe, and then in the next, and so they fly, like a phantom, before us.

The leaders of war parties also apply the epithet of cannibals to their enemies in order to inflame their warriors going into battle: "You go to fight a set of cannibals—to conquer or to be eaten!"

Some of the most recent travellers in Africa (and the most recent ought to be the most reliable) assure us that several of the tribes they were amongst were cannibals, and that they eat the very aged people, "killing them to eat them, and eating those who die of old age." Grandfathers and grandmothers I should scarcely think would be very good eating. If these people eat each other for the pleasure of eating, one would suppose they would take the middle-aged or the young and tender.

If these travellers would merely tell us that these people eat each other, we might believe it *possible;* but when they qualify their statements by telling us that they only eat the very aged ones, they weaken their own evidence. They leave us as history, assertions, without proof, relative to the existence of a custom both against nature and against taste; raising presumptions formidable enough to stand against very strong positive proof.

As a ceremonial—in the celebration of victories, religious rites, &c.—human flesh is sometimes eaten; and the practice, by custom, observed as a necessary form; but this is not cannibalism.

That savage tribes may sometimes eat their enemies whom they have slain in battle, one can easily believe. Savages always go to war on empty stomachs; and at the end of a battle, after many days' fasting and under great exhaustion, and having no commissariat to supply them with food, it would be easy, and almost natural, to use their enemies for food.

But that any race of human beings, with humanity enough to treat unprotected strangers amongst them with "kindness and hospitality," and to "help, and to protect and feed them" in travelling through their country, will kill and eat their own people for the pleasure of eating, I don't believe it.

The poor Indian's remark above quoted ("we have not got to be so poor as to have to eat each other yet; though we may some time be reduced to that necessity") is not without its significance.

White men have in some instances been reduced to the dire necessity of eating each other, and have cast lots to decide which of the party should be killed first for food; but this is not cannibalism. If this were cannibalism, it might with truth be predicted that by the system of robbery and abuse practiced on the American frontiers, thousands of the poor Indians will soon be compelled to become cannibals.

Some very respectable and accredited early travellers and explorers averred that they saw the Patagonians on the Atlantic coast, seven, eight, and even ten feet high! but modern travellers who go and live amongst them find the tallest of them to be but a little over six feet. It is evident that the atmosphere, under certain circumstances, has a magnifying power, and becomes a very uncertain medium, and particularly so when persons are frightened. The first Indian I ever saw, my little readers will recollect, was a giant; but a little familiar acquaintance made him much smaller.

Some writers (who take a peep into the Indian's wigwam without knowing the meaning of things around them, see little balls of clay piled away, which every Indian stores up for cleaning his dresses and painting his body and limbs, and of which he sometimes swallows a small pill to cure the heart-burn, just as my good old mother used to make me do when I was a boy) have reported some of the tribes as *"dirt eaters,"* asserting that "when they are in a state of starvation, they live for some time upon dirt, eating a pound of clay per day." What!—a pound of clay per day on a famished stomach! what an absurdity! And what a pity the revealers of such astonishing facts should not live a while in some of these poor people's wigwams, and learn what the Indians do with these little balls of clay, before they prepare such astounding information for the world's reading!

But stop! dirt is much more digestible than stones? I was a *"stone eater"* a little way back—both are "giants"—and one story has just as much truth in it as the other.

We were near the head of the Trombutas—on its beautiful and grassy plains? Yes. Well, let us sit down here too, a while, in the shade of these beautiful bananas—but no; these are not bananas—the pride and grace of the forest—such as we saw on the banks of the Essequibo and the Orinoko. No, but they are palms, nevertheless; and oh, how charming and elegant, with their leaning, bending stems and pinnated foliage! The graceful banana of Guiana, I think, has not yet made its way over the Tumucamache; I don't see it anywhere. All the rest seem to be here.

How beautifully and gracefully these bespangled prairies wind and roll their sloping sides down to the river shore!—what a beautiful lawn for a nobleman's mansion, with this very clump of trees for its center —with these myriads of wild flowers, and all these gay and cheerful songsters in it! But look! What snake is that? That's not a rattlesnake, with a white ring around its neck? Oh, no; it's quite a harmless creature; it never bites; it's only a pilot. A pilot! I don't understand. Why, it's the rattlesnake's pilot—always with him, looking out the way. What a gentleman! Then the rattlesnake is close by us? Undoubtedly—most likely behind us: they always lie in the shade during the heat of the day. Let's move off!—can't say that I fancy the company of such gentlemen.

Our little boat rolls and glides along from day to day, and palms, and enamelled rolling prairies, and gay and chirping birds are everywhere. The river enters the deep and shady forests, and we enter with it. Who knows what we shall see when we turn the next point?—and the next?—and the next? Each turn is new, each is beautiful, and more and more grand.

The dense and lofty forests, into which the sun's rays can never penetrate, are before us. Twining and twisting vines, like huge serpents, are rising to their tops; some clinging to their trunks, others hanging suspended in the air like broken cordage, and on them, in clumps and bouquets, the most beautiful parasitic flowers. Crowded out from these thickets of trunks and branches, leaves and vines, so thickly grouped that neither sun nor wind can penetrate, we see the strangled palms and other trees pushing their heads out, and bending over the river for a breathing-place.

And through and above these matted forests, the tall and straight trunks of the lofty palms are seen in distance, like the columns of vast and boundless edifices, and spreading over and above all, their pinnated heads show us a *forest above a forest*—the one apparently growing out of the other. How sublime!

These, with all their grandeur, are reflected in the mirrored water; and thus we have four forests all before us at one view—the one just as distinct in form and color as the other. How grand the mirage! The touch of the oar upon the boat comes back from these solitudes with a redoubled sound; every cough and every "whoop" is echoed back, and with them "who, who!" from the wilderness; but we don't know from whom. Every crack of the rifle sets a hundred squeaking and chattering voices in motion. A hundred monkeys are shaking the branches in the tree-tops ahead of us, and taking a peep at us, and the sleeping alligators tumble from their logs into the water leaving their circular waves behind and around them.

But these solitudes are not everywhere. We turn another bend, and before us we have, on one bank, a vast and beautiful meadow, and on it a forest in miniature. The grass, some six or seven feet high, and filled with twisted and knotted vines, and dotted with wild flowers; and above and through it, like the stately palms in the forest, the tall and straight shafts of the sun-flowers, with their graceful yellow and leaning heads, forming a forest of black and gold above the green, and red, and pink, and blue below.

What myriads of bumble-bees and humming-birds and butterflies are working here! But—this path! this path? Why, it's the tiger's walk! Let's go on—push off!

We sleep in hammocks here. Not in these prairies? No, but always in the timber. We sling our hammocks between two trees, and build a fire on each side of us. The fire protects us from animals and reptiles; both are afraid of it.

We stopped our boat one day for our accustomed midday rest, in the cool shade of one of these stately forests, where there was a beautifully variegated group of hills, with tufts of timber and gaudy prairies sloping down to the river on the opposite shore. Our men had fallen asleep, as usual, in the boat, and I said to my friend Smyth, who, with myself, was seated on top of the bank, "How awfully silent and doleful it seems!—not the sound of a bird or a cricket can be heard! suppose we have some music." "Agreed," said Smyth; and raising the old Minié, he fired it off over the water. *Sam* followed with three cracks, as fast as they could be got off!

The party in the boat were all, of course, upon their feet in an instant, and we sat smiling at them. Then the concert began—a hundred monkeys could be heard chattering and howling, treble, tenor, and bass, with flats and sharps, with semitones and baritones and falsettos, whilst five hundred at least were scratching, leaping, and vaulting about amongst the branches, and gathering over our heads, in full view, to take a peep at us. We sat in an open place, that they might have a full view of us, and we rose up to show ourselves at full length, that their curiosity might be fully gratified. With my opera-glass, which I took from my pocket, I brought all these little inquisitive, bright-eyed faces near enough to shake hands, and had the most curious view of them. I never before knew the cleanliness, the grace, and beauty of these wonderful creatures until I saw them in that way, in their native element and unrestrained movements. Where on earth those creatures gathered from in so short a time, in such numbers, it was impossible to conceive; and they were still coming. Like pigeons, they sat in rows upon the limbs, and even were in some places piled on each other's back, and all gazing at us.

To give the inquisitive multitude a fair illustration, I fired another shot—and another! and such a scampering I never saw before! in half a minute every animal, and every trace and shadow of them, were out of sight; nor did they come near us again. The woods were ringing at this time with a hundred voices—"Tsocano! Tsocano! Go on, John!" came from the tops of the highest trees; the hideous roar of a tiger was heard, not far off, and when done, another answered on the other side of the river. The howling monkeys, who only open their throats at night, gave us a strain or two; the white swans were piping in the distance, and the quacking ducks and geese were passing to and fro in flocks up and down the river. The gabbling parrots and parroquets and cockatoos, with their long, and red, and blue tails, were creeping out and hanging on to the outer branches to get a look at what was going on.

So far we heard but the notes of alarm, of fear, and they were soon done—there was little music in these. But then the songsters came—the joyous, merry pipers (when fear was over, and curiosity not satisfied); they now began to venture out from the thickets and the towering forests, and in hundreds were seen sailing over the river from their shady retreats in the copses and little groves on the hillsides, and lighting on the trees around us. Curious and inquisitive little strangers, with your red breasts and throats, your white cockades, your blue jackets and purple tufts, and piercing eyes, and turning heads, I wish I knew your hundred names!

All yet were silent. As we sat still, gazing and ogling were the first impulses—they with their piercing little sharp eyes, and I with my opera lens; but a chirp or two opened the concert. One song brought on another, and another, as an announcement that danger was passed; and no aviary that ever was heard could produce such a concert and such a chorus of sweet sounds as was here presented.

They swelled their little throats to the highest possible key in the din of their concert; and after it gradually died away, some hangers-on gave duets, and others solos, each little warbler hopping nearer and nearer to

42

us, and dropping his last notes with a bow of the head and a "There, there! they *can't* beat that!—mine is certainly the most beautiful!"

"But hark!" said I, "Smyth; music is contagious." The crickets and grasshoppers were singing in the grass, and at length, "P-r-r-out! p-r-r-out!" said a huge frog, whose snout and ears were raised a little above the surface of the water, amongst the water-lilies and rushes near the shore; and then, another, a smaller one, "Peut! Peut!" and another, a big fellow, "El-der-gin! el-der-gin!" and then a terrible bull-frog, his mouth the size of the clasp of a lady's reticule, "Kr-r-r-ow! kr-r-r-ow!" and at least five thousand more, on both sides of the river; for, by the custom of frogs, when one sings, all must join in, large and small, no matter what time of day or night, as far as their voices can be heard by each other.

All animals and birds sing in this country—it is the land of song. Music is the language of happiness and enjoyment!—what a happy community this!

Now for the "pigs." Pigs, in this country, are peccaries, a species of wild hog, resembling, in color and in character, the wild boar of the continent of Europe. They are not more than one-half the size, but have all the ferocity and sagacity of that animal, and are equally pugnacious. An individual one is not able to cope with the strength of a man, but when in groups they are able to tear a man to pieces in a little time.

Immense numbers of these animals are found throughout the whole valley of the Amazon and the Essequibo, living chiefly on the great quantity of mast that falls from various trees. They often run in groups of several hundreds, and unite in terrible conflicts with man or beasts for their own protection.

We had taken our dinner one day on the bank in a large and open forest, when Smyth took his rifle in his hand and said he "was going to take a walk down the river, and see what he could murder." His passion was for shooting; and it seemed to be little matter with him what it was, if he could hear the "old Minié speak" (as he called it), and see his game fall.

He strolled off down the river-bank, and after he had been gone a quarter of an hour or so, I heard the crack of his rifle; and in the half of a minute another—and in the quarter of a minute another!—and after the lapse of two or three minutes he commenced firing again! I began to fear that he had met hostile Indians or some other dangerous

43

enemy, and seizing up my rifle and taking one of the Indians of the boat, with his quiver of poisoned arrows slung, we started for his assistance; at this time the firing stopped, and we heard him calling out at the top of his voice for help. We then ran as fast as we could, and getting near the place, we began to advance with caution, and I at length discovered him standing on the trunk of a fallen tree, the branches of which had lodged against others, preventing it from coming quite to the ground; his rifle was in his left hand, and by the other he was holding on to a branch to balance himself, and underneath and around him a dense mass of some two or three hundred peccaries, with the bristles all standing on their backs, as they were foaming at their mouths and whetting their white tusks and looking up at him.

Smyth saw us approaching, and called out to me to take care of my life. These sagacious little creatures knew, from the direction that he was giving to his voice, that he had help coming in that quarter; and a hundred of them at least began to turn their attention to us, and were starting to come towards us without having seen us, and without our having spoken a word to notify them of our approach.

The only shelter for us was the trunk of a large mora tree, behind which we took our positions. I stood so as to look around the tree, and getting my rifle to bear, and my position to be right for firing, and the Indian with his bow drawn behind me, we waited till the foremost of this phalanx of little warriors came advancing up slowly and whetting their tusks, not having yet seen us. When within some seven or eight rods, I began upon the nearest—and the next—and the next—and having shot down four of the leaders, the sagacious little fellows, seeing their foremost and bravest falling so fast—and thinking perhaps, like the Indians, that this was to last *all day,* they gave a grunt and made a wheel, which seemed to be a signal understood by the whole troop, for in one instant they were all off at full speed, and were soon out of sight; leaving the four I had shot, and some eight or ten of the leaders which Smyth had killed, on the field of battle, when his powder had given out and he was obliged to call for help.

He told me that he had discovered some parts of the group whilst they were scattered about and hunting nuts; and having no idea of their numbers, he had shot one, when the others, from all quarters, gathered around him, and that if he had not luckily found the fallen tree close by him, or that if his foot had slipped after he got on to it, he would have been torn to pieces in a very few minutes.

I had not a doubt of this fact when I saw the manner in which they had cut and marked with their tusks the log on which he had stood, and also the mangled bodies of those he had shot; which, by their custom, they had fallen upon and torn to pieces in their fury.

CHAPTER 4

The Amazon

(CHAPTER XVIII FROM *Life Among the Indians*)

LET US NOW for a while leave beasts, and birds, and reptiles for a subject of far greater interest and importance. The studies of my wanderings have been the looks, condition, character, and customs of *native man;* and these their incidents or accessories merely. These are not without their interest and importance, however, but they can be seen in the wilderness alive, and in our museums, for hundreds of years to come, as well as now; but native man, with his modes, is soon to disappear from the American forests, and not even his skin will be found in our museums.

The hand of his fellow-man is everywhere raised against him, whilst the grizzly bears, the tigers, and the hyenas are allowed to live—and why? because he is unfortunately a land-owner, and has the means to pay for rum and whiskey.

Much the same system of traffic and dissipation, which I have before alluded to, is destroying these poor people in this country, but without the devastation which it carries with it in some parts of North America; because there are no immigrating masses here to push forward a frontier so rapidly, dispossessing the Indians of their country.

A sort of civilization has been longer established in this country, and more generally and more gradually infused amongst the savage races, without so completely destroying them. By this process, a greater mixture of races and languages has been produced; and though there is little high civilization, and seldom extinction, there is yet an immense existence of demi-races, and very seldom full-bloods. The true original looks and customs of the Indians in this country are therefore, most generally, very difficult to see.

From the warmth of the climate, the Indians in these regions, semi-civilized or not, are almost too naked to paint. Their character and customs are nevertheless equally full of interest; and in this country, as in North America, I have aimed at gathering everything pertaining to a full and just account of them. In doing this, the reader can imagine that I have had many long and tedious journeys by land and by water; some of which have been already briefly told, and most of the others (though we may journey together yet a little further) must be left for a larger book.

We were at Pará? Pará is a large and flourishing commercial town, of forty or fifty thousand inhabitants, on the south side of the great estuary of the Amazon, and one hundred miles from the coast of the sea.

There are the remnants of several Indian tribes living around Pará, who bring into its market fish and oysters, and fruits of fifty kinds, from the palms and other trees and shrubs of the forests. In the dense and lofty forests of palms on the islands and shores between Pará and the ocean, we see again, as we saw at the mouth of the Orinoko, the Canoe Indians living in "nests" built in the trees. These constructions, though exceedingly rude, are nevertheless comfortable and secure for the people who live in them, and whose modes in many other respects are equally curious.

These are very properly called Canoe Indians, for they live exclusively on fish and oysters, and to obtain them, and to travel anywhere and on any errand whatever, they must necessarily be in their canoes. They cannot step out of their houses, except into their canoes. In their canoes they dart through the dense forests of lofty palms with a swiftness which is almost incredible. They never travel in any other way, and very many of them seldom set their feet upon the dry land.

These stupendous forests of palms (called *miriti*) constitute one of the curiosities of the Amazon, and perhaps of the world. Hundreds, and thousands, and tens of thousands of acres around the mouths of the Amazon and the Orinoko are completely covered and shaded by these noble trees; their trunks, almost perfectly straight and smooth, without knot or limb, rise like the columns of some lofty temple to the height of one hundred or more feet, and then throw out their graceful branches, somewhat in the form of an umbrella, which are interlaced together so thick that the sun seldom shines through them.

At low tide these trees may be said to be rising out of the mud, and at high tide they are rising out of the water. They are so far from the sea that no waves of the ocean, or even of the river, reach them, and the water of the rising tide creeps in and around them as quietly and unruffled as if it came out of the ground, and actually has that appearance.

At low tide the Indian's canoe lies in the mud, and he is as sure to be lying, and eating, and drinking or sleeping in his wigwam of sticks and leaves. But when the tide rises, it lifts his canoe to the steps of his wigwam, when, with his gay red feathers in his head and his varicolored paddle in his hand, his nets, his spears, and his black-headed little pappooses in his canoe, he steps into it and darts off amidst the myriad columns of this mighty temple, echoing and re-echoing the happy notes of his song as he glides, and those of the thousand songsters above his head and around him.

How curious it is that a part of mankind should build their houses in the trees!—these *are,* strictly speaking, odd people. You will recollect I told you [in an earlier book] of the *Skin-builders,* the *Dirt-builders,* the *Bark-builders,* the *Grass-builders,* and the *Timber-builders,* and here we have the *Nest-builders!* and what sort of builders shall we have next? We shall see.

In the neighborhood of Pará, on the Rios Trocantins and Zingu, I visited a dozen or more tribes, and then, on a steamer, started to see others. Lay your map of South America on the table, and see what I had before me! look at the rivers, and realize their lengths. I took the largest first, the Amazon—rode to Tabatinga, 1,800 miles, the western boundary of Brazil; and from that, between Peru and Equador, to Nauta, 350 miles, at the mouth of the Yucayali, and yet 400 miles further, and leaving the steamer, crossed the Andes to Lima, the most beautiful city in the world!

But this is travelling too fast again. I passed several things on the way, and we will go back and take a look at them.

From Pará, I started on the steamer *Marajo,* the second or third voyage she had made, and the first steamer that ever ascended the river. There were on board several Portuguese gentlemen from Rio de Janeiro, and several others from Pará, with their families; forming together a very pleasing and agreeable travelling party no doubt, if one could have spoken their language.

The first day at noon brought us into the bay of the Amazon, with its hundred islands; and the second, to Santarem, at the head of tide-water. Above this we began to stem the current, and, for the first time, had evidence that we were ascending a river; and for the first time, also, that we were fully sensible of the majesty and grandeur of its movement.

I had a few months before crept and drifted along its shores and sluices in a humble craft, from the mouth of the Trombutas, without being able to see or to understand it. But we were now lifted upon the deck of a steamer, and stemming the current and viewing it on both sides at once, which gave me some basis for its measurement.

From the middle of the river, the distance was so great that the forests on either shore settled into monotony and tameness; but with my knowledge of their actual grandeur, this only served to inspire me with the real magnitude and magnificence of the sweeping current intervening. But when the vessel was running near the shore, which was generally the case, to evade the strength of the current, no pen or pencil can describe the gorgeousness and richness of the overhanging and reflected forests that changed every moment as we passed.

Every length of the boat was in itself a picture to stop and look at; but why stop? for the coming one was just as beautiful. Conversation was at an end, for exclamations and interjections took its place. A never ending mass of green, of yellow, white, and pink and red; and that without monotony, unless, from the never ending changes, *change* itself became monotony!

Here the rounded tops of the lofty trees, some white, some pink with blossoms, were crowding out their flowery heads amongst the mass of green and extending their long branches down quite into the river, and a hundred twisting vines hung in knots and clumps, and festoons of parasitic flowers were jetting down from the tops of the higher trees— the overhanging, gorgeous, rolling, and impenetrable mass, sweeping the sides of the boat as we passed, seemed to be tumbling down upon us, while they hid from our view the lofty bank on which their stately trunks were standing.

And *there,* an opening! We see the high and sloping bank, spangled to the water's edge, and into it, with pink and purple flowers—and the graceful palmettoes, like a thousand open fans, leaning and bowing around—and above the bank, the straight and lofty trunks of palms and other stately forest trees, like the pillars of some mighty portico, supporting their dome of branches interlocked—and further on, but a part of this, an "upper forest"! The wind has done this. Huge trees have been uprooted, and, tumbling halfway down, have lodged their branches in the crotches of others; falling vegetation has lodged on these until a super-soil has been formed; descending vines have taken root in them and clambered again to their tops, and interwoven and lashed the mass to the encircled trunks and branches; nuts and fruits have fallen on

49

these and taken root, and trees and flowers are growing in a second forest from fifty or sixty feet above the ground!

And do these look like loathsome ruins—like a wreck—like a misfortune? No, they are rounded; they are hidden; they are looped and festooned and embraced with clinging and hanging vines, supporting bouquets of beautiful flowers and fig trees bending with their blossoms and ripened fruit at the same time.

But how gloomy and desolate? Not so. This is Nature's temple; its roof is not tiles nor slates, but a bed of flowers! and man is its tenant. Blue curls of smoke are seen floating around amongst the trees, and from underneath, a hundred pair of black and sparkling eyes from behind the logs and trees, and a dozen or two of the bravest and boldest of both sexes, as naked and as thoughtless as Adam and Eve (and from appearance as happy), come leaping to the brink of the bank, to salute us as we pass.

Man's abode! how splendid, how grand, how cheap, and how comfortable! Man wants but a roof in this country; the open air must be around him. How splendid a roof he has here bespangled with flowers and dropping ambrosia! and how delicious the air that he breathes, rustling through the blossoms and spices with which he is encompassed.

We see hundreds of canoes as we pass on, gliding along the shores in different directions, filled with red heads and red shoulders, but when we get near them, they dart into the mass of overhanging branches and leaves and disappear in an instant. Sometimes their villages stand upon the bank, and in hundreds they are yelling and saluting us as we are puffing along by them.

They have no fears; they are at a safe distance; but my little opera-glass brings them near enough to shake hands. What a beautiful sight! Men and women, wild and simple as Nature made them. It's a long time since; why have they remained so? What gleaming, laughing, happy faces! Oh, that human nature refined were half as happy, and sinned as little!

Thanks! thanks to you, my little opera-glass! the best of all travelling companions, that reveals so much and asks no questions. What do you show and interpret to me on such a voyage? All nature in this country will let me come within rifle-shot, but you move me near enough to shake hands! One day's seat with you, upon the deck of this boat, is worth a week of nights in Her Majesty's Opera House.

The little reader who runs his eye through the pages of this book, and should at any period of his life make a tour to the Trombutas or the Amazon (and I believe there will be such), should by no means forget to take such a companion with him. It is no incumbrance in the pocket, and with it he can converse with animals at a distance; with the birds and the fruits and the bouquets of beautiful flowers in the tree-tops. He can scan the ugly looks of the staring tiger, or the silvery texture of the basking alligators, or the gazing multitudes of painted, streaked, and feathered Indians. He can see the bright eyes of the cunning little monkeys peeping down from the branches of the trees; he can scan the beautiful colors of the tocanos, bowing their heads from the tops of the lofty mora. He can see what he never can see in museums amongst glass eyes and wiry attitudes—the little humming-birds, as they are balanced on their buzzing wings, and glistening in the sun as they are drawing honey from the flowers; and so all the feathered tribe of songsters, straining their little throats, giving aid and expression to their music.

With it he can explore the highest and most unapproachable cliffs and rocks in the Andes, and by lying on his back, may almost imagine himself lifted in the claws of the soaring condor.

Obidos, at the mouth of the Trombutas, is where my friend Smyth and myself first launched out into the broad Amazon—a little Spanish town of 1,500 or 2,000 inhabitants. Our steamer was alongside and moored. Some passengers got out, and others came on board. The inhabitants were all upon the bank, and amongst them several groups of Indians, and all gazing in wonder at us. Here was work for my pencil, and groups of them were booked as I sat upon the deck. And just before the vessel was to start, as I was walking on the deck, a sudden outcry was raised amongst the squaws and then amongst the men, and all eyes were upon me, and many hands extended towards me.

It seems that amongst the crowd were a number of the Indians, men and women, whom Smyth and I had joined in the turtle-hunt six months before,[1] who now were down in their canoes, on a visit to Obidos, and who, having recognized me, were calling to me to come ashore and shake hands with them. This compliment I could not resist, nor could I deny *myself* the pleasure of shaking hands with these good creatures— these "Amazons"—these "Cannibals" of the Trombutas.

I leaped ashore, to the great surprise of all the passengers, and of the Captain also, and the boat delaying a little, gave me time for the

[1] Not reprinted here.—EDITOR'S NOTE.

51

interview. No one can imagine the pleasure which these poor people felt in discovering me and then seeing me come ashore to shake hands with them. I told them I was glad to see them, and not now being quite so poor as I was when I was among them, if the Captain would wait for me a few minutes, I would make them some little presents.

I explained my views to the Captain, and he granted me the time. I opened a box in my luggage, and supplying my pockets with a quantity of knives, fish-hooks, beads, &c., which I had laid in for such occasions, I went ashore and distributed them, when several of the men embraced me in their arms, and all, both men and women, shook me by the hand, wishing me farewell.

This scene excited the sympathies of the ladies and other passengers on board, who threw them many presents, in money and other things.

The boat was ordered to go ahead, and just as the wheels began to revolve, a little lad ran to the water's edge and handed to the Captain, who was standing on the wheel-house, a beautiful *"blow-gun,"* and made signs for him to hand it to me.

Oh, how pleasing such meetings are to me! how I love to feel the gladdened souls of native men, moved by natural, human impulse, uninfluenced by *fashion* or a *motive!* Mine, I *know,* has something native remaining in it yet.

Ten days from Pará brought us to Nauta, having passed some fifteen or twenty small Spanish towns and missions, and at least one hundred encampments and groups of Indians on the islands and shores, who seemed to have got notice in some way of our approach, and had assembled to take a look at the boat and salute it. They stared at us with uplifted hands, and raised their voices to the highest pitch, but fired no guns, for as yet they neither have them nor know the use of them.

From the immense numbers of Indians we saw gathered on the banks, it would seem as if the country was swarming with human inhabitants, while in the whole distance these interminable forests and shores showed us not a monkey or a parrot, nor a tiger! The former were led to the river-shore, no doubt, in the extraordinary numbers which we saw, by feelings of curiosity; whilst the latter, from fear at the puffing and blowing of the steamer, hid themselves in the forests in silence as we passed; but no doubt a grand chorus was constantly raised behind us after we had got by.

It is estimated that there are over one hundred tribes, speaking different languages, on the shores of the Amazon, from its rise, at the base of the Andes, to its mouth; and at this point we have probably passed something like three-fourths of them. I could give the names of near one hundred tribes that I have already learned of in the valley of the Amazon, but the list would be of little interest here.

If it be true that there are one hundred tribes on the banks of the Amazon; which I doubt, we may easily get five hundred different names for them, and be ignorant of their own, their real names, at least.

Bands of the same great family or tribe are often improperly called tribes, and have languages very dissimilar, and therefore the endless confusion in classification.

There is a general system of civilization teaching by the Catholic missions throughout all parts of South America, to which all the tribes have had more or less access, and from which they have received more or less instruction in Christianity, in agriculture, and in the Spanish and Portuguese languages.

The soothing and parental manner of the venerable *padres* who conduct these missions is calculated to curb the natural cruelties of the savage, and have had the effect in all parts of that country to cut down the angles that belong to all natural society unaided by the advances of civilization.

These missions are everywhere; and around them, in their vicinity, always more or less extensive settlements of Spanish and Portuguese, called in the Spanish language *Gauchos* (Gautchos), who live by a mixed industry of agriculture and the chase. This population mixes easily with the native races, and with this amalgamation ensues a blending of languages, which is one of the most extraordinary features to be met with in the country; and particularly so on the lower half of the Amazon and its tributaries, and also throughout the whole northern and eastern portions of Brazil, where the three languages—the Spanish, the Portuguese, and Indian languages—are all about equally mixed, and in such a way as sometimes to appear the most laughably droll and ridiculous, and at others the most absurd and inexplicable of all jargons on earth.

This language, which they call *"Lingua-geral,"* is spoken by all—by Spaniards, by Portuguese, and by the Indians much alike; and though it no doubt is a handy language for the country, it is exceedingly perplexing and embarrassing for the traveller, who may think that his Spanish and his French which he has learned for the occasion are going to answer him through the country. He must employ an interpreter or learn to speak the Lingua-geral, or be as mum as if he were in the deserts of Siberia.

George Catlin

At Tabatinga, eighteen hundred miles above Pará, two steamers were building by Americans, who had brought the whole machinery from the United States complete and ready to be put in. These vessels were being built to run on the Amazon, and a few years will no doubt show us a fleet of these and other vessels at that place, which will be the great commercial depôt of western Brazil and eastern Peru and Equador.

In the vicinity of Nauta are a great many Indian tribes, amongst which are the *Zeberos*—the *Urarinas*—the *Tambos*—the *Peebas*—the *Turantinis*—the *Connibos*—the *Sepibos*—the *Chetibos*—the *Sensis*—the *Remos*—the *Amahovacs*—the *Antis*—the *Siriniris*—the *Tuirenes*—the *Huachipasis*—the *Pacapacuris,* and at least a dozen others; their languages all dialectic, and their physiological traits and color altogether proving them to be only bands or sections of one great family, and that family only the fusion, perhaps, of *Ando-Peruvian* and *Guarani.*

It would be next to impossible for any stranger to trace the Amazon from its mouth to its true source in the space of his lifetime, and it would be ten times more difficult to trace the savage races in South America, through all their displacements and migrations, to their true fountain.

Of the South American tribes there are none nearer approaching to their primitive state than many of the tribes about the heads of the Amazon, and amongst these I spent some time. They have forests full of game and rivers full of fish, and all the varieties of palms with their various kinds of fruit; and also the immense plains or *pampas,* stocked with wild horses and wild cattle for food, and for their skins and hair, which are articles of commerce with them; and from these combined advantages they insure an easy and independent living, and have therefore the fewest inducements to adopt civilized modes.

CHAPTER 5

Pampa del Sacramento

(CHAPTER XIX FROM *Life Among the Indians*)

A RIDE ACROSS THE *Pampa del Sacramento,* and a passage of the Yucayali in a canoe, afforded me some of the loveliest views of the country I ever beheld, and some of the most interesting visits I have ever made to Indian tribes; the shores of the Yucayali are not unlike those of the Trombutas—the animals, the birds, the trees, the flowers, everything the same.

The *Connibos,* of some two or three thousand; the *Sepibos,* of three thousand; the *Chetibos,* of an equal number, and the *Sensis,* inhabit its shores. These tribes are all much alike, and their languages strongly resemble each other, yet they are constantly at war, though the river only separates them.

The Connibos live upon the borders of the pampa, but build their villages in the edge of the forest. A village generally consists of but one house—but a curious house it is; it is a *shed,* and sometimes thirty or forty rods in length, constructed of posts set in the ground, to the tops of which are fastened horizontal timbers supporting a roof most curiously and even beautifully thatched with palm-leaves. Houses in this country, I have said, have no sides, no walls, except those of the Gautchos, and the sides and partitions in those can be perforated with the finger, as they are but a web of palm-leaves.

The Connibo wigwam, or shed, contains sometimes several hundreds of persons, and the families are separated only by a hanging screen or partition made of palm-leaves suspended across the shed. Like all the tribes in the valley of the Amazon, they sleep in hammocks slung between the posts of their sheds, when at home; and when travelling, between trees, or stakes driven into the ground. . . .

The *Sepibos* and *Chetibos,* though only separated from the *Connibos* by the river, have no communication with them except in warfare, and that is very seldom; each confining themselves in their canoes to their own shore; and their boundary line being so definitely established, it is less often passed over than those of tribes who have only an ideal line of division, which is most generally the case.

The *Chetibos* and *Sepibos* may properly be said to be Canoe Indians, their country being a dense and impenetrable forest, throwing them, from necessity, upon the river for subsistence and the means of travelling; and in their narrow and light little dug-out canoes, they are indeed one of the prodigies of the world. When they all strike with their paddles at once, they may almost be said to *bound* over the waves. They ascend and descend the foaming rapids which in some places are frightful even to look at, and where they are at times entirely lost to the view from the foaming spray that is rising around them. They descend the Yucayali to Nauta—the Amazon to Tabatinga—to the Barra, and even to Pará and back again, against a strong current for the distance of two thousand miles, in less time and with more ease than they could do it on horseback, provided there were roads.

The *Chetibos* are much like the *Winnebago* and *Menomonie* Indians on the Great Lakes in North America, and if placed by the side of them would scarcely be distinguished from them. Like all the Indians in this country, they wear very little dress. The men always wear a flap or breech-cloth, and the women wear a cotton wrapper that fastens about the waist and extends nearly down to the knees. The necks and wrists of the women are generally hung with a profusion of blue and white beads, which have a pleasing effect, and also, in many instances, brass and silver bands around the ankles and around the head, fastening back the hair.

Both men and women daub and streak their bodies and limbs with red and white and black paint, much in the same way as the North American tribes. In this custom I see but little difference. The *Connibos*, the *Remos*, the *Amahovacs*, and all other tribes on the Yucayali and the upper and lower Amazon, have the same fondness "for dress," which is paint, according to his or her freak or fancy.

The *Pacapacuris*, the *Remos*, the *Antis*, and a dozen other small tribes, and the *Connibos*, who dwell around the skirts of the Pampa del Sacramento, lead a different life from the Canoe Indians I have just mentioned, and in appearance are more like the *Sioux* and *Assinneboines* on the buffalo plains in North America.

Pampa del Sacramento

The Connibos interested me very much. They are one of the most curious, and ingenious, and intelligent tribes I met with. They seemed proud of showing me their mode of manufacturing pottery, which was in itself a curiosity, and in some respects would do credit to any civilized race. They have a place somewhat like a brickyard, on the edge of the prairie near their village, where the women mix and beat the clay with a sort of mallet or paddle, and afterwards mould (or rather model) it into jars for their *turtle butter,* and also into a hundred different and most ingenious forms—into pitchers, cups, pots, and plates; and what is actually astonishing to the beholder, these are all made in the most perfect roundness and proportion, without the aid of a wheel, but by the rotary motion of the hand and adjustment of the fingers and mussel-shells which they use in giving form.

After these are dried in the sun sufficiently, the painting operation begins, which is a curious scene, and performed by another set or artists, and some of them, evidently, with a talent worthy of a better place. With red and yellow, blue and black colors which they extract from vegetables, and brushes they make from a fibrous plant they get amongst the rushes at the river-shore, these colors are laid on and often blended and grouped in forms and figures that exhibit extraordinary taste.

Painted, they are then passed into the hands of old women, whose days for moulding and painting have gone by, but who are still able to gather wood and build fires on the sands at the river-side where they are carried and baked; whilst the old women are tending to them, with hands clenched, they dance in a circle around them, singing and invoking the Evil Spirit not to put his fatal hand upon and break them in the fire. Those that come out without the touch of his fingers (uncracked) are then removed to the village and glazed with a vegetable varnish or resin which they gather from some tree in the forest.

This pottery, though it answers their purpose, is fragile and short-lived, being but a temporary proof against cold liquids and no proof against those that are hot.

The sole weapons of these people, and in fact of most of the neighboring tribes, are bows and arrows, and lances, and blow-guns, all of which are constructed with great ingenuity and used with the most deadly effect. My revolver rifle, therefore, was a great curiosity amongst these, as with the other numerous tribes I had passed. I fired a cylinder of charges at a target to show them the effect, and had the whole tribe as spectators.

George Catlin

After finishing my illustration, a very handsome and diffident young man stepped up to me with a slender rod in his hand of some nine or ten feet in length, and smilingly said that he still believed his gun was equal to mine; it was a beautiful "blow-gun," and slung, not on his back, but under his arm, a short quiver containing about a hundred poisoned arrows. (The reader will recollect that just such a weapon was presented to me on the steamer when we were about leaving Obidos.)

The young man got the interpreter to interpret for him, as he explained the powers of his weapon, and which, until this moment, I had thought that I perfectly understood. He showed me that he had a hundred arrows in his quiver, and of course so many shots ready to make; and showed me by his motions with it that he could throw twenty of them in a minute, and that without the least noise, and without even being discovered by his enemy whose ranks he would be thinning, or without frightening the animals or birds who were falling by them, and the accuracy of his aim, and the certainty of death to whatever living being they touched!

This tube was about the size of an ordinary man's thumb, and the orifice large enough to admit the end of the little finger. It was made of two small palms, one within the other, in order to protect it from warping. This species of palm is only procured in certain parts of that country, of the proper dimensions and straightness to form those wonderful weapons. They are manufactured most generally, and the most extensively, by the *Maycas* and *Zeberos* tribes on the Amazon, more than two hundred miles from the *Connibos,* and two hundred miles above Nauta; and they are sold to the *Connibos,* as well as the *Sepibos* and all the other tribes in those regions, and also to all the other tribes in those regions, and also to all the tribes of the lower Amazon, and even taken in large quantities to Pará and sold in the market-place. The prices that these blow-pipes command in the country where they are manufactured are from two to three dollars; and on the lower Amazon, at the Barra, at Santarem and Pará, from three to five dollars each.

Opening his quiver, the young man showed and explained to me his deadly arrows, some eight or nine inches in length. Some of them were made of very hard wood, according to the original mode of construction; but the greater and most valuable portion of them were made of knitting-needles, with which they are now supplied by the civilized traders. They are sharpened at the end and feathered with cotton, which just fills the orifice of the tube and steadies the arrow's flight. The arrows are pushed in at the end held to the mouth, and blown through with such force and such precision that they will strike a man's body at sixty yards, or the body of a squirrel or a small bird on the top of the highest tree.

The ends of these arrows, for an inch or more, are dipped into a liquid poison, which seems to be known to most of the tribes in those regions, and which appears to be fatal to all that it touches. This liquid poison dries in a few moments on the point of the arrow, and there is carried for years without the least deterioration. He explained to me that a duck, or parrot, or turkey, penetrated with one of these points, would live but about two minutes; a monkey or peccary would live about ten minutes; and a tiger, a cow, or a man, not over fifteen minutes. Incredible almost as these statements were, I nevertheless am induced to believe, from what I afterwards learned from other abundant information, that they were very near the truth. One thing is certain, that death ensues almost instantaneously when the circulation of the blood conveys the poison to the heart, and it therefore results that the time, instead of being reducible to any exact measure, depends upon the blood-vessels into which the poison is injected. If the arrow enters the jugular vein, for instance, the animal, no matter what size, would have but a moment to live!

The interpreter assured me that neither the bodies of birds or animals killed by these poisoned arrows were injured for eating, and that the greater part of the food of the Indians was procured by them; the poison being a vegetable extract, and the quantity at the same time so exceedingly small that it becomes neutralized, so as not to interfere with digestive action.

I was anxious to witness some experiments made with it, and observing that these people had a number of young peccaries which they were raising for food, I bought one of them by giving the owner a couple of papers of Chinese vermilion, and allowing him the carcass of the pig to eat. He was much pleased with the arrangement, and brought the pig out. I got the young man to aim an arrow at the neck, explaining to him that I wished him to strike the jugular vein, but, missing that, it passed some five or six inches into the neck. The animal made no signs of pain, but stood still, and in two minutes began to reel and stagger, and soon fell to the ground upon its side, and in six minutes from the time the arrow struck it, it was dead!

I was then informed that there was another animal which I might like to kill. An immense rattlesnake had been discovered a few days before near their village, and as their superstitious fears prevent them from killing a rattlesnake, they had made a pen around it by driving a row of stakes, preventing its escape, until they could get an opportunity of sending it on some canoe going down the river, to be thrown overboard, that it might land on the banks of some of their enemies.

We proceeded to the pen, and having excited the reptile to the greatest rage, when it coiled itself up and was ready for a spring, I blew the arrow myself, and striking it about the center of its body, it writhed for a moment, twisting its body into a knot, and in three minutes straightened itself out upon the ground, and on its back, was quite dead!

This might be considered a very fair test of the horrible fatality of this artificial poison; for I have often held the enraged rattlesnake down with a crotched stick until it has turned and bitten itself; and even then, excited to the most venomous pitch, and giving itself several blows, it will live some ten or fifteen minutes.

I bought the young man's blow-gun and his quiver of arrows, and I have procured several others from other tribes, and several sacks of the poison, for experiments on my return, which may lead to curious and possibly important results. How awful and terrific would be the effects of an army of men with such weapons, knowing their powers and skilled in the manner of using them!

This poison is undoubtedly a recent discovery. From the facts that I gathered in this and many other tribes, I learned that anciently the Indians went to war much oftener than they now do; but they then fought with lances and shields and large bows, but since the discovery of this poison for their arrows, they dare not come so near as to use those weapons; and that it had almost put a stop to warfare.

The young Connibo assured me that his tribe had resolved not to use these arrows upon any of their enemies, unless they began to throw poisoned arrows, and, in that case, to be ready to kill every one of them. And to convince me of the cruelty and horror of warfare waged with these weapons, he related to me, as matter of history, much as it seems to partake of the marvellous, that—"Some time after the poison was discovered, and these blow-guns were made, the war parties of two neighboring tribes met in a plain, all armed with these weapons, and their bodies were afterwards discovered where every man was killed on both sides. Getting so near to each other, every man was hit; for each one, after he was hit, had time to strike his enemy, or half a dozen of them before he was dead."

Pampa del Sacramento

Poisoning arrows has been a very ancient custom amongst savage tribes, and no doubt has been practiced for many centuries amongst the South American as well as amongst the North American races, and too generally known and used to be any longer a secret; but the acme of poison, which seems to be that now used on the points of these little darts, I believe to be very different from that used by the same people on the blades of their lances and arrows, and a modern discovery.

This poison is no doubt a vegetable extract, or a compound of vegetable extracts; and though so extensively known and used by the Indian tribes, seems to be by them treasured as a secret so important and so profound as to have, so far, baffled all attempts to obtain it from them. It admits of no chemical analysis which leads to anything, except that it is a vegetable extract. The *vegetable,* and the *mode* of the extract, the analysis does not show.

Amongst the *Macouchi* and other tribes on the Essequibo, in Guiana, I obtained similar blow-guns, and, I believe, the same poison (though the color is different). The Indians there call it *waw-ra-li*. Many travellers, French, English, and German, have made great efforts to obtain the secret, and though some have thought themselves in possession of it, I still very much doubt the fact.

I, like many others, followed the *phantom* a long time, but in vain; and if I had found it, what good would it do? I don't wish to poison anybody! and game enough *"Sam"* and I can always kill without it—powder and ball from Sam are *rank poison.*

Amongst the *Chetibos,* the *Sensis,* and other tribes, I had painted a considerable number of portraits, which surprised them very much, and gained me many compliments and many attentions as a great *medicine man;* and of the *Connibos* I had also painted several portraits, and passed amongst them for a wonderful man; but in the midst of all my success, my *medicine* met with a sudden reverse.

The *Great Medicine,* whom I had heard much of, and who at that time was absent, returned from a tour on the Pampas with a party of young men who had been out with him to visit a neighboring tribe. He was an ill-looking, surly, wrinkled-up old gentleman. Of myself and my works he soon had a view, and from his people, no doubt, a marvellous account. He soon had his face painted black, and was parading about with his rattle in his hand, and singing a doleful ditty—his death-song, I was told; telling his people "this wouldn't do—that it was very fortunate for them that he had arrived just as he had—that here was

61

something, to be sure, very wonderful, but that it would do them no good."

"These things," said he, "are great mystery; but there you are, my friends, with your eyes open all night—they never shut; this is all wrong, and you are very foolish to allow it. You never will be happy afterwards if you allow these things to be always awake in the night. My friends, this is only a cunning way this man has to get your skins; and the next thing, they will have glass eyes, and be placed amongst the skins of the wild beasts and birds and snakes! Don't hurt this man—that is my advice; but he is a 'bug-catcher and a monkey-skinner'!"[1]

One can easily see the trouble that was here brewing for me, and easily imagine, also, how quickly I lost caste from the preaching of this infallible *oracle* of the tribe, and how unavoidable and irrevocable was the command when I was informed that my operations must cease, and the portraits which I had made all came to me, and told me they would rather have them destroyed, for if I took them away, they might have some trouble. I told them we would let them remain over another night, which would give them time to think more about it (give my pictures more time to dry), and if on the next day they still continued in their resolve, I would destroy them as they desired.

I had yet another motive for this delay—the hope of being able, by a little compliment and flattery, to get the old doctor to change his views and to take up the right side; but in this I entirely failed, almost for the first time in my life. He had been to Pará, or other places, where he had seen the stuffed skins in a museum, with glass eyes; and the poor old fellow had got the idea fixed in his mind that I was gathering skins, and that by this process the skins of his people would find their way there, and soon have glass eyes!

I luckily found in the bank of a little stream some white clay; and the next morning, when the Indians came in with the doctor, I had a good quantity of clay on my palette, mixed with water and some water-colors. I then said, "There are your portraits; I am very sorry that you don't let me have them to show to my friends amongst the white people; but you have resolved to have them destroyed. There are three ways—you may burn them! or you may drown them! or you may shoot them! You can destroy them in your own way. Your *medicine man,* who has

[1] A term of reproach which they apply to naturalists and other scientific men, who they often see making collections of natural history.

frightened you about them, can tell you, most likely, which way will be the *least dangerous!*"

The old doctor lit his pipe, and they all sat down and smoked and talked a while, when he informed me that they were a little afraid to do either.

I then said there was another way I had, that of *unpainting* them, from which there could be no possible harm, but it required each one to sit a few minutes for the operation. This seemed to afford them a great relief, and in a few minutes they were all unpainted, covered in with a thick coat of clay, which would perfectly preserve them until I wanted to see them again. All were satisfied. I took my canoe and came off, all good friends. . . .

~~~~~~

The Rio Paraguay and the Rio Uruguay
(CHAPTER VI FROM *Last Rambles*)

DESCRIPTIONS OF LONG VOYAGES in a short book must necessarily be discursive and disjointed; and with jumps like those of kangaroos, they must *leap,* not *creep,* from point to point, that voyage, incidents, and the end of the book may terminate together.

Under this necessity . . . I have had the somewhat painful task of inviting the reader to *imagine* the intervening incidents, which the want of space has often prevented me from narrating. In this dilemma we now are. After a long and interesting voyage—or series of voyages—we are at Rio de Janeiro, in Brazil: a beautiful apron, in front of it. Its foaming and dashing cascade of the Corcovado is a fixture, and, like the rest, an ornament eternal. But what are more beautiful—or, at all events, more exciting and interesting—are its grand, and mighty, and impenetrable forests, and rivers, and swamps, and mosquitoes, and fireflies, and butterflies, and alligators, and tigers, and monkeys, and parrots, and Indians, that lie west and south of it.

Rio, I have said, is a beautiful city; its rocky walls are grand, its Botafogo charming, its Plaza amusing, and its museum; its inhabitants are gay and rich, and its ladies are beautiful; its civilization is of a high and noble cast. But what of all this? why should we stop here? The Bay of Botafogo, and these dark and frowning escarpments of rocks, and the glistening cascade of the Corcovado will be the same a thousand years hence; and the Plaza will be better built, its inhabitants will be more rich, its civilization will be higher; and its ladies, not more beautiful, but there will be more of them. Then why detain us now? We travel to see the *perishable,* not the *eternal.*

These grand and sublime forests which we are to enter soon fall by the axe; these beautiful, crouching, creeping, spotted, and glistening tigers, and the muddy alligators, will soon be seen, with glass eyes, in our museums; these thousands of leaping, vaulting, and peeping monkeys, and chattering parrots and parroquets, and gilded butterflies, and anacondas will be there also; and all those endless clusters and bouquets of wild flowers, and everything else of Nature's blossoming and breathing works, including the wild and frolicsome Indian, who now exultingly smiles as he draws his long and unerring bow amidst the jungle, and paddles his light canoe, are soon to be metamorphosed—to be spoiled, if not obliterated, by the ruthless march of civilization.

Why, then, stop to see the imperishable and the progressive, which can be seen a hundred years hence as well as now? We are of a different caste and a different taste. We travel to see the perishable and the perishing; and let us see them before they fall; let us hie away, then, to Buenos Ayres. There are no Indians, no tigers, no alligators, no anacondas, here. The steamer leaves tomorrow for Buenos Ayres. I'll take this little book along, and my pencils. The Uruguay, with its clear and blue waters, comes in there, and on it, in their light canoes, the tall and handsome *Payaguas,* the *Tobos,* the *Lenguas,* and the *Bocobies,* and the *Botocudos.*

The mighty Paraguay comes rolling along there, also, with the waters of the long Paraná, both rising in the mountains in the center of the empire; and, in the course of 1,800 miles, afford a highway and food for more than fifty tribes of Indians, and their waters and their shores, localities for 50,000 tigers, 150,000 alligators, 1,000,000 monkeys 5,000,000 parrots, tens of thousands of anacondas and rattlesnakes, and, now and then, a boa-constrictor.

What a delightful field have we, then, before us at Buenos Ayres! And yet, not far off, to the south, the *Aucas,* the *Puelches,* the *Auracanos,* the *Patagons* and *Fuegians.* Oh, how inviting and how exciting! I cannot crowd them all into this little book, I am sure of it; but I will abridge when I can, and go on while the paper lasts. . . .

My friend Thomas, in whose house I was made welcome whilst in Buenos Ayres, recommended to me a faithful servant man— José Alzar (pronounced Althar)—whom he had employed for several years and whose native place was Corrientes, some hundreds of miles up the Paraguay, and at the mouth of the Rio Paraná. His knowledge of the country, and of several of the Indian tribes and of their languages, was just the thing for me; and, with José Alzar, I was again soon ready, by steamer and canoes, and without horses, for Indian peregrinations.

I put into Alzar's hands the now famous Minié rifle, first carried on the Essequibo and the Trombutas, as has been described, by my worthy companion Smyth, and afterwards by Caesar, for more than ten thousand miles. I reduced the number of cartoon portraits in the portfolio to about a dozen, and, strapping it on his back, we started on a steamer for Corrientes.

Of Corrientes, which is a large and flourishing town on the right bank of the river, I have little other recollection than that of seeing from the deck of the steamer, before we landed, several groups of tents of Indians lining the shore of the river, above and below the town.

I recollect landing and taking my luggage to an hotel; but my subsequent and stronger impressions were got in the wigwams, to which I was a quick and constant visitor.

One can easily imagine the facilities and the confidence rendered me by my new *employé,* who was now in his native town, and with the Indians of his personal acquaintance around him. Three families of the Payaguas tribe were there, and several tents of the Botocudos, who had made long voyages in their canoes, and were soon to return to their native countries.

The Payaguas, the representatives of a tribe nearly extinct and whose modes were purely primitive, were chiefly naked—both men and women wearing but a "fig-leaf" the width of the palm of one's hand, made of cotton cloth or of bark—and made a new impression upon me, of native man in psysiological development and dignity. Not even the Osages or the Shyennes of North America were equal in stature to them, nor men whom I ever saw in any society. Six feet and nine inches, and six feet and seven inches, and six feet and six inches were the meausurements of the three men of the party, and six feet the measure of a boy of sixteen years.

My interpreter, who had seen the whole of the tribe, assured me that these were about an average of the tribe; and these men told me there were many others taller than themselves. And, until I shall see the Patagons, I shall believe them the tallest race in America. They are Canoe Indians, and, like all of that class, from the constant use of their brachial and pectoral muscles, are broad and muscular in the chest and shoulders, but, in proportion, slight in their legs, from their habitual squatted positions and little use of their nether limbs.

The *Payaguas* live on the right bank of the Paraguay, and have, on the opposite bank, the *Chacos,* a race of horsemen who have extensive prairies for the chase, and consequently, like the prairie Indians of North

America, exhibit a different symmetry in proportions. These two tribes, although always at war with each other and inveterate enemies, have been unable mutually to inflict more than partial injuries on each other—the canoe-men too wise to be caught upon the prairies, and the horsemen unable to contend upon the water.

The Payaguas live chiefly in one long cabin or tent (*tolderia*) in the form of a shed, standing on the bank of the river, of some thirty or forty rods in length, built of upright posts at equal distances, set in the ground, and covered with a curious and beautiful thatching of palm-leaves—a roof merely and no walls, with a curtain of palm-leaves or of rush mats forming a hanging partition between the different families. A community excessively droll, and too closely associated to be otherwise than social and peaceably disposed.

They live principally on fish and turtle, with which the river abounds, which are easily taken and at all seasons of the year without the slightest danger of default.

The Botocudos, who come from near the sources of the Uruguay, are quite a different race in appearance and in language; the remnants of a warlike and numerous tribe, recently reduced to a few hundreds by those universal pests of the American Indians—rum and whiskey and the smallpox. Of ordinary stature, they are a better-proportioned race than the Payaguas, and with an approach to civilization, are in a measure clad with tunics and ceintures of cotton cloth, which they barter for with the border traders.

Both the Botocudos and Payaguas wear the block of wood in the under-lip as an ornament, like the Nayas Indians of Queen Charlotte's, in North America, already spoken of. How surprising this fact! that, on the northwest coast of North America and on the southeast coast of South America, almost the exact antipodes of each other, the same peculiar and unaccountable custom should be practiced by Indian tribes, in whose languages there are not two words resembling, and who have no knowledge of each other. Such striking facts should be preserved and not lost, as they may yet have a deserved influence in determining ultimately the migration and distribution of races. . . .

Who can imagine, who can understand, but myself, the astonishment and also the amusement which my portfolio produced amongst these poor people, when I showed them a couple of portraits of the Nayas Indians, with the block in their under-lips, whom, as I told them, I had recently visited, and who were at least three hundred days' march (their only mode of computing long distances) from them, and also on the exact opposite side of the earth, which was round—a new idea to them!

What a pity poor Caesar lost this! By the portrait which I showed them, I explained also that the custom of slitting and elongating the ears, and wearing in them oval blocks of wood, was precisely the same, when a chief of the party pronounced them "brothers," and a facetious old *medicine man,* with his head painted white, disposed to be witty, observed that he thought "the Nayas Indians were very *distant* relations."

By going to my hotel and opening my luggage, I was able to return in a little time to these astonished people, with three of the blocks which I had brought from the Nayas tribe, and which were polished by long use. At the sight of these, which they could take in their hands, they seemed to draw more practical proof, and all the men set up a terrific howl, started by the medicine man, whilst the women covered their mouths with both hands. This, my interpreter told me, was their mode of recording a truth, an *established, proved* fact, which no one was allowed afterwards to deny. A *recorded fact.*

I explained to them the slight difference in the shape of the blocks—those of the Nayas being of an oval form, and concave on the upper and lower sides, and grooved around the rim, whilst those of the Payaguas and Botocudos were round, and both surfaces and the rim perfectly plane.

The chief replied to this, that he could recollect perfectly well when the Payaguas shaped their blocks in the same manner as the Nayas; but, for the greater facility of slipping them in and out and also to save the labour of excavating them, for which their tools were very bad, they changed their shapes to what they now are. On inquiring what their object was in wearing such things in the lip and in the ear, I met at once some difficulty, which seemed to be raised by the fidgety old *medicine man*. He seemed to meet the inquiry with some suspicion, or to treat it, at least, as he suggested, as a thing which I ought to have learned from my friends, the *Nayas,* "on the other side of the world"—a queer thing running still in his head; which, as I learned through the interpreter, had led him to doubt, in some measure, my strict sanity.

The chief, however, took a different view of the affair, and gave me in a very few words, as well as he could, an answer to my inquiries. He said, in the first place, he believed the reason why the custom was practiced was that their ancestors had practiced it before them; that he had always thought it a very foolish practice, and, as it was chiefly confined to the women, it was not likely to do any harm; that the women seemed to think it improved their appearance, and that, in such things, the men generally let the women have their own way.

He said, there was now and then a man to be seen with the block in his lip, but that in such cases it only got him the name of "old woman." The men of his tribe, he said, all have the under-lip pierced, so as to wear ornaments of various kinds. "This we can't avoid," said he, "for it is done by our mothers when we are infants, and under their sole control; and there are many men in our tribe whose ears and lips have been thus cut, and who never have worn an ornament of any kind in them; and I think it is much the best way."

In speaking of this strange custom amongst the Nayas Indians of British Columbia, I described the manner in which the orifice in the lip was produced, as well as the mode of slitting and elongating their ears, by wearing weights in them, and the mode seems to be precisely the same here.

After having expressed my surprise at finding two peoples, on opposite sides of the globe, practicing alike this unaccountable custom, it is not less surprising that the Rev. Dr. Livingstone should have found a native tribe in the center of Africa wearing blocks exactly similar in shape and dimensions in the *upper-lip,* and called by the natives, *Pé-lé-lé* (pronounced *Pay-lay-lay*).

From his description, the blocks are from one and one-half to two inches in diameter, and the modes of perforating the lip in childhood and increasing the size of the blocks as the wearer advances in age are the same as I have described above; and he adds that the only object for which they are worn, as far as he could learn, was that of ornament.

Now, if, in my eccentric peregrinations, I should stumble on to a tribe, or meet an individual Indian lady, ingenious enough to have united the two—wearing a block both in the upper- and the under-lip—what a beautiful and useful improvement it would be, and what a wonderful addition to the honorable discoveries of my roving life—*a double Pay-lay-lay!* The very thought of its being a possibility ahead of me stimulates me, and Alzar and I will move on.

A sort of barge, not unlike the keel-boats of the Missouri, propelled by eight oars, and freighted, not unlike the crafts of that river, with stuffs and hardware, &c. (and, no doubt, in the bottom of the hold, with rum and whiskey), was starting for the upper waters of the Paraná: and Alzar agreeing to handle an oar, and myself to lend a hand in rapid water, got us an agreeable and amusing passage to the mouth of the

Iguazu River—a distance of five hundred miles—from which point we designed to cross the country to the upper waters of the Uruguay, and descend that river to Buenos Ayres, visiting many tribes of Indians on its banks, and killing some of the black tigers that fatten on the peccaries and soft-shelled turtles that abound along its shores.

Alzar, with these boatmen, was at home; and his acquaintance with them and their modes of life made the boat, though a rough one, an agreeable home for me.

I had promised him, at the end of our campaign, in addition to his monthly wages, to leave him, as a present, the Minié rifle; and one can imagine better than I can describe it the infinite pleasure he was taking in cleaning, polishing, and handling it, and "heaving his lead ashore," as Smyth used to do on the banks of the Trombutas and Essequibo. Alligators, peccaries, swans, wild geese, and ducks were constantly marks for him; and his long and deadly shots were not only amusement, but astonishment for his comrades, who never before had seen a Minié rifle, or even dreamed of its long range and accuracy.

The high and perpendicular walls of red sandstone and overtowering forest of lofty trees, alternating from one side to the other and fronted by islands, and the opposite shore covered with forests of orange and wild peach trees, bending down with their yellow and red fruit, and interspersed and interwoven with the deep green of rhododendrons and the massive purple of thorn blossoms, presented a picture as new to me as if the river and mountain scenes of my former voyages I had passed blindfolded.

"Sam"—a name not made known even to Alzar as yet—"Sam Colt," a six-shot carabine, made expressly for me by my old friend Colonel Colt, and which has answered to the nick-name of "Sam" in my former travels, had been so far under cover; but the constant flapping of wings about and over us, and the total nothingness else for me to do, brought it out, and a new excitment and a new astonishment amongst the boatmen, who had barely heard the word *"revolver"* pronounced, but never in those days had had the chance of seeing one.

But why should I spend time and space here, with the thousands of incidents that took place on this beautiful river? We have a long journey before us, Indians in abundance, and, perhaps, a double *Pay-lay-lay;* and, getting towards the end of my little book, I may have yet to strike out the fifty last pages that have been written. One thing, however; by the way, rowing against the stream, we saw few tigers—not even their heads—for, at the grunting of our boatmen and the noise of their oars, they lowered themselves in the weeds, and peccaries stood in the shade as we passed; but the wild-fowl, unused to the sound of a gun, sufficient for our larder, I daily seduced with "Sam," from my comfortable seat— a keg—which made me a sort of "figure-head" in the bow of the boat.

Rapids became frequent, and laborious, and tedious, and were said to be more so ahead of us, and the sun insupportably hot; and, before our five hundred miles were finished, we were at Candeloria, a small town on the east bank of the river, where our trading companions had business to do, and an encampment of Botocudos promised work for me, and Alzar and I halted. After a couple of days, our trading companions continued on their course, and we got conveyed across the *"Entre Rios"* mountain to the small village and mission of Conception, on the upper waters of the Uruguay.

Alzar renewed old acquaintances there, and with the "old Minié" in his hands and the portfolio of Indian portraits on his back, and the tact and facetiae of a son of a Portuguese father and a Creole mother, one can easily imagine rapidly gaining new ones, and raising a sort of *furore* in the peaceable and silent little village into which we had entered.

No Indians were there, and after sleeping two days ahead, whilst Alzar was stipulating for a "dug-out" canoe, and laying in salt meat, coffee, sugar, salt, &c., for our voyage down the river, I stepped with him into our lazy, ugly, but solid and steady little craft, in which he had seated a stout and first-rate paddler of his old acquaintance, who was wanting to go to Buenos Ayres, and was willing and glad of the chance if he could be allowed to "work his passage."

To this lucky occurrence there was no objection; and with three good paddles and three good paddlers (not peddlers) from *Conception*—a very good starting-point—we started off.

To go down stream in a solid and dry canoe, in such a climate, and on so clear and beautiful a river, with hard biscuits enough, and coffee, and sugar, and salt, and a few pounds of salt pork for cooking, and plenty of powder and ball and fishing-tackle, is one of the delightful things in the world. To paddle or to sleep, as we choose, we still go on, and the stillness with which we can travel brings us within pistol-shot, if we wish it, of the staring tigers, whose heads are above the grass and weeds on the bank.

As Smyth and I had been tiger-shooters on the Trombutas, so Alzar and I, with the same weapons, were tiger-slayers on the shores of the Uruguay. And why not? It costs nothing, no apprenticeship is necessary; no courage, or rashness or recklessness is called into question; no great skill in shooting is requisite, for they hold their heads perfectly still—there is a beautiful mark in the center of their foreheads, the right spot exactly, where the black lines radiate—the smooth current does not in the least interfere with our range, and brings us within fifty paces if we desire it.

The whole cost, therefore, is the price of a conical ball and a charge of powder. And for these, if the animal be fat, which is generally the case, the tail itself pays a hundred times over, and leaves us the skin, which is worth twenty dollars.

"A tiger's tail, ha! You eat a tiger's tail?"

Yes, to be sure, a tiger's tail; but it cannot be cooked in a kitchen—it would be useless to try it. It must be bandaged in the leaves of the wild cabbage (or *wapsipinnican*), and roasted under the embers of a camp fire, on the ground. Nothing that ever was cooked exceeds it in deliciousness of flavor and pleasure of digestion. These often weigh some six or eight pounds, and an evidence that they are by the Indians considered the choicest of food is, that, in my South American travels, I have met at least a dozen Indians of the highest rank surnamed the *"Tiger's Tail,"* from some peculiar excellence; and I have myself twice received this high and flattering distinction from these poor people, who have hearts, but no decorations, to give.

Like the Rio Trombutas, the banks of this beautiful river are chiefly covered with dense and magnificent forests, abounding in monkeys and parrots, and peccaries and tigers, and the bed of the stream, from their emptied shells on the beach, would seem to be paved with soft-shelled turtles. Fish of many kinds and of delicious flavor, and for the names of which I was obliged to appeal to Alzar, were constantly raised by our trolling lines. And ducks and geese—and swans and pelicans if we wanted them—were constantly at our service, and an easy prey; and the islands of the lower half of the river, like those of the Paraná, covered with oranges and wild peaches of delicious flavor.

We generally slept on islands, for on them tigers more seldom walk, and rattlesnakes generally fail to reach them; but on these, as on the main shore, like the islands and shores of the Missouri and the Amazon, those invulnerable and unconquerable pests, as universal and as omnipresent in that country as the air itself, the relentless mosquitoes, were always at war with us as soon as the sun was down.

The Rio Paraguay and the Rio Uruguay

On the shore at that time it was necessary to be, to boil the pot and cook our food, but that done, and each one armed with a bunch of bushes, our provisions and culinary articles were taken into our canoe, and pushing into the stream, and whipping off, the flying, whirling cloud was soon ashore; and casting anchor, we had till ten o'clock, or thereabouts, a quiet and delightful time to get our first nap in the canoe. At that hour, by some police that these creatures have, and which I never could exactly understand, hungry or not hungry, they are all housed until near sundown of the next day.

So at ten o'clock, or a little after, we always went quietly to the shore and slept—"Where?" Not in hammocks, but in our strong and dry canoe, ready, at a moment's warning, if danger was at hand, to push off upon the boiling current. And if it rained, covering the canoe from stem to stern by an unrolled mat, constructed of palm-leaves by Alzar and his passenger, as we floated along, we were perfectly protected from the entrance of a drop of water. The heaviest thunder-showers pelted us, and poured on to us, but in vain; but against mosquitoes our roof was no proof, for where air comes, in South America, there *will* come (during their daytime) mosquitoes also.

And how strange! What a mysterious order of nature! The billions on billions of millions of these saguiniverous insects created to exist but a few weeks of time, with a taste for blood, and a proboscis for boring and for drawing it through the thickest of hides, and, probably, not one in a hundred millions ever tastes the food they were made to procure and enjoy; and from which, if they are allowed to be gorged by it, they are known to die in a few minutes.

How strange, also, that the beautiful provision of nature, given them for penetrating the skin and drawing the food which nature has indicated for them, should inflict such insupportable pain as completely to defeat their efforts to procure it! No animals of the country allow a mosquito to bite; and man, at the few points where he is exposed, though he often feels the sting, allows the insect no time to draw his blood.

Is it then that here is an order of nature frustrated, or was it the intention of nature that the probosces of these murderous creatures should have been used for a different purpose, and that the cruel and sanguinary use they are making of them is but a wicked perversion of an instrument intended for a different object?

How strange, also, that the proboscis of this insect, which will go through the thickest clothing and the skin of a white man, and even at

73

times through his buckskin leggings, has little or no effect upon the naked Indian, not that it lacks the power or that the blood is not as easily drawn, for the Indian's skin is as soft and as thin as that of a white man.

There have been various theories advanced on this subject. Some have supposed some peculiar quality in the Indian's blood makes it unpalatable to the mosquitoes. And others have thought that the Indians had some oil or drug which they rubbed over their bodies and limbs as a protection; but it is more probable that the constant smoke they live in, and which mosquitoes always avoid, forms a surface on the skin repugnant to the olfactory nerves of the insect.

The Indians of South America, and particularly those of the Amazon, sleep under sheds, in the open air, unmolested by mosquitoes, where a white man, naked, could not possibly exist one hour; not loss of blood but inflammation would be the death of him. And if the whole human (civilized) race of the globe were spread over the valley of the Amazon and its tributaries, and exposed in the same way, one day, from sundown to ten o'clock at night, would end the whole of them.

But enough of tigers and mosquitoes. I fear I shall have to strike them all out of my little book before I get through, for want of space. We are travelling with the Indians. However, I will venture to insert here the following recipe which I wrote out to please Alzar, and after that we will proceed on our course.

How to Make Mosquito Soup

Recipe.—Descending the Missouri or Arkansas rivers in North America, or the Corontyns of Uruguay in South America, run your canoe ashore in a thick bottom, just at sundown, having filled your kettle about half-full of river water, which is very pure and wholesome. Before landing, however, throw a couple of spoonfuls of salt (or, what is better, if you have it, half-a-pound of salt pork) and one of black pepper into your kettle, and a dozen or so of the small prairie (*cop-o-blos*), a sort of wild onion about the size of a rifle-bullet, and which no travelers in those regions should fail to gather and carry along, as important aids in cooking. In fact, a wild turkey or goose cannot be well roasted without them, as your *stuffing* otherwise will be a complete failure.

All these things be sure to arrange before you land, as it might be difficult to arrange them on shore. Also, before being put on shore, if you be the cook, you should draw a pair of Indian buckskin leggings over your pantaloons, tying them very tight around the ankles. Leave your hat or cap behind, covering the head with a large silk handkerchief or shawl, passing under the chin and covering the face as high as the bridge of the nose, and tie it firmly in the back of the neck: then, with a bunch of willow boughs in your left hand to protect your eyes (keeping it constantly in motion), whilst your right hand is free to work with, a thick pair of buckskin gloves or mittens on your hands, and your pantaloons' pockets turned inside out, your person is tolerable secure from all approach, and you may venture to step ashore, but keeping your body and limbs constantly more or less in motion, which will defeat the aim of such probosces as may occasionally have found their way through the imperfect seams or otherwise vulnerable parts of your dress.

In these heavy-wooded bottoms there is always plenty of dried mulberry limbs and trees, which gather as quick as possible; they burn free, with a light flame and little or no smoke to frighten the mosquitoes away. Set your kettle exactly in the middle of the fire, so that the flame will rise equally all around it, and some twelve or fourteen inches above its rim, which is abundantly high.

The rest of the party, having left you ashore, should then lose no time in paddling into the stream, each one with a bunch of willow boughs whipping ashore all the insects that are attempting to follow the canoe, and leaving you, the cook, alone to "walk the kettle," as one alone concentrates the flying cloud better than several.

The cloud beginning to gather in promising quantities around you, you may commence walking at a regular pace, with short steps, around the fire and boiling kettle; the swarm will follow in your wake, and, to shorten the distance, they will constantly be flying over the fire, when, their wings being singed, they fall into the kettle; and whilst keeping your eyes clear with the willow bough in your left hand, if you aim your blows right, a great many may be thus knocked into the kettle that perhaps are too wary to get their wings burned.

There is no limited time for this operation, nor any end to the arriving multitudes; but you must be guided entirely by the apparent quantity, by lifting off the kettle occasionally, when the boiling ceases, and their carcasses rise in a large clotted mass on the surface, which, with a large wooden spoon, you should throw off, as the fat is all extracted from them, and their bodies should give way to a fresh supply, in order to obtain the requisite richness of the soup.

75

George Catlin

If you observe occasionally a gallinipper or a mosquito-hawk falling in, which is very apt to be the case where they are so confusedly grouped together, all the better, for they are always gorged with a fresh supply of these insects; and if in the desperate struggle any part of your dress should have given way, and the mosquitoes should have succeeded through the breach in getting a few ounces of your blood, no matter—never mind it; it will add to the richness of the soup.

The boiling operation being finished and the canoe called ashore, the kettle should be handled as quickly as possible, and taken on board; all hands, as they are armed each with a bunch of willow boughs, will be able to whip the following swarms ashore as the canoe enters the current, over which they never venture to fly more than a few rods.

The landing on some barren sand-bar which has no vegetation, and consequently is uninhabited by these torments, a comfortable night's rest may be enjoyed; and the soup, when it is sufficiently cooled, and the again-collected mass of their light and emptied carcasses floating on the surface are again skimmed off with the spoon, and some hard biscuits crumbled in, your kettle of "Mosquito Soup" is ready for use.[1]

Geo. Catlin, Rio Uruguay.

From Conception, where we started, to the little town of Santa Cruz, two hundred miles, and from that to San Pedro, on the west bank of the river, two hundred miles farther down, here and in the neighborhood were Indians a-plenty. But *one* incident more—*a tiger story*. It never again can be told, and should be history. I can tell it in a few words, and then we will go on with the Indians.

On the Missouri, with Batiste and Bogard to paddle, I always steered; but on the Uruguay, the steering-paddle was in the hands of Alzar, and I sat about the middle of the canoe, whilst our passenger "working his passage" was near the bow, with his propeller always at work, like a machine.

Some thirty or forty miles below the town of Santa Cruz, and whilst we were passing great quantities of turtle-shells, and half-devoured carcasses of turtles lying on the sandy beach, signs incontrovertible of tigers.

[1] If from any undue prejudice the superior quality of this soup should be questioned, it at least has this advantage over most other kinds, that it costs nothing, and is always at hand, and easily obtained in all the great *western* valleys of *North* and in *all* the valleys of *South* America.

I had charged Alzar to keep a bright look-out, and to let me know if any game was discovered, and I had fallen asleep. In the midst of this (I forget what I was dreaming about), Alzar whispered in my ear—"Señor, there's a beautiful tiger ahead—stands out whole neck and head above the grass!"

Before getting my eyes fairly open, "Slip back," said I, "to your seat inch by inch, and keep your paddle down, and both hands close to the water's edge, and steer the canoe a little in; we are rather too far from the shore."

Before he retreated, he had given me, with his forefinger, the direction, and I was beginning to see the staring, glaring round head of the villain above the grass on the top of the bank.

But why, by the way, should I say "villain"? These poor creatures slay only for food; we kill for amusement, not for food, not for the carcass—and for the *tail,* we sometimes don't even take that. But a "Tiger ahead!" is a poor place for moralizing or sympathizing. "Sam" was in both hands, and, of course, near my cheek! The smoke cleared away. I could see nothing; but both of the men exclaimed—"Dead shot, dead shot! Señor."

I told Alzar to steer the canoe in and put me ashore. He landed me a few rods below where the animal had sat, and advancing along the edge of the stream until I got opposite to the place, I directed him to keep the canoe a little out from the shore, and in front of me, and his rifle up and ready in case of any necessity.

Though my men had seen the animal fall, I took this precaution, as I was about to ascend the bank, of some thirty or forty feet, and covered with tall grass and weeds, under a sort of conviction, from the rather slow fire of my rifle, that I had missed, or only grazed the creature's head, and that it might be lying in the weeds and ready to make a spring upon me; or, if the animal were dead, as my men believed, its mate might be lying by its side and ready to do the same thing for me.

I had five shots left in the cylinders, however, and ready at the instant, and was ready to run all risks of mounting the bank alone, imprudent as it was. The bank was something like thirty feet higher than the river, and from the water's edge rose at an angle of thirty degrees, and was covered with grass and weeds as high nearly as my head. I ascended very slowly, and with my rifle raised; and when near the brink, I was no doubt soonest discovered, being in motion. And, as if shot from a cannon, the beast struck me, its breast meeting the muzzle of my rifle,

77

which was thereby thrown over my shoulder, and quite into the river—and myself backwards and headlong to the water's edge! It was a blow and a rebound; and the animal, at one leap, was out of sight!

I was paralyzed by the shock, and in that condition was taken into the canoe; and might as well have been taken and lugged into the thicket, the helpless prey of my adversary. When consciousness came, beyond the shock, I knew nothing of what had transpired except what my men related to me, nor had I then the slightest recollection of having seen the animal, in its flight, coming upon me, probably from the quantity of weeds between us hiding it from my view.

We got into the stream and floated off, all hands (judiciously, no doubt) agreeing to a drawn battle rather than risk anything further to gratify curiosity.

The animal that I fired at might have fallen dead, as my men still declared, and its mate, lying by, might have sprung upon me; or I might, as I think, from the dampness of my powder, have grazed its head, and brought it, in the manner described, upon me; but, whichever might have been the case, we were quite willing to leave it to tigers to decide.

Whilst exulting in my lucky escape, I began to feel pain in my left arm between the wrist and the elbow and the blood beginning to issue freely from it, I was convinced that the animal, though instantly as it had rebounded, had had a grab at my arm; and getting at it, the incisions of two of its teeth were visible on the upper and one on the opposite side. And, as proof that the creature intended to have taken me along with it, one paw had gone over my left shoulder, and, failing to take me along, had opened my cotton paletot for a considerable distance, and left the furrows of two of its nails in the flesh. My wounds, therefore, like those of a woman's fight, were but scratches and easily dressed, and were quickly forgotten, though the marks of them still remain.

At San Pedro I said we should find Indians, and in it and its vicinity we found plenty of them. The *Tobos,* the *Lenguas,* and the *Bocobies*—small tribes, the survivors from rum, and whiskey, and smallpox, by which the greater portion of those once numerous and warlike people have been swept away.

Of these the *Lenguas* and *Tobos,* which seem to be an amalgam of two tribes, are the most numerous and the most interesting. Their village (*tolderia*) is all in one long shed, standing on the bank of the river, and forty rods in length, and built much like the *tolderia* of the Payaguas, which has been described; and resembling also the sheds of the Connibos and Sepibos, on the Rio Yucayali, in Peru, and already described in [an] earlier [part] of this work. The *people,* also, in their personal appearance and customs, resemble the Connibos enough to be their brothers; and yet they resemble the Botocudos, of which people they are no doubt a part. Like the Botocudos, they wear the block of wood in the lip, and slit and elongate the rims of their ears.

This extraordinary and curious custom, of which I have spoken in former chapters, I had opportunities of more closely examining in this tribe, and which examinations will justify a few further remarks in this place. The greater portion of the tribe have long since abandoned so useless and so ridiculous a custom, and others still study eccentricity by keeping it up.

In several instances I was permitted to examine closely the orifice in the lip, when the block was not in, and to my surprise, in each instance, such is the elasticity and contraction of the lip, that from the moment a round block of wood, of two inches in diameter, was taken out, the lip contracts to its natural shape and proportions, and the orifice is so perfectly closed that not even the saliva from the mouth escapes through it; and to the passing spectator the mark of it is scarcely visible in the face.

From one of their medicine men, whose portrait I was painting, with a block in his lip, I got many curious particulars relating to the custom, and amongst others, he put his finger on several holes in his cheeks, from which he told me he suspended strings of beads and feathers, and other ornaments, on certain occasions, in their dances, masquerades, &c. And I pointed to one that I discovered in his *upper*-lip—

"Yes," said he, pulling down the lip and running his thumb through it, "and I have sometimes worn the block in it."

I had just before bartered for a couple of these blocks, which I had at the moment in my pocket; and handing him one of them, he knew my object, and in an instant it was adjusted in his upper-lip! Here it was that I *"stumbled* on a *double pay-lay-lay."* It made a great laugh amongst the Indian bystanders, which showed that it was an eccentricity of the moment, not a custom. The droll old doctor found, however, that he could talk better with the two than he could with the one only, and the clacking and clattering sounds of his wooden lips, and the curious grimaces of his face, produced a short spell of excessive laughter and amusement.

Besides this singular mode of *ornamentation,* and the modes of *deformation* already spoken of, practiced by the Flatheads and Peruvians, there are yet many others, not less curious, which I have witnessed, and of which the world are as yet not generally aware. And of these none are more curious and extraordinary than those practiced by the numerous tribes on the upper Amazon and its tributaries, whom Caesar and I visited several years before, and of whom I spoke very briefly in the earlier [part] of this work.

Of all the tribes on the continent of America, those of the Amazon and its affluents are the most nude, the most ill-shaped, the least ornamented, the least warlike, and the least hostile.

The equatorial climate in which they live, almost absolutely denying the use of clothing of any sort, and their fisherman's modes of life, living almost constantly in their dirty and wet canoes, destructive to costumes of all sorts, present thousands of these people almost in a state of nudity.

Ill-looking as many of the Amazon tribes are compared with the other American races, there are still tribes amongst them that remind the traveller of the Winnebagoes, the Menomonies, and other Canoe Indians of North America, and are quite their equals.

On the Amazon and its tributaries, from the mouth of the Rio Negro to Nauta, which constitutes but a half of that river, there are more than one hundred tribes speaking different or dialectic languages; and though ugly enough from Nature's hands, they have been caricatured in a manner that reflects little credit to Art, and stigmatized as *Cannibals* in language as little worthy of historians.

The whole country, a distance of eight hundred miles, if it were possible to traverse its vast forests and swamps on both sides of the river, might be travelled in security by a man with his wife and his children, and unarmed, without harm from the Indians; and amongst them he would find helping hands whenever difficulties were in his way. These people are friendly to the whites, because there are no buffaloes nor beavers in their country to excite white man's cupidity—because they have nothing with which to buy rum and whiskey, and because their lands are so vast and covered with such unmovable forests of timber that white men do not want them. Hostility amongst themselves is little known—the tribes are too small to wage desolating warfare—they have no defined boundaries to protect or hunting grounds to defend. They cannot hunt; the denseness of their forests forbids it; and living by fishing, the rivers which they fish upon admit of no boundaries, and are alike free to all; and the movements of their canoes, propelled only by the muscles of the warrior's arms, are less inspiring to deeds of war than the movements of the horse, which often lead the crazed warrior into rash and mortal combat.

Like most Canoe Indians, the peculiar modes of their lives, sitting in their wet canoes or wading in the water, forbid their dressing their feet and their legs, and, unlike the Indians who ride the prairies or travel on foot amongst the rocks, they are generally bare-footed; and the labor of propelling their canoes without the use of their nether limbs gives them physiological disproportions—an over-development of the muscles of the arms and chest, and a narrowness in the hips, and a lankness and deficiency in the legs.

The horsemen on the prairies, on the other hand, who always exercise astride of their horses' backs, and using their arms only for their light bows and the bridle, beget a lack of symmetry almost equally striking: an over-breadth in the hips, expansion and curvature of the upper legs, and comparative lightness and slightness in the arms and chest.

The fisherman is beautiful as he glides along in his canoe; but placed upon his naked feet, he cringes and looks to the ground before his steps, and loses the dignity and grace of the moccasined man, who fearlessly and solidly sets his foot and uses his eyes for the distance.

These circumstantial departures from the natural symmetry of man and his movements are plainly exhibited amongst all the horse and Canoe tribes of America; but there is another, the Mountain Indians, who have neither horses to ride nor canoes to paddle—who have no fish to catch and no buffaloes to chase, who draw their sinewy bows— whose steps and leaps, upwards and downwards, and climbing amongst the rocks, exercise alike all the muscles of the body and the limbs, where perfect symmetry of form alone can be found.

The numerous tribes on the *haute* Amazon—about the mouth of Rio Negro, and from that to Nauta, and upon the shores of the Yucayali, of whom I have spoken as Canoe Indians, deserve a few further remarks in this place relative to the curious modes of *pendant* and *pigment* ornamentation which they practice, and with effects perhaps more *bizarre* and more droll than even the blocks of wood worn in the lips in the tribes where we are now halting.

Besides the ordinary way of painting with vermilion, and other colors daubed on with the fingers, several of these tribes have a mode of *printing* the colors on their faces and bodies in the manner somewhat of theorem painting. On a certain sort of palm-leaf, or a piece of parchment-dressed skin, the most curious and intricate arabesque devices are drawn and cut out, and this laid on one cheek and the other, and the forehead, and the color, mixed with grease, covering the palms of the hands of the operator, a gradual pressure prints the intricate designs through the theorems upon the face.

There are often different patterns printed on the breasts, the shoulders, and arms, and legs, bewildering the beholder who does not understand the process with astonishment at the apparent labor and artistic effect produced on a figure in the morning, to be washed off at night, little thinking that the whole effect has been produced in five minutes.

These theorems are prepared with oil and glue, so that they bear washing and, being once elaborated, can be used a thousand times; and the mystery that astonishes an artist is, that two or three colors are sometimes printed over and between one another, like chromo-lithographic printing, and the colors rubbed in with the fingers, effects being often produced that would test the skill of the best artist to copy.

The fat and round and solid cheeks of these people, and their peculiar color, form the best possible ground for this curious art, which I am quite sure could not be practiced with equal effect on any other substance.

The pendant ornaments of the face and ears in most of these tribes are not less surprising, and certainly are more completely unaccountable. Of the tribes that I have visited in that region, the most remarkable for these modes are the *Muras,* on both sides of the Amazon, above the mouth of Rio Negro, the *Iquitos,* the *Omaguas,* the *Ticunas,* the *Yahuas,* the *Marahuas,* the *Orejones,* the *Mayorunas,* the *Connibos,* and *Sepibos.*

These tribes all sever the rims of the ears and elongate the lobes, by wearing heavy weights in them which accomplished, enables them to wear enormous blocks of wood and other ornaments in them, precisely like the Botocudos and Lenguas, whom we are yet amongst. By the process of elongating the lobe, it becomes enlarged, and oftentimes is seen descending quite to the shoulder, and, from appearance, of half-a-pound or more in weight.

I have given copies of [two] of my portraits made amongst these people, illustrating the principal and most curious of the above-named modes. A *Mura* chief, his ears curiously mutilated and elongated, with ornaments attached, round plates of silver fastened to his cheeks, his chin, and his nostrils, and long thorns standing out from his cheeks and his chin.

For the supports of these singular ornaments of the face, incisions are made in the flesh in childhood, into which a large bead is forced, with a slight thong hanging out. The flesh heals around the cicatriced wound, and the bead is withdrawn. The elasticity of the flesh is such that the orifice is scarcely perceptible; and, at the times of ornamentation, for galas, festivals days, &c., a bead, into which the butt-end of the thorn is pressed, is slipped into the orifice, and supports the thorns in the positions in which they are placed, and so the silver plates are supported on the cheeks and the chin, and feather and other pendants.

They dance, and sing, and yell with all these ornaments attached, and if any one of them becomes the least deranged, the mere touch of the fingers adjusts it again. [Another] portrait (i.e., an *Orejone*) is still more curiously ornamented with long feathers run through the cartilage of his nose, two splinters fashioned from the branches of palm, attached by beads to the nose, and quills and beads suspended from his under-lip by the same means, and blocks of wood in the cartilage of his ears. . . .

I have given a copy of a portrait of a medicine man (sorcerer) in the Omagua tribe, who uses the perforation through his lip alternately for suspending strings of beads or shells, or beautiful plumes, or for suspending a boulder of flint of a pound or more in weight, supported by a large bead on the inner side of the lip, which he assured me was the habit that he could not dispense with, from the pleasure it gave him at times, and always after eating, of drawing the cool air upon the gums and through his teeth!

The habit of suspending strings of beads and feathers from the under lip is also practiced by the females in many of the tribes, not only on the Amazon, but in various parts of South America, amongst the women of Venezuela, of Guiana, of Paraguay, and the mountains of Peru. A copy of a portrait of a *Gooagive* unmarried girl of Venezuela illustrates this mode amongst the females; and the long thorns projecting from her cheeks might almost be recommended for young ladies in the economy of civilized life.

Finishing this curious episode amongst the Amazons, we return again to the Tobos and Lenguas, whom we left on the Uruguay.

The passion for ornamentation seems to belong to all the human race much alike; whether they are clad in beautiful and costly stuffs or are naked, the passion seems to be the same. The Indians in the northern latitudes of North America, who dress in skins, wear their ornaments in paintings and embroideries on their dresses. The Amazons, who wear no dresses, are equally vain, and expend their ingenuity and exhaust their means in ornamenting their naked limbs. They load their wrists and ankles with bright and costly bracelets and rings, and their necks and breasts and hair with beads, and paint their limbs and faces with beautiful colors. And what can be more beautiful? what more proper?

But blocks, and thorns, and weights! What a mistake in taste! And last of all, to flatten and elongate their skulls, like the Flatheads and Peruvians, in order to look beautiful! O Vanity, thy name is (certainly) —Indian! "Everything has its cause." It is easy to account for the love of ornament with paint and beads, and even blocks and thorns, but who can guess the cause of changing the shape of the skull to beautify "the human face Divine?" There *must* be a cause for this.

The Flathead tribe at the mouth of the Columbia, whose portraits I have shown (and also their mode of flattening the head) and the ancient Peruvians, as we learn by their skulls, are the tribes that have ventured to *deform* nature for a form they imagine more beautiful. And is it exactly so? I do not believe it. I do not believe that any part of the human family would venture such a stride from nature as to flatten the skull as the Flatheads do, or to compress it into a sugar-loaf as the Peruvians have done, without a model, without a fashion to follow—an Indian *beau-ideal* to which they have aspired. . . .

Not to make this chapter too long, I shut my note-book on the Lengua and Tobos Indians around us; and shaking hands with them, a few days down stream showed us the little band of Bocobis at the mouth of the Rio Negro of Uruguay, and after that the beautiful city of Buenos Ayres, and—where next?

"Patagonia and the Patagons, of course." The "Giants of Patagonia— ten feet high"! and the "Cannibals"! I did not believe such things, but would go and look for them through the center of Patagonia and Tierra del Fuego. But here this chapter ends.

~~~~~~

Buenos Ayres

(CHAPTER VII FROM *Last Rambles*)

HERE, IN A boarding-house, in a comfortable room looking on to the Plaza, and at home, of course, I was at work on my sketches.

Alzar came in, and softly, behind him, and wrapped in a scarlet mantle, a handsome young man, a half-caste, rouged to the eyes, and his glossy hair, parted on his forehead, falling back upon his shoulders, and without a quill upon his head; and in his wake, and more softly and timidly still, a young woman of the same color, in a calico dress, her hair dressed in the same manner, the two looking effeminate enough, and enough alike to have been sisters.

Alzar, with his hat in his hand, "bowed and scraped," and introduced them as brother and sister, of the *Auca* tribe, living on the head waters of the Rio Salado, to the south of Buenos Ayres. Such was the suavity and gentleness of their manners as they advanced and both shook hands with me, that I felt almost embarrassed. Alzar had no doubt given them a high-colored description of me and my works, and they were approaching me with a profound respect.

Alzar could speak somewhat of their language, and, what was better, the young man spoke Spanish very well, and his beautiful and modest sister well enough to be amusing and agreeable to me. They had learned enough from Alzar to know the object of my travelling and the sincerity of my views, to enter into undisguised conversation about their own and other tribes of Indians in the vicinity, and conversation took the place, for the time, of my painting, and my brushes were laid down.

I expressed my surprise at meeting red people in the city of Buenos Ayres, and particularly so beautiful a young lady, when *Til-tee* ("The Firefly"—I found that was her name) replied quicker than her brother was able to do, "Oh, we often come here, señor, and there's a plenty of us here now; my father, and my mother, and my sister are all up town."

Alzar then said, "This is a very respectable family. *Señor Gonzales Borroro,* he is a Portuguese gentleman, and his wife is an Auca woman. They live on the Rio Salado, and these are some of their children; and if you will permit me, Señor—I know they will be glad to see your paintings."

"Most certainly, Alzar. Go and fetch them." Alzar was off, and I went to amusing my visitors with my sketches.

My portfolio of Indian portraits was giving so unthought-of and so exciting a pleasure to the two, and particularly to that beautiful little creature, who became more beautiful every time she turned, that I was in the midst of a peculiar satisfaction myself, when Alzar came in with the rest of the family.

This was the first day after my arrival in Buenos Ayres, and though I had several letters of introduction which I had not yet delivered, I spent the whole of that day with this interesting family, having learned, in the early part of my conversation with them, that their business was all settled, and their arrangements all made to start for their home on the Salado at an early hour the next morning.

I gained from them a great deal of valuable and reliable information respecting their own tribe, and of their neighbors on the south, the *Puelches* and *Patagons,* with both of which tribes I found they were well acquainted, and with which they were living on terms of friendship. The Puelches and Aucas, both come freely into Buenos Ayres, and trade for guns, ammunition, clothes, hardware, cutlery, &c., which they sell at a profit to the Patagons, who are sworn enemies to the Buenos Ayreans and never see them except on the field of battle.

My cartoon portraits, which they could not see enough of, gave an unspeakable pleasure to these people; and those with flattened heads, and those with blocks of wood in the lip, seemed to excite, with a people who wear few ornaments, equal disgust and astonishment. They told me they never had thought that any Indians were such great fools.

Borroro and his son gave me such a glowing description of the country where they lived, of the beauty of the forests, the lakes, the prairies, and *pampas;* of the chasing of ostriches, wild horses, and wild cattle, which they kill for their hides and their hair, as well as the beautiful games of the Indians, and, at the end of all, so pressing an invitation to come and see, and to join in them, that I told them distinctly that Alzar and I would ride there before a fortnight was out.

This evidently gave him great pleasure, and the father said that both he and his son would join me in any or all of the sports of the country, if I would come. I told him I had long had an intention of making a journey through the middle of the Puelche and Patagon tribes to Tierra del Fuego, and he believed that from that place on the Salado, which would be 150 miles directly on the route, would be the proper point to start from; and that, if I chose, his son, who was an excellent horseman and hunter, and knew well the Puelches and the Patagons, should be one of the party, and could easily get me any number of first-rate young men around him to join me.

"Well done," said I. "Alzar, my troubles are all over. I see our way now clearly. We'll go through the center of Patagonia."

Borroro was himself half an Indian (his father a Portuguese planter), and, therefore, with all the vanity that usually belongs peculiarly to the half-caste class, and with the strict traits of honor that generally characterize them also; and I thereupon said to him and his Indian wife, "There is one thing, now, that I want to ask of you—I want you to allow me to make a sketch of Til-tee, your beautiful daughter. The day is half gone, and I will not have time to finish it very well, but I will bring it with me and finish it when I come to see you. She is so pretty that I don't wish to forget how she looks."

The extreme overjoy of the mother seemed as if she had, in a measure, misunderstood the arrangement I had asked for; and no objections being made, and no conditions named, I went to work. The timid little girl said she was sorry that she had not her prettiest dress on. I told her that was no matter, it was not the dress I wanted, it was her pretty face and neck only, and if I could paint that part now, the dress could be painted when I should see her again.

When my work was done, "one thing more" I wanted, and they granted it. I wanted to walk with them to a jeweller's shop in the corner of the plaza, where, old man as I was, I could not forego the pleasure I had of buying, and placing in her ears with my own fingers, a brilliant pair of pendants, for which she prettily tried to express (but could not well enough in Spanish) what her brother interpreted to me, "that her heart was thankful for the rich present I had made her." Night was at hand, and *"Buenas noches," "a Dios,"* &c., and we parted.

I had commissioned the young man Gos-brok not to buy, but to look up and have ready for my negotiation when I should arrive, the best horse in the country for my tour through Patagonia; an animal of the best bottom and speed, and well trained in the chase of ostriches, horses, guanacoes, or anything else; and the two or three weeks previous to our start, I passed by working on my numerous sketches and making the necessary preparations for our campaign.

My spirits were a good deal depressed during this time by reports, made to me by my friends, that there was a prospect of an approaching war between Buenos Ayres and the Patagon Indians, which would render my expedition to Patagonia impossible, as these people know no white people but the Buenos Ayreans, and would make no distinction between me and them, provided I were endeavoring to enter their country under such circumstances.

I nevertheless got my preparations made, even against the advice of friends, and, with Alzar, started for the banks of the Salado. Our ride was a severe one, and much longer than we had apprehended, but the country one of continued interest as we passed. Not on the bank of the Salado, but a great way beyond it, we found the *rancho* of our new-made friends, and by and around them many families of the small and handsome *Auca* Indians.

The tribe is small, having been decimated by whiskey and the smallpox, and, though partly civilized, are still living principally by the chase. Game of many kinds is always abundant in their country, and easily killed; and wild horses and wild cattle in countless numbers, which they kill for their hides and hair, which find a ready market in Buenos Ayres.

All were rejoiced to see us in performance of the promise I had made, and particularly so the pretty little "Firefly," who was parading her sparkling eardrops—and also the rather unfortunate mother, who, we learned (but not till some time after) had overheard, but misunderstood, the arrangement made between her husband and myself in Buenos Ayres, as to hunting ostriches, &c., and which arrangement, fearing an announcement of it for two or three weeks ahead would bring an unwished-for assemblage of Indian sportsmen around him, he had charged his wife *to say nothing about.*

Under the wrong impression which the poor woman got when I asked permission to take her daughter's portrait, which was that I had asked her hand in marriage, and afterwards under the injunction "to say nothing about it," she was keeping (as will be seen) the supposed important secret profoundly safe, and, as can be imagined, was not the least joyful of the family on our arrival.

The Aucas are not only a small tribe, but a tribe of small people; and, a singular fact, the men and women near the same size, and resemble each other so much in stature, form, and features, and in the mode of arranging their hair on their always naked heads that it is often difficult to distinguish one sex from the other.

They wear but little dress in the summer season, and that chiefly of civilized manufacture; of calicoes and other cotton cloths. The men often wear ponchos, and the women, in the warm season, are naked as low as the waist, from which drops an apron of cotton, extending as low as the knee; and wear a sort of sandal or half-moccasin, made of goat's skin, or skin of the guanaco. In this really pretty way I found the handsome little "Til-tee" dressed, and freed from the horrible folds of pictured calico, she was free and graceful, and more beautiful than ever.

The young man Gos-brok lost no time in informing me that he had found the best horse in the country for me, without the least trouble; that it belonged to his father—a mustang, taken by his own hand on the *pampa,* and trained in the chase by himself; that his father had ten horses, and this one, his favorite, he had resolved to sell to me. I gave him his price 150 piastres, and the lasso was in my hand. A noble creature—an entire horse. I could imagine him "Charley" [Catlin's horse in the Far West]—but he wanted the color; he was a silver grey, his mane and tail were black, and the latter swept the ground.

The sagacious animal seemed to know, from the moment his owner put the rein in my hand, that he had got a new master; and from my caressing, and combing, and trimming, evidently was soon convinced of the fact. A mutual understanding was soon established between us— several little excursions we made together about the neighborhood, and yet there was one unthought-of and necessary condition to be understood and arranged, which neither "Yudolph" (that was the name he answered to) nor his former master had probably ever heard of.

Horses in that country, and ostriches, and guanacoes, and other animals are taken with the lasso and bolas, and no guns are ever fired from a horse's back for anything. Colt's revolvers had not at that time travelled so far, and horses knew just as much of them as their masters; the amusement of which remained yet to be afforded to the one, and the alarm and astonishment to be presented to the other. In short, Yudolph had got to smell gunpowder, and the Aucas to understand revolvers.

"Sam," for the first time in that region of country, was taken from its case, and in the wigwam, in a little time, was partly comprehended; but for Yudolph, it was to become a more inexplicable mystery. In the rashness and thoughtlessness of my *inexperience,* being then only fifty-seven years of age, it had not occurred to me that Yudolph, though a bold hunter and warrior, as he had been, had probably never heard the sound of a gun; and, under this lack of intelligence, I mounted him with "Sam" in hand, in presence of his former master and Alzar, and the pretty little Til-tee, to see, as I said, how he would "stand fire," for *my* game had got to be taken, and my battles fought, not with lasso and bolas, but with gunpowder.

I certainly was a pretty good rider, as well as a good shot, by this time; and galloping him round in a curve or two, I fired a cylinder to the left!—and the next thing that I was sensible of was, the Borroro and Alzar had hold of me, and were carrying me towards the *rancho.*

I said, "Hold on—I am not hurt.—Where's Yudolph?"

"He's yonder, Señor."

And at a distance of thirty rods I saw him standing broad-side—his head and tail up—a beautiful picture, as he stood gazing at us and wondering what had taken place. His master walked towards him and called, "Yudolph!" when the faithful creature advanced, and met him half-way. He led him up and put the rein again in my hand, and the trembling brute, seeming to think there had been some *accident,* followed my motions as willingly as before.

"Where's 'Sam'?" said I.

"Here!" said Alzar, as he handed it to me in two pieces!—the stock broken off below the guard, not injuring the lock in any way.

"Where's the saddle?"

"Here, Señor," said Borroro. "The girth is broken and by that means you fell."

"I know that—saddles have thrown me many times, but no horse can do it."

"Is your rifle loaded, Alzar?"

"Yes, Señor."

"Just give it to me, then, and your bullet-pouch and powder-cartridges, if you have any."

Alzar handed me his rifle and three or four powder-cartridges, and placing my nose to the nostrils of the trembling animal, and exchanging a few breaths to inspire him with confidence, I threw myself upon his naked back, and galloping the same rounds as before, I fired the Minié to the left—kept the horse upon his course; reloaded, and fired again, and again, as if I were in a buffalo chase on the Missouri, or in mortal combat, and as easily, and with as accurate an aim, as if I had been firing from the back of "old Chouteau," my buffalo chaser at the mouth of Yellow Stone.

"Huzza! huzza! bravo! bravo!" exclaimed the bystanders; and trembling Yudolph, as I rode him up, seemed to take one-half at least of the applause to himself. And last, though not the least complimentary and welcome, came the nice old lady from where she had sat in the door of her house, who extended her hand, and showed me, by the expression of her face, that she was taking to herself a *peculiar* satisfaction at the successful and laudable feats of her (as she still supposed) approaching son-in-law.

Yudolph now understood something of gunpowder, and was ready for the chase. He had long since, under his former master, learned how to run and how to approach; and I, who had long since learned how to shoot, with "Sam" in hand and a six-shot revolver in my belt, was considered equal to a war party. But where was "Sam"? Sent off by a little son of mine host to a small village on the river, some twenty miles distant, where a country blacksmith bound the two parts together, and it came back, not as handsome, nor as light, but quite as strong as ever.

After a few days spent in and about the little Auca village, the appointed day approached for a "grand hunt"—an *ostrich chase*. The young man Gos-brok had told me in Buenos Ayres that he knew of a fine brood that had been hatched and raised within a few miles, as yet unmolested, and just about old enough for sport. This he had told me in my painting room when the father and mother were sitting by, and just when I had obtained their consent to *have the daughter* painted; and the old lady, from her imperfect knowledge of Spanish, understanding by a word or two of what he had said, nodded assent, as in the other cases, supposing we were still talking of Til-tee, whilst the rest of us were thinking of ostriches.

This "hatch" was also known to Gonzales Borroro (his father), who now told me they would be found in the edge of the thistles, near the head of the "red water," one of the extreme sources of the Salado, and in the *pampa*.

The *pampas* in various parts of South America are vast level plains, not unlike the great prairies of the Platte and the Arkansas, excepting that they are covered with high weeds instead of short grass; and amongst these weeds, of which there are many kinds, there are wild flowers of all colors. And on the eastern borders of the great *pampas,* stretching off from Buenos Ayres to Patagonia on the South and to the base of the Andes on the west, there are vast forests of thistles, which, sometimes for a great many miles together, though they grow in patches and as high as a horse's back, are almost impassable, even for a man on horseback.

These thistles are the covers and asylums for the ostrich, which feeds mostly out in the open plains and in the ravines; and when pursued runs to the thistles for cover, where it is excessively difficult to follow it.

The plan of our day's sport was to ride about ten miles before sunrise, and break upon the brood whilst they were feeding in the open plain; and if not successful in that, to drive a thistle patch of several miles in circumference, forcing the game to cross an intervening prairie of two or three miles to enter another thistle cover, and in which plain our run would take place.

Borroro laid the plans and took the lead, riding a beautiful pied horse, his bolas coiled upon his left arm, and a lasso, in loops, round his horse's neck. His son, Gos-brok, and two other young men, well mounted and equipped in the same way, and Alzar with his Minié rifle, and I with "Sam" in hand, and a six-shot revolver in my belt, formed the "hunters" of the party; and some six or eight Indians, mounted but not armed, followed in our train, as drivers of the thistles.

I have before said that sportsmen in this country hunt without guns. The bolas—the "deadly bolas!" a thing imagined in the powder-burning world and yet but little understood. Let us know more about it and its deadly powers before we go further—before we see these true sportsmen playing with a flock of birds before us. (We will come back to this play-day anon.)

"Borroro lives by killing and by catching horses, and others of my people live by killing cattle." So said Borroro to me; and two weeks after this play-day on which we have commenced, I went with Borroro and a party of ten to see the deadly work of the bolas amongst a band of wild horses that had been reported on the plains near the head of the Río Saladillo.

Driven by drought upon the vast *pampas,* these animals often come in thousands together to the extreme sources of the rivers rising in the plains, to get water; and sometimes, the Indians tell us, die by thousands and rot upon the *pampas* before they reach it.

A circuit of ten days, in which I lost much flesh, though I had flesh to spare, satisfied all the passion I ever had to witness the extreme of

Indian endurance, the deadliness of the bolas, and its havoc amongst the noble tenants of the *pampas*.

The bolas is a rawhide cord (and, of course, of great strength, though very small), somewhat in the form of the capital letter "T"; each of the three branches being some eight or ten feet in length, and having a leaden ball of half-a-pound weight at its end. This is carried in a coil on the rider's left arm, or on the horse's withers, and when in the heat of the chase the rider raises it and swings it in a rotary motion around and above his head, by holding one of the balls in his hand. His horse is trained to approach its game on the right-hand side, that the missile may be thrown with its fullest force and accuracy; and, at the proper distance, the balls are sent forward with a force and tact that keeps them revolving in the air, and their centrifugal force keeps the cords straight, till one or the other of the cords strikes the animal's neck, it matters not which, for in an instant they all wrap around its neck and legs, and binding both and all together, the animal falls upon its head, and generally the neck is broken by the fall; if not, before the instant is out its hamstrings are cut by a long and semi-circular-bladed lance, and its chances for life are ended.

In battle, an enemy's arms are thus wrapped to his sides, or his body wrapped to the neck and the legs of his horse, and both go to the ground together!

In this hunt (or massacre), to which I have no more space to devote, twenty horses were killed; their skins, with the manes and tails attached, were stripped off, and, on the backs of mules, were transported to the Indian village.

This chase was for skins and hair only, and the lassoes were not used. When death is wanted, the bolas is taken in hand. When the Auca or the Puelche Indian wants a horse for service, the affectionate lasso is dropped over its neck, and it is broken in and domesticated much in the manner of the North American Indians described in [an] earlier volume.

Mounted and equipped, as has been related, for the ostrich chase, we assembled at and around the *rancho* of Gonzales Borroro, a little before the dawn of day.

Til-tee was up and dressed (the little she had was soon put on), and her fond mother was there too, and, from a wooden bowl, filled my pockets with dried prunes, delightful to eat in the chase when water is scarce. She patted Yudolph on the neck and the nose, examined the girth of my saddle closely, and saluted me with a wave of the hand, and a long "ya—ya—a" as I rode off, evidently afraid that I should be thrown from Yudolph's back, and perhaps my neck broken.

At that time I could not more than half-comprehend such marked kindness and such *peculiar* solicitude, but gave the good woman credit for it, and received it as a *very strong expression* of hospitality.

We were off, and galloped over our ten miles pretty quick, and getting near to the ground for our sport, it was necessary to follow up for a mile or two the bed of a small stream, forming a little grass-covered valley, lower by some twenty or thirty feet than the surface of the level platform on which our game was expected to be discovered.

Borroro and myself, leaving the rest of the party in the valley to await our signals, rode up the embankment as quietly as we could, under cover of some hazel-bushes and thistles standing on a projecting point, to reconnoiter the plains about, of which we had a perfect view for several miles.

Discovering nothing, after a careful search, we stepped our horses out into the open prairie. Hearing the signal whistle of his son, which he understood, "Here they come!" said Borroro, as he was wheeling his horse about, and the whole troop, with their necks stretched and their wings up, were breaking from a copse of willow on the bank of the stream, where they had been for water, had passed our companions, who were mostly dismounted, and were now steering for the thistles, exactly in a straight line towards us, and with our fellow-sportsmen in their wake, as fast as they could get their feet in the stirrups.

"Stand!" said Borroro. "We can do nothing in meeting them—we must get behind them." And moving his horse back into the bushes, at his signal I followed him.

It was a beautiful sight—there were about twenty in the troop, two coveys united. They rose the hill within a few rods of us, and the plunging chevaliers were a long distance behind them. "Now!" said Borroro, "don't try to shoot, but lay out Yudolph to his utmost—we must cut them off before they reach that thistle patch, or we lose them!" Both Borroro and myself were at our extremest, and side by side, as if on a race-course. The "thistle patch" was half a mile or more. Yudolph headed him by several lengths, and yet the running-flying troop, on their tip-toes, turned the point of thistles before us, and were out of sight in an instant.

All hands again together, and out of breath from the sudden brush, a dismount and a "council of war" was the next thing. That we should have passed the whole troop in so thoughtless and careless a manner within two or three hundred yards, in the valley, was an affair so provoking and so humiliating to all that the first part of our counsel was taken up with groans and exclamations of disappointment and regret, and afterwards we proceeded to plans for bringing our labors to better results.

If Borroro and I had been a few rods farther ahead in our chase, we should have cut them off from the thistles, and turned them loose upon an open prairie of several miles, where the ground was good and where our sport would have been of the first order. "However," said Borroro, "we'll have it all right yet—there's the south prairie—we'll turn them into it—it's just as good."

The "south prairie" (or *llano,* as they call it) was another open, grassy plain of several miles in extent stretching off between the forest of thistles into which our game had plunged, and another similar forest farther to the south. Our plan now was for the hunters of our party to ride round some five or six miles, and in this prairie, on its northern border, to take our positions at equal distances, under cover of the edging thistles, and await the breaking of cover, which was to be produced by our staff of "drivers," who were to enter the thicket, and work their way through it from the north.

Signal whistles were to be blown when the birds were well entered on the prairie, for the drivers to appear as soon after as possible on the prairie's border, to prevent them from returning to the thistles, and not until their appearance was the chase to begin.

We all sat close and silent, and at length (it was a curious sight) the older and wiser birds appeared first, and led the way, tilting and crouching along as they cautiously emerged, and their long necks stretched, examining the prairie before them to see if an enemy was on it. Moving as if they suspected the plot, and the younger of the broods following, they advanced a long distance into the prairie, and lay down, some upon their bellies, and others upon their sides, hiding their heads behind bunches of leaves and tufts of grass, whilst the whole of their fat and round bodies loomed up in full view and exposed.

Our "drivers" came out and showed themselves at different points, and at the sound of Borroro's whistle we all started. The poor birds (which Borroro subsequently assured me had all shut their eyes), from the tramp of our horses, which announced our approach and which they heard with their heads on the ground, were up and off. We were now in the chase—"an ostrich chase."

They started in a group, and ran, not in a circuit or a curve, but stretched their necks in a straight line to the nearest thicket, perhaps at a distance of two miles. No maneuvring, and nothing but a fair and a straight race offered us any chance, and the first half-mile was thus contested with equal speed, when the tremendous strides of maddened Yudolph, in spite of all the poor creatures could do, brought me into the midst of them, with Borroro but a length or two in arrear, and on their right flank. At my first cylinder one of them fell, and, probably from the sound of the gun, they broke and ran in all directions. The sport then became beautiful, each rider, crossing their curves, came upon them. I saw them writhing and struggling in the deadly coils of the bolas, and recognized the "old Minié's" voice in the mêlée. It was now a "running fight," a leaping and dodging for life with some, others were leading off in straight lines for the thicket, and some got there—but few. Every one was attending to his own business, and it was difficult to see or to know exactly what was actually progressing.

When the field was cleared, however, and there was nothing more to be done, though we were separated, in some instances, several miles apart, we got breath by resting awhile in our saddles, or by dismounting and lying on the ground, and at length got together on the field, our drivers having been whistled up to carry our game.

I have joined in the buffalo chase in all its forms, but never before took part in a chase so difficult as this. After the brood was separated, they ran in all directions, darting in zig-zag and curved lines before and around us, leading our horses into angles difficult to turn, and the rider into positions from which he could not use his weapons. Our horses, at the end, as if they had run a five-mile heat, like ourselves, were ready to lie down upon the ground for rest.

My first two shots killed, but I discharged the other four cylinders all upon the same bird, but without effect, owing to its shifting courses, and the consequent irregular and violent motions of my horse. My two first shots, which were fatal, were given while both the bird and the horse were running in a straight line, which made the aim more steady and more sure. My third bird worried me and my horse by its crooked lines until it reached the thistles, and I returned without it.

Borroro picked up three, and his son brought in two. The other two Indians had three between them, taken with lassoes, and Alzar had fired once, and missed.

Our birds, therefore, counted up, were ten. The ostriches that we killed, called in that country *"nandu,"* were about one-half the size of the African ostrich, with three toes instead of two; and their feathers comparatively of little value. Their wings were cut off and carried, and their legs for sinews; and the skins of several of them were taken for sacks, useful for many purposes, and their carcasses were left on the field.

The ten pairs of wings were elevated on two long poles by two of the Indians, as we rode triumphantly into the village under shouts of applause. Little Til-tee's voice and hands were raised amongst the number, and the good mother, when she heard from her husband how I had performed, patted me on the shoulder, exclaiming, *"Bueno! bueno!—* muy *bueno,* Señor!" thinking perhaps to herself of what nobody but herself had yet thought of.

The grand features of this vast and untilled country, in addition to its *pampas* and prairies, are its lakes, its salines, and its sables. Its sandy (or "cedar" ridge, lying off towards the Rio Negro, is full of guanacoes, a species of llamas, beautiful for chasing, and almost the only sport and living of the Puelches and Patagons. Its flesh is equal to that of venison, and the skins form leggings and robes for clothing, and, sewed together, form coverings for their tents. We planned a run amongst them, but now are taking a look at the "Grand Saline."

Gos-brok, the chief's son, was to lead us. Alzar was going, and two Indians. The ride was thirty miles—one day's work. One day to be spent there, and two days to come back, examining the "talking lake" and shooting ducks on our way. We laid in salt (we actually required nothing else). I promised the little Til-tee to bring her some beautiful feathers, which could not be reached by bolas or lasso, and she was in raptures; and the mother again stuffed my pockets with dried prunes.

Our horses were led up, but not yet saddled, and Alzar's nag from Buenos Ayres, ruminating perhaps on the uncouth manners of people in this part of the country, slipped its head out of its bridle, and evidently was turning its face towards the civilized city. Alzar mounted on to one of the Indians' horses, and, with a lasso in his hand, with which he was tolerably expert, galloped off after it. A broad prairie was before us, and making a circuit to get ahead of his eloping horse, he made several passes at it, but the cunning animal showed its heels, and effectually kept out of his way.

The scene was an amusement for all, and all were astonished at the desperate bolts and curves made by both, to no effect excepting the complete discouragement of Alzar, who seemed to be abandoning the chase in despair to return to the village.

I stood at the moment holding Yudolph, yet unsaddled, with the bridle in both hands crossed behind me, and feeling a gentle pressure upon the rein, I looked round and met the sparkling eyes of the smiling little Til-tee, by their very expression emphatically and silently asking consent as she was timidly drawing the rein of Yudolph out of my hand. The instant allowed me just enough to yield consent, and to see that she had a lasso coiled on her left arm, when Yudolph had her astride of his bare back, and was off, in his clear and flying bounds!

A shout of surprise was raised, but no one had fears but myself. The father smiled, the mother gazed, and the child rode on! And as her floating black hair and narrow shoulders of demi-red were alternately rising and sinking above and in the waving grass, I thought, "O lucky, envied horse! Were I in Yudolph's place with such a prize, I would gallop to the golden coast." She seemed troubled; her hair had lost its pin, and fell in two parted waves over her shoulders; and, dropping the rein to adjust it (for it was in her way), oh, how gracefully she balanced as she was wrapping and tying it round her neck!

Yudolph, though knowing his errand and his rider, had kept his speed, but not exactly his course. The rein was lifted again, and the mile that she and Yudolph then made in a straight line was like a flying arrow, leaving a tinged train from its reddened feather. Alzar was passed, and stood astounded, as if a meteor had gone by him! The Buenos Ayrean steed, aware of what was behind him, steamed at his highest, and just before they would have slipped from our view, the delicate arm of the little Amazon (for with my pocket-glass I could see it distinctly) made a circuit round and over her head, and the fatal noose was seen to fall! A shout was raised, but she was too far to hear it. Yudolph was seen galloping a curve or two with the Buenos Ayrean nag by his side, like a boat picked up on the waves of the sea, and, taking Alzar in tow, all came trotting in together.

Alzar looked distressed, but said the Indian horse he rode knew he was not an Indian; his Buenos Ayrean steed showed an expression of utter despair and a full conviction of Yudolph's mettle; and ever beaming little Til-tee dismounted, and with her smiling cheeks and heaving breast received the applause of *all*, and from *me* a kiss—I could not help it—and a beautiful pocket looking-glass set in silver.

Buenos Ayres

Our ride to the "Grand Saline" was yet before us, and, our saddles on, we started. An hour or so, and we were at the shore of another branch of the Salado; into it, and through its clear water, and over its pebbly bottom we waded—reminding me of Caesar and me in the Snake River. As we passed over these clear and transparent waters, quietly on their way to the ocean, I contemplated the vast and unknown solitudes of grass and thistles in which they had their origin, and mounting the retraced banks also and slopes on the opposite side, the ancient turns and motions of the elements when these vast excavations were dredged out.

We were beyond it, and on an elevated plain of grass, with wild flowers that no pencil could portray and no pen could describe. We were evidently on a divide—a water-shed; and looking to the south convinced us. A vast and interminable lake or sea seemed to be lying in the distance before us, here and there spotted with green, like islands, which proved to be shrubbery, but at last terminating, like everything else, blue in the distance; and yet not all blue—there were streaks of white. And in the sky—what's that? Soldiers are not in the sky. It's a mirage. It's the mirage of a war party; and yonder is another, drawn out in Indian file! It must be so! But stop!—these soldiers are pouring down like a stream into the lake of blue and white below; and now this shadow passing by us!

Now look up, Señor; here is another war party right over our heads!"

"And so it is. And now I understand: these are the beautiful birds, the *flamingoes,* that you are taking me to see."

"Yes, Señor. That blue lake you see in the distance is the *'Grand Saline,'* and the streaks of white are the beautiful birds hatching out their eggs. This is just the season, and tomorrow you shall have fun enough."

From the summit of the graceful swell upon which we had mounted we gradually and almost imperceptibly descended for several miles, until we were near the border of this vast saline; when, whispering, Alzar begged us to halt a moment. I held his horse as he dismounted, and cautiously advancing a few rods, he raised his rifle and shot down a solitary guanaco that had stood its ground and was looking at us, precisely at the place where we were going to sleep and when fresh meat was wanted.

We were now on a level with the saline, and could see little but the constant flocks of flamingoes sailing about like infantry, or like war parties on the march. These, constantly rising and getting high into the air, were steering off to other parts or were streaming down into the saline to spend the night.

We collected great quantities of dried willow-stalks for fuel, and with a rousing fire on each side of us and a smoke from burning rotten grass, we kept off the mosquitoes, but greatly to their disappointment. Their hour, about ten o'clock, arrived, but they were silent, and we walked forth in the cool air unmolested, and unattracted or amused, except by the clacking and chattering of the wild-fowl of these saline solitudes and the incredible beauty of the firefly halos that were here and there glowing like the light of hidden lamps.

Everywhere and all around us these little insects, each one carrying his beautiful phosphor lamp, were making their curves, and swinging and dancing under our noses, and sometimes against them; and here and there, in the distance, swarms with myriads in a little space moving the air, or settled and hovering in the grass and around the bushes, where my note-book was read as easily as by daylight, or under the brightest lamp.

These swarms, some stationary and others travelling, could be seen in the distance until their numbers became countless, and a general flood of light near the ground almost extinguished the darkness of night.[1]

The salines, of which there are many on the head waters of the Salado and Saladillo, and also farther south, near the Colorado, and between that and the Rio Negro, are evidently the remains of salt lakes, in time filled in with growing and decaying vegetation. There are still, around the extreme sources of the Salado, a great number of salt lakes without any connection with running streams, either into or out of them.

These salines, in the winter season, are generally covered with several feet of salt water, which rises from the earth, and in the summer season this water is evaporated by the rays of the sun, leaving an incrustation of the muriate of salt over much of the surface, and other parts a slimy mud associated with salt, so excessively difficult to travel on and so nauseous that no animal whatever will venture into it, and none of the feathered tribes except the stork species, of which are the flamingoes. They build their nests and hatch their young in it, in perfect security from molestation by animals of the country.

[1] What an ornament these beautiful and harmless insects would be to a nobleman's or gentleman's grounds in England; how beautifully they would light up his lawn. They could easily be imported, and the climate of England would, no doubt, be suitable for them.

It is probably owing to this perfect security to their eggs and their young, that incredible numbers of these birds are seen in that country, often settling down, and rising, and wading in these salines, and sailing about over them in millions at the same time.

The flamingo, which is one of the most delicate and beautiful birds in existence, varies from four to five feet in height; its chief color is pure white, with parts of its wings of the most flaming red, and another proportion jet black.

They gather grass and weeds, with which they build their nests on the ground, and stiffen them up with mud, much in the manner that swallows build. These nests stand in the mud, and are generally about one foot high, open cones, and from two to three feet apart; and sometimes cover hundreds of acres, looking from a distant elevation like a mass of honeycomb.

In the winter season these nests are all under water, and not seen. In the summer, when the water is evaporated, they reappear, and the birds, taking possession, fit them up and hatch their broods in them again. The birds are always paired, and the male is busily engaged in hunting and bringing food, or standing by on one leg and sleeping whilst the female is sitting on her eggs. Domestic rights seem to be guarded with the greatest jealousy, and, from their frequent encounters, one would suppose they were protected with the most obstinate and heroic gallantry.

From our bivouac we saddled up in the morning, and rode to a slight eminence, the nearest we could see to the nests, and from that, overlooking the scene with a good field-glass, the picture was one of interest for hours to look upon; it was truly a "Grand Exposition"— grand for its industry of millions, all busy, building, hatching, and feeding—grand for the beauty of its colors; for the sun was just up, and its horizontal rays, catching upon the bending columns soaring in the air, and on the never ending group, where thousands were constantly playing on tip-toe with upspread wings, and all, the red, the black, and the white, glistening, like the slimy mud they walked and ran and played upon, with the sun's refracted rays.

My glass was good, but perhaps I am more inquisitive than other folks—I wanted a nearer view. Reconnoitering the ground closely, though we were full a mile from the nearest part of it, I discovered a sort of promontory of grass and bog, with now and then little tufts of willows, extending into the saline and very near to where the nests commenced. One of the little Indians who had accompanied us (half-Negro) told me he could lead me near enough to shoot amongst them. He said he had sometimes walked up so near to them as to catch them with the bolas. "Come on, then," said I. We left the rest of the party to overlook us; we were in the chase (or rather ruse).

Advancing about half the way, we came to a bunch of alder and willow bushes, and in a few minutes he had cut and so arranged a screen of these, to carry in both hands before him, as completely to hide him from their view and also to screen me, as I was to walk close up to him, stepping in his footsteps. My hat was left behind, and my belt was filled with boughs rising higher than my head, and with others descending to my feet, so that we were ostensibly (at least for silly birds) nothing but a bunch of bushes.

My cylinders, which my friend Colonel Colt had shaped expressly for shot and ball, I had filled with duck-shot, and we began to move forward in a straight line, but very slowly. Full half a mile, almost inch by inch, the bunch of bushes moved. Sometimes we were on or astride of bogs, and sometimes up to our waistbands in mud, and ignorant of the moment that might have taken us to the chin.

However, "nothing risked, nothing won." We kept on, and at length came within some five or six rods of the nearest nests, where the females were sitting on their eggs, and the husbands standing on one leg by them and fast asleep, whilst others were gathering worms from the mud and bringing to feed them!

The silly things looked hard at us as an unaccountable appearance, but the bunches of bushes not apparently moving, they seemed to think it was but the natural. I had no chance to sketch, as "Sam" was before me in both hands, and motions would have been imprudent; but I had the most perfect chance to see and to study (to sketch in my mind) every attitude and every characteristic.

At length one of the tallest of the throng, with his mouth full of collected worms, seeming to be suspicious, advanced quite up to take a good look at us, and poked his long neck forward, and began to walk round to get a side or back view of us. His motions and expressions were so droll, as I saw him across the bridge of my nose, that I burst (which I could not avoid) into a loud laugh. He screamed, and I fired through the group, a raking fire, and another cylinder as they were getting on the wing; and of all the curious hunting or other scenes that I have seen on earth, that scene was the most curious. Those that were near were wheeling about in the air, like a cloud above us, and shadowing the earth around us; and as the alarm was general, those rising more slowly in the extreme distance looked like a white fog streaming up from the ground. We stood still, and the whirling multitudes in the air formed into lines like infantry, and each, with its leader, was moving round and over our heads, not knowing what the matter was, or where the danger was, or where to go.

One of these lines came so near that I brought the leader down. He descended with outspread wings, and fell within ten feet of me, and down came his troop, faster than I could count them, all in a mass, one upon the other, not knowing what was the trouble, stretching down their long legs and flatting their scarlet wings actually against me and in my face! At the struggling of their dying leader, they all saw there was some mistake, took the alarm, and were off in confusion. Still, brigade after brigade came sailing round us, and I soon discharged all my cylinders, bringing down one at each fire.

From my two first raking shots, where in range they looked like a solid mass, seven or eight were lying dead, and others were hobbling off with broken wings; and of all together we picked up thirteen. But, before picking up my birds, I had been obliged to pick up my Negro Indian boy. He had had no idea of my firing more than once, and in my agitation and somewhat of confusion in turning to fire right and left, being withed up in a bunch of bushes filled with smoke, the sharp breech of my rifle had struck him on the temple, and knocked him down helpless, without my knowing it. He had fallen backwards, entangled in his bushes, and was lying on his back, imploring me to be merciful. He thought I had shot him and that I was going to shoot him again.

I got him up, and soon explained, by signs, the accident, and then we observed our companions, without their horses, coming at full gallop to join us. We were a nasty group, up to our waistbands in the mud and slime, on which the birds walked with scarcely wet feet.

The scene now before us was strange in the extreme, a landscape, a perspective of nests, with the heads of young birds standing out, as far as the eye could discern, and nothing else. Nests with eggs, and nests with young; the very young heads up and gazing, the older young, but without wings, pitched out of their nests, and sprawling, and trying to fly or to hide themselves on the ground. We replaced the little chicks about us in their nests as well as we could, and left them.

Two pair of the handsomest wings I cut off with my own knife for little Til-tee, and the rest were taken by the others of the party. These wings, for military feathers and other uses, are objects of commerce, and always find a ready market in Buenos Ayres and Rio de Janeiro.

Now, why should I lose space by telling how we got back; how we spent the day amongst the birds, the worms, and snakes that infest in myriads the shores of the "Grand Saline"—how we recrossed the sandy plains, rode to "talking (echoing) lake," and after shooting ducks and geese till we were tired, returned to the happy little Auca village.

Til-tee was the first to meet and to greet us, half a mile from the village. I then gave her the beautiful red wings of the flamingoes, and others, of green and blue, of the wood-ducks I had shot at the "lake that talks." Yudolph knew the little maid, and he trembled with his love for her when she came up and patted him on his nose. She bounded with joy, and was in the village before us.

The villagers were gathered around us, and what was the first news we heard? Borroro had gone to Buenos Ayres, with two Puelche chiefs, who had arrived from the Colorado with information that a large war party of Patagons was assembling on the Rio Negro for a war with Buenos Ayres! Borroro had left word that I must not think of going to Patagonia yet, and that his son Gos-brok should accompany me to Buenos Ayres.

I was very liberal now with the little store of presents I had laid in for the Patagons. Til-tee got many strings of beautiful beads, of ribbands, needles, &c.; and her mother several vari-colored cotton shawls, for which she had a peculiar passion; and, with Gos-brok for our guide, we started for Buenos Ayres.

And what in Buenos Ayres? All was for war. "War, war, with the Patagons!" Men were enlisting, and soldiers were drilling; and I saw at once the impossibility of a tour through Patagonia under the present circumstances. And why should I say more of my dreamed and fancied expedition which did not, and could not take place?

Faithful Alzar, who had become very much attached to me, and I were obliged to take leave of each other, and shaking hands for the third and last time, he was saved, perhaps, from shedding any tears by the "old Minié," which I had promised him, and now placed in his hands.

~~~~~~

Tierra del Fuego

(CHAPTER VIII FROM *Last Rambles*)

MY "OCCUPATION (AGAIN) GONE," I dwelt no more on Indians, but thought again of *"Rocks."* "How much more grand, how sublime! Indians are, after all, poor things, and soon to become extinct—but rocks! *rocks!* the eternal landmarks and boundaries of the globe!"

"Tierra del Fuego (the land of fire), the perpetual *snow-covered* mountains of the *land of fire!* how harmonious and how inviting. And the fire-vomiting Cotopaxi (Cotopaçi), that coughs up a rock of sixty tons weight, and only throws it fifteen miles! and six hundred miles the greatest extent to which its awful bellowings are heard; and the snow and cloud capped Chimborazo! (Tchimboràcho); these are said actually to exist, and the great Baron de Humboldt has even said so, and also that he saw them; but how much more satisfactory to go and see and *feel* them."

With such contemplations, could I stop in Buenos Ayres? I was going on board the *Gladiator*. She was bound to Valparaiso, on the Pacific coast. From day to day the palisaded coast of Patagonia, like the cliffs of the Kentish coast in England, were tantalizing us as we passed them. And the ragged and black and white, and smoking heaps and piles of lifted mountains and mountain peaks of *"Magellan"* and *"Fuego"* were ahead of us, but as yet in imagination. Cartoons were ready, and colors and pencils, and two days of sleep ahead, so as to be wide awake whilst passing them.

We are in the Strait of Magellan—and those mountains, blue on our left and before us, and some over them and higher, glistening like the tin roofs of Montreal—the sun's rays are on them, and they are covered with snow!

"Captain, you know all about these?"

"Well, I ought to know something of them; I have seen them from all sides."

"And these black and frowning walls on our right, they look as if they had been broken off with mighty sledge-hammers; and these two, right straight ahead—how immense and how grand! They look as if they had been shoved up from the bottom of the ocean on the back of some terrible monster! Surely the Andes has been broken in two here! What an awful struggle there has been! The Indians tell us that the Andes was once a great serpent—that its tail was here, and these huge rocks were its rattles! How sublime! What a rattlesnake! I have crossed over the back of this reptile, and also of its mate, in North America, the Rocky Mountains, in their largest parts."

"I think you are fond of rocks and mountains, sir?"

"Yes, Captain. There is nothing else on the earth's surface so sublime, so grand, and so interesting for the study of man. I think of nothing else—but here—how is this? you are anchoring in this cove—what for?"

"Why, sir, the wind is dead ahead round that point yonder, and blowing fresh—we'll have to lie by a bit here. We are in 'Pecket Harbor.' Vessels are often wind-bound here, and take in water and provisions. There's a sutler here, and he's just come on board, and this is he, sir."

"Ah! where's your town, sir?"

"That's all that you see yonder, sir, and a few houses round the point. There's nothing here but a few of us, and some poor creatures, Indians, encamped around us—"

"What! Indians? Well, that's droll; I thought I had finished with Indians. What Indians are they?"

"Well, sir, there's a little encampment of Patagons, and a dozen or so of Fuegians."

"Captain, I am going ashore, and you must send the yawl with me after breakfast; and let me have one of the cabin-boys to carry my portfolio."

"They shall be at your service, sir."

Ascending the little hill at the back of the village to reach the Indians' camp, and near it, with a mulatto boy carrying my portfolio, I met a large and a very fine dog hobbling along towards me, and yelling in the most piteous manner, with an arrow driven into its side quite up to the feather, and two Indians following it with guns, and evidently intending to shoot it. My first impression was that it was *mad,* and I was raising my rifle for self-defense when I observed by its crouching position and the wagging of its tail as it was approaching me that it was seeking a friend in me, and evidently was approaching me for protection.

I answered its supplication by beckoning with my hand, and the poor creature understanding me, crept up and lay down at my feet; but the link of sympathy was severed the next moment, by one of the Indians advancing and shooting the poor creature through the head!

I had no interpreter, and of course no means of getting an explanation; and taking it by the legs, the Indians dragged it into the camp. This was entering an Indian village for once in my life under an excited and rather hesitating feeling, but it would not do to turn back at this point, where the eyes of all were upon us.

I was met, however, and luckily, in this dilemma, by an interpreter who was sent to speak with us.

The first thing I asked, and the first thing explained, was the object for which the poor dog had been shot. It was required, by the singular custom of the country, to be placed in the grave with its master, whose body was then just being buried, and whose tent, at a little distance, containing all its furniture, clothing &c., was then burning!

In the middle of the night before, the poor man had gone out from his tent to move the picket of his horse, when he was bitten in the leg by a rattlesnake that he had disturbed. The villagers were all up, with torches in their hands, and the reptile being found, was killed, and the man died in a few hours.

I had sat down with this interpreter, who was a Portuguese half-caste and also spoke Spanish tolerably well. I told him I feared it would be an unlucky time to visit their little camp, and he said, "No; the occurrence which has just happened would present no difficulty whatever"; and he then conducted me to the chief's tent, where I was politely received, and easily explained my views—that I had come ashore from a vessel just arrived, and having learned that a party of Indians were there, I had come to make them a short visit, probably for the day only.

I told him that I had spent the best part of my life in visiting numerous tribes of red people like himself, in various parts of the world; and, like a practical and reasoning man, and a real gentleman, he evidently appreciated my motives in an instant, and began to ask me questions about the various races I had seen faster even than I could answer them.

This man, though a chief, was but the chief of a band, or perhaps only of the little encampment over which he had control. His questions were rational and judicious, and after answering them awhile, I took the initiative by opening my portfolio of portraits, which seemed to answer a thousand questions and evidently to suggest as many more.

I explained to him that I had visited more than one million of red people in their various villages; and on a small map of North America I pointed out, so that he clearly understood their relative positions and distances from where we were then sitting. He expressed no astonishment whatever in his looks or actions, nor made ejaculations, but calmly told me there was much more for poor Indians to learn in this world than he ever before had thought of.

By this time his tent was becoming too small for the crowd that was getting into it, and it became necessary for my mulatto boy to hold up each portrait in turn, so that all could see them, whilst I, with the aid of the interpreter, descanted on them.

These people never flatten the head, nor cut and maim the flesh in any way for the purpose of ornamentation, and when I showed them the Flatheads, and explained the process of flattening the head, and the Botocudos and Nayas portraits, with blocks of wood in their lips, a tremendous laugh was raised, and the chief very coolly remarked that "they were very great fools."

For want of space I was now obliged to take up a position outside of the chief's tent, where all comers could see and hear; and amongst others that appeared there soon came from two grass-covered wigwams, at a little distance, several Fuegians, and amongst them an eccentric character whom the interpreter told me was a medicine man (a sorcerer), his body and limbs curiously painted, and his head and neck as white as pipe-clay could make them and surmounted by two white quills of the largest dimensions. This strange-looking being, either from jealousy of my works (which, of course, were considered great *medicine*), or from disbelief in my wonderful relations, took it in his head to raise objections to the "spectacle" that was going on. The chief, however, telling him I would most likely have his frightful face put in my book, caused him to haul gradually off, whilst the crowd were laughing at him.

I felt at once amongst this little group as if I were amongst a group of Comanches of North America. Not only are they counted, equipped, and armed, like the Comanches, with bows and arrows, and long lances, and like them in their modes of dress and ornament, but strikingly resemble them in physiognomy and physiological traits.

The men chiefly divide their long hair in two parts, separated on the forehead and thrown on to the shoulders and back by a silver-plated band or hoop, which is crowded down from the top of the head and over the hair, near to the eyebrows, holding the hair in its place, clear from the face and back of the ears. Their faces (in full dress) are always painted red from the eyebrows to the mouth, including the ears, and the other parts of the face painted in a variety of shapes and bright colors; and they wear no head-dresses, and very seldom ornament the head even with a single quill or feather.

Their dress at this season—the middle of January, and therefore midsummer—is very slight. The men wear a breech-cloth round the waist, and the women a sort of apron of cotton cloth or of bark, extending down to the knee, and moccasins beautifully embroidered, made of the skins of deer or goats; and in the colder season, both men and women dress the leg with skins of guanacoes, and curiously painted; and their tents, which are small and light for the convenience of transportation, are made of the skins of the same animal, or of wild cattle and horses, with which the vast plains of their country abound.

Observing on the chief's face the marks of smallpox, I questioned him about it, and he informed me that when he was a boy he was near dying with that disease; and he told me that, about 1812 or 1815, as near as I could ascertain, that awful disease was communicated to his people by some white people on the coast, who were selling rum and whiskey and other things to the Indians, and that more than one-half of the great and powerful tribe of Patagons were destroyed by it.

"We are poor," said he; "we want many things that the white people make—their clothes, their knives, their guns, and many other things— and we come here to buy them; and many of my people, who are foolish, will buy whiskey, and it makes them mad, when they will kill even their own mothers and their little children. We do all we can to prevent this, but still it is not stopped, and we are afraid of getting the awful disease again."

One can easily see that I had enough to do this day without painting, and we returned on board full of fatigue and hunger, the chief having agreed to sit for his portrait the next day, if the vessel would wait for me.

My conditional appointment with the chief being explained to the captain, and the portfolio opened to him, which he had not before seen, he agreed to wait another day, whatever the wind might be, for the satisfaction of gratifying me and the pleasure he would have ashore with me.

Captain Ford proved to be a real *"bon homme,"* and, becoming as much taken up with me as the Indians were, went ashore with me the next morning, on condition that he could have the pictures to lecture on amongst the women and children, who had not yet seen them, whilst I was sketching my portraits. And when night came, and we were safe on board again, and our craving stomachs pacified, he said to me that this had been to him the happiest day of his life that he ever had spent.

My sketch of this rational and intelligent chief was followed by that of his wife and a warrior; and then hasty sketches were made at the little and more humble *demeure* of the Fuegians, at which the famous doctor, with his white head, was *minus,* he having withdrawn himself, probably with absolute disgust.

The reader will easily imagine with what excitement, and with what *éclat,* and with what security and success, from this point I could have penetrated and passed through the center of Patagonia, with the introduction of this little returning colony, had there been no rumors of war and I had my faithful Caesar, or even Alzar, with me; but here I stood alone, and the barren coast could have furnished me no reliable companions. But it may happen yet that I shall be able to see the way and a proper time to pass through the midst of these interesting people; and then if it happens, I shall be able to say more of them and their customs than I now can.

Yet, from this little caravan, which had travelled several hundred miles to visit the coast, I learned many things of interest, and was enabled to learn them in a little time. As to the fabulous accounts of "giants," men "eight and ten feet high," as related by some early writers, I learned from this chief that there actually existed no such monstrous persons in the tribe, though there were some parts of the country where the men were very tall, considerably taller than himself.

From this man I learned that the government of the Patagons resembled very closely that of most of the North American tribes—a head chief and a council of subordinate chiefs, or chiefs of bands, forming the government of the tribe. He told me they could muster eight thousand warriors, well mounted and well armed, and were abundantly able to defend themselves and their country from assaults of any enemy they had. That the tribe of Puelches on the north of them, between them and Buenos Ayres, were their relations, and that through them they traded horses and hides for guns and ammunition to the Buenos Ayreans, and in that way could equip all the warriors of the tribe. They catch their horses wild on the prairies, and train and ride them in the same way and as well as the Comanches do.

Their saddles and stirrups are made with great skill, and the stirrups for women (who ride astride, as boldly as the men) are suspended by a broad and ornamented strap crossing the horse's neck; and for both men and women these stirrups, which are made of wood, and curiously carved, admit but the two largest toes to enter, to guard against fatal accidents, which too often befall horsemen in the civilized world.

Their dead are always buried in a sitting posture, and with them their pipes and their weapons, and by the side of them their dogs and their horses and everything else that they possess is burned with their wigwam.

The Fuegians are a tribe of some five or six thousand, inhabiting both sides of the Strait of Magellan, living entirely on fish and wild-fowl. Their lives are spent chiefly in their canoes, made from bark of trees, sewed together and glued, somewhat like the canoes of the Ojibbe-ways of North America. In the summer season, both men and women wear only a flap covering the hips; and in the winter cover their bodies with robes made of the skins of the sea-wolf, which they kill with their spears and arrows.

Their manufacture of flint spear and arrow heads is not surpassed by even the Apachees or Snakes, or any other of the North American tribes, and they are made in the same forms and by the same process which has been described. And their wigwams, which are very small, are made by setting a number of slender poles in the ground in a circle, and bending the tops in, forming a cone, which is covered with long grass, or with skins of the sea-wolf.

These people are unquestionably a branch of the Patagon family, speaking a dialect of the Patagon language and living in harmony and friendship with them; and living by the side of and adjoining them, and still so entirely unlike, both in physiognomy and in symmetrical proportions, furnish one of the most striking and satisfactory proofs of the metamorphose of *man* by men's different modes of life. . . .

PART II

North American Indians West of the Rocky Mountains

~~~~~~

CHAPTER 9

Along the Pacific Coast of North America

(CHAPTER III FROM *Last Rambles*)

THE "GOLD FEVER" having thus been cured, and two weeks of delightful convalescence passed in the hospitable hacienda of Senor N——, an ascending steamer snatched Caesar and myself, with scarcely a moment to shake hands, from this scene of enchantment to the "Barra," at the mouth of the Rio Negro; from thence we went to Tabatinga and to Nauta; and after visiting the surrounding tribes, the *Muras,* the *Marahuas,* the *Yahuas,* the *Orejones,* the *Angosturos,* the *Mayoroonas,* the *Iquitos,* the *Omaguas,* the *Ccocomos,* the *Ticunas,* the *Connibos,* the *Sepibos,* the *Chetibos,* and a dozen other *"bos"* and *"guas"* of the Yucayali and Upper Amazon, we crossed by the mail route, with many jovial and agreeable passengers, the rocks, the snows, the ravines, and the frightful dog-ways of the Andes, to Lima . . . "the most beautiful city of the world." . . .

Now we start. The field is new, and vast, and fresh, before us. Between Lima and San Francisco there are many Indians inhabiting the coast, but we go by sea, and necessarily must leave them, at least till we come back.

San Francisco is a highly civilized place, so we have little interest there. There are plenty of books written about it. They are all for gold there, and I am *shy of gold,* having just recovered from it. Some straggling Apachee Indians come in there at times; but we will probably see better specimens of them by and by, on our return. We are now on our way to Oregon, the mouth of the Columbia. Our craft is small, and sails slow; and when the sea is smooth, gives me a good chance to finish up my sketches, and to prepare my cartoons for others to be made.

The schooner *Sally Anne* (she was built in New York) doubled Cape

Horn in 1843, and is now sailed by Señor Pedro Pasto, a Spaniard, who goes once-a-year to Astoria, to Victoria, to Queen Charlotte's, to the Alaeutian Islands, and to Kamskatka, and returns with sheepskins, wool, dried fish, and other products of those countries.

J. Paulding, of New York, L. Simms, of Missouri, J. Stephens, of Ohio, then living in San Francisco (who had got an idea in their heads that *nuggets of gold* were larger on the Columbia coast, and perhaps in the Alaeutian Islands), and I (who was quite sure that *Indian portraits* in any quantity could be got there) agreed to pay to Captain Pasto $200 each to take us safe to Queen Charlotte's Island—to Liska, on the Alaeutian Islands—and to Kamskatka, and back to Victoria, on Vancouver's Island (my man Caesar to be carried free, but a servant to all, when required). And did Captain Pasto do it, and what did we find, and what did we see?

Before we enter further upon this, it will be well for the reader to understand upon what conditions we sallied forth on the broad ocean for so long and so critical a voyage. An *"understanding"* (as agreements are called in that country) was definitely agreed to, and an off-hand article for all to sign was drawn up, in the following form and words, by Simms, whose extraordinary tact and despatch in draughting contracts and other documents of those countries, to be executed by revolvers and bowie-knives, if not otherwise, will be visible on the face of it.

Understanding.

Agreed—the *Sally Anne,* Captain Pasto, bound for Nishnee Kamskatk, to take us 4, and found, whole way and back to Queen Charlotte's Sound and Victoria, at 200 dols. each, one-half down; salt pork and beans to last; owner's risque; and Catlin's nigger to go free.

(Signed) *J. Paulding.*
V. Simms.
J. Stevens.
Geo. Catlin.
Pedro Pasto, Capt. *Sally Anne.*

Each contracting party, armed with a copy of the above "agreement," a six-shot revolver, a rifle, and a bowie-knife in the belt, in a country where there are no courts of justice, or even magistrates, feels abundantly able to defend his rights, and to enforce the performance of all engagements so solemnly and *definitely* undertaken as this.

These documents pocketed (which, by the way, were not rights, but only indications of rights), we move on; all is jocularity, mutual confidence, and good fellowship, or sure *to be* so, at least, in the outstart.

A long voyage, with no other absolute misfortunes than the total exhaustion of all our "salt pork and beans" and alarming symptoms of scurvy, brought our little bark to the mouth of the Columbia, with the safe harbor of Astoria close before us. Here, however, when the dangers of the sea seemed over, our difficulties began.

Captain Pedro Pasto (for the owner was captain of his own craft), about to glide from the rough waves of the ocean into the smooth waters of the Columbia, ran his ship upon the bar—her bow in the sand, and the waves dashing against her stern, and driving her farther on, as the tide was rising.

Night approaching, our position was critical; but morning showed us, at full tide, driven quite over the bar, and at anchor in the quiet water of the river, with loss of rudder only.

Captain Pasto, with Paulding and Stevens, in a small craft, went up the river to Astoria for ship-carpenters to make repairs, and to replenish the exhausted requisite of "salt pork and beans" and other provisions, and Simms and myself remained on board.

At low tide the schooner lay upon her side on the sands, and Simms, with his hawk-eye, in walking around her, discovered that the name of the vessel, the *Santa* (I forget what) *de Callao,* in large yellow-ochre letters, was chiefly all washed off by the force of the driving waves against her stern, and the remainder of them peeling off under the rays of the sun, and underneath them, covered with a thin coat of paint, the *"Sally Anne, of N. York"* was quite conspicuous.

I opened my paint-box, and with a brush, and a tube of yellow chrome spread upon my palette, I touched the letters up a little.

When the Captain returned, the vessel was afloat, and Simms, taking him around astern in the yawl, said to him, "Look there, sir, I can disfranchise you, when we get back, for changing the name of your vessel when at sea. It is a very grave offense."

Getting on deck, Simms said, "We have no idea, Captain, that you stole the vessel, and *Sally Anne* being a favorite Yankee name of ours, we shall christen her so, for this voyage at least, and you bringing out a couple of bottles of wine for the occasion, we will agree to say nothing about it."

With his wine, the good-natured captain brought on to the table his papers, showing that he bought his schooner of a couple of Americans in the port of Callao; and it was at this moment that the famous *"understanding"* on the previous page was first reduced to writing and signed.

A few days making the necessary repairs, and we sailed out, all in good humor, passing outside of Vancouver, and coasting along its western shore of huge rocks and pine-covered mountains, towards Queen Charlotte's Sound, the grand anticipated field for the gold-hunters, and also for the operations of my brush.

Nootka Sound took us up. A strong northwest wind, increasing to a gale, held our schooner three days wind-bound in this snug and quiet little shelter, with the picturesque island of Nootka on one side of us, and the dark green pine forests and overtowering black piles of up-heaved rocks, and blue, and then snow-covered mountain peaks of Vancouver, on the other.

Nothing ever surprised me more than the information I here got, and demonstrated to my eyes, that mountains covered with perpetual snows were standing in the island of Vancouver! And nothing that I ever before heard, or ever should have heard, would have conveyed to me an adequate idea of the singular appearance (and beauty, I may say) of its vast and ever changing (in form, but not in color) hills and mountains and ravines, not only *clothed,* but *robed* and *mantled* and *belted* with dark-green and gloomy pines and cedars, throwing out their long and drooping arms over rocks and streams, and even over the waves of the ocean.

The first day that we lay here we had amusement enough on deck of our little vessel in studying the scenery around us, and the darting (and seemingly *leaping*) canoes that were passing around, and the *Klah-o-quat* Indians, and their wives and little pappooses, that we invited on board.

A remarkably fine-looking man, whom I supposed, from his appearance, was a chief, with his wife, carrying her infant in its cradle on her back, and their daughter, came on board, after getting permission, for which he asked by smiles and intelligible signs. His manner was that of an intelligent man and a gentleman; and when he raised his hand and presented its palm towards the throng that was endeavoring to follow him, I was convinced that he was a chief, and was going to use his authority to protect us from an uncomfortable crowd on deck.

It was but half an hour's sail from here to the place where the *"Ton-*

quin," Jacob Astor's brig, was destroyed, some years before, by the Indians, and the crew destroyed, and Captain Pasto began to feel fears for ourselves and his vessel. The chief seemed evidently to be aware of this from the Captain's manner, and leading his wife and daughter up to me, easily explained by signs that he would leave them with me until he would go in his canoe and bring someone who could talk with me. And I said to Caesar—

"This is a fine old fellow; jump into his canoe with him, and take the wife's paddle, and help him; and if he runs away with you, I will hold on to his wife and daughter, and easily get you exchanged after a while."

"Agreed, massa! I no fea!"

They paddled off rapidly, and soon turned round a point and were out of sight. And in half an hour they came back, with a brigade of canoes following them, and bringing with them an intelligent mulatto boy, who spoke English very well and also the *Klah-o-quat* and several other Indian languages of the coast.

This young man told me that he swam ashore there from a whaling vessel two years before, because they flogged him too much, and was now making his living by interpreting for the Indians, and for vessels coming into the Sound; and that he lived most of the time in one of the Indian villages; and that the Indian who had come for him was the chief, and a very good man.

Then, said I, the first thing I wish you to tell him is, that I knew by his actions that he was a chief, and by the expression of his face, that he was a good man. And tell him that I am very much obliged to him for going in search of you. This being interpreted, a hearty shake of the hand took place all around.

My three gold-seeking companions, who had rather shunned him at first, now came forward, and shook hands with him also, and Simms went to his luggage, and brought and gave to him a bundle of about a dozen cigars. The chief was so pleased with the present, that he seized hold of Simms, and embraced him in his arms.

"Well, Catlin," said Simms, "that's a very fine old fellow—that man is a gentleman! I'd trust myself anywhere with that man!"

Always carrying with me a quantity of little trinkets and ornaments for the Indians on such occasions, I went to my trunk and got a handsome string of blue and white beads, which I placed on his daughter's neck; and a little looking-glass, which I gave to his wife in return for his kindness in going for the interpreter. This explained to the chief we were all friends, and under a sudden and tolerably good understanding.

There were at this time a great number of canoes from the Vancouver shore around the vessel, and the crowds that were in them were generally a poor-looking set—poor-looking as to clothing, weapons, &c., but at the same time with faces full of sprightliness and intelligence. A great proportion of the women had their heads flattened; and occasionally a man was seen with a flattened head, but very seldom.

They were beckoning and whining, and some of them were crying to be allowed to come on board; but the chief, by showing them the palm of his hand, quieted them and kept them back. I told the interpreter to say to him, that if there were any whom he would like to indulge by permitting them to come on board, he could do so, as the captain of the vessel had agreed to it.

He then called to several whom he thought deserved the privilege, and they came on board, and amongst those there came several with baskets of dried salmon, whale blubber, and oysters, to barter, and the captain and mate at once had something to do in replenishing our larder.

The interpreter I engaged to be with us long as we should remain in the harbor, and he agreed to take us the next day to the *Klah-o-quat* village, where the chief had invited us to go.

Leaving Caesar to amuse the Indians on deck and in their canoes around the vessel, I got the chief, with his wife and daughter and the interpreter, below, and as each of us *compagnons de voyage* had laid in at San Francisco a certain number of bottles of cognac brandy for emergencies, I uncorked one of these on this special occasion. I explained to the chief that we were all temperate men, but that we carried a few bottles for medicine if we got sick, and once in a while, for those whom we loved, not to make them drunk, but to give them a pleasant drink, as a mark of respect.

He replied, through the interpreter, that he perfectly understood my meaning, and, taking up his glass, took me by the hand, and bowing his head, "My friend, I drink your love." This was a little different from the usual form of salutation; but what could be better—more expressive? Simms, whose heart was always ready for anything *from the heart,* was quite touched at this, and swore it was something "new, and ten times better than the old and hackneyed and worn-out expression."

I learned from this intelligent man, to my great surprise, that there were about twenty different tribes of Indians on the island of Vancouver, and containing some six or seven thousand persons, though after all, they are but different bands of the great flat-head tribe, and speaking languages, though dialectic, oftentimes almost entirely different.

The greater portion of these practice the abominable custom of flattening the head, which will be described anon.

"On that western coast of Vancouver," the chief continued, "besides the *Klah-o-quats,* there are the *To-quahts* living in Barclay Sound, farther south, and several other tribes living on the coast between Nootka Island and Cape Scott, the northern cape of Vancouver; that they all believe in a Great Spirit, who created them and all things; and that they all have times and places when and where they pray to that Spirit, that he may not be angry with them. That they live chiefly on fish of various sorts—salmon, halibut, blubber of whales, oysters, clams, &c., which they can always get in abundance; and that they had but one fear, that was, that 'King George,' as they had been told, was soon going to drive them all from the coast into the mountains and rocks; and in that case," he said, "they would all get sick, and soon starve to death."

I told him "King George" had long been dead, and that there was a queen in England, who was kind-hearted and good, and I knew she never would allow her Red children to be treated so cruelly; which seemed to please him very much; and his wife, hearing it translated, cried out in a most expressive tone, "La—la—la—a" (good, good, good).

After the chief had drunk about half of his wine-glass of brandy, and which he told me he never had tasted before (though he had sometimes drunk whiskey), I took a large glass, and with brandy, and water, and sugar, made a "brandy toddy," which he said he liked much better, and which I got him to share with the old lady and her daughter. All were delighted with it, and after that I opened my portfolio of cartoon portraits of Indians. These surprised and amused them very much, and after an hour or so the interpreter took canoe with them and paddled toward their village, as night was approaching, the interpreter having promised to come on board the next morning and conduct Caesar and me to their village.

The next morning, if we were still wind-bound, the Captain had promised me the use of the yawl; but at the hour appointed, the chief himself came with the interpreter, paddling his own canoe, which was a compliment that I could not decline; and Caesar and I got into it, taking the portfolio and my sketching apparatus, and leaving my gold-hunting companions at cards with Captain Pasto, and the gale outside of the Sound still blowing.

George Catlin

The *canoe*—the canoe of the chief, in which we were riding—*floating,* not flying, though it seemed so, was a *shell,* apparently as thin and as light as bark, and made from the trunk of a huge cedar— a "dug-out"—yes, *strictly* a dug-out. And I must tell you *how* it was dug out. Large enough and strong enough to carry thirty men, yet its sides so thin and light that the paddles of two men, with us four in it, sent it like a bird flying through the air. The gala-boat, the gondola, the water-phaëton, of a nobleman, kept dry except on fête days, saluted by the multitude when it passed, and a beautiful ornament for a palace park or a royal museum.

"Dug-out," I have said; but how? not from the patriarchal cedar as it *stands* in the forest, on the mountain-side—it must lie prostrate on the ground for that; it must be "chopped down." But how? These people have no axes! Listen, and say if there is not industry and tact in this? Wapiti, a noble animal and shy, with immense horns, feeds under these stately cedars on the mountain-sides; *they* must be brought down to bring the *cedar* down. And how? not with rifles (these people know nothing of gunpowder and of rifles), but by motive power *sinewy*—not explosive. Missiles are designed and shaped in wood, made light, and steered in the air by feathers on their sides, and their points of flint or bone—one about as good as the other. Bows are made to throw them, and strained by sinews, not by gunpowder. The stately elk (or wapiti) falls before them. His horns—the broadest, hardest parts—are cut with knives and hatchets of flint into the form of chisels. With these chisels in the left hand and a heavy mallet made of stone encompassed in a withe for its handle, the axe-*men* and axe-*women,* on their knees, set to with "hammer and chisel" at the trunks of these stupendous trees; and, doomed, they are cut near to the center, and then left; and when the wind is in the right direction to lay them on the ground best suited for their excavation, a few blows with the hammer and chisel send them tumbling to the ground.

The monster tree is down! What next? Why, a hundred laborers, both men and women, with the same tools and others, mount upon it and work at the same time. The bark is stripped off, and the work laid out and marked by master-workman, and all—even women and children—dig, and cut, and drill to the lines marked out, and no farther.

For digging out, a species of mussel-shell of a large size, found in the various inlets where fresh and salt water meet, are sharpened at the edge and set in withes of tough wood, forming a sort of adze, which is used with one hand or both, according to its size, and the flying chips show the facility with which the excavation is made in the soft and yielding cedar, no doubt designed and made for infant man to work and ride in.

But, felled and dug out, this is but brute force and industry. The beaver can do this, and all Indians; but the architect, the naval constructor who conceives in the log and lays out those beautiful lines that are to balance and ease it through the water—those "lines of beauty"—what artist? Where did he get his art? And where is he? Is he gone? He can't be a savage. And the soft and smooth and polished finish, outside and in, how done? And the painter—the artist who designed and drew those ornamental lines and figures on its sides, its bow, and its stern; and for what, and what do they mean? Maybe we shall find out.[1] At present we get in and we ride; and a chief who "drinks my love" paddles me to his house—his humble dwelling. What is it? It is a shed made of heavy posts standing in the ground, with long and immense timbers resting on their tops, and covered with planks for a roof. Its floor is the ground; trodden and swept, it becomes hard and dry and polished. The fire-place is a circular enclosure of stones in the center, and the chimney the raising of a short plank in the roof directly over it. Their food is served and eaten on the floor, and their beds—without feathers—cribs eighteen inches above the ground, made of small elastic poles and covered with rush mats; and pillows made of a solid block of wood excavated so as to receive the head, with soft matting underneath—the best sleeping contrivance ever yet invented, as it holds the head elevated and inclined forward, and keeps a man in his sleep always on his back, as he ought to be.

This chief, not like the chiefs of the Crows, the Sioux, or Mandans, clad in skins fringed with scalp-locks and ermine, with painted robes of buffalo skins, and head-dresses of war-eagles' quills—but with a simple breech-cloth around his waist, and a blanket over his shoulders, his hair parted on his forehead and falling over his shoulders without ornament. He is quite their equal in war or in councils, and no less the gentleman.

What evidence of this? In his hospitable wigwam, where he had invited me, he had assembled the worthiest of his tribe who were at the time near him; and when I entered, he brought them to me one by

[1] This beautiful canoe was a present from a Nayas chief, of Queen Charlotte's Island, to the Klah-o-quat chief; though the interpreter informed me that, amongst the Klah-o-quats and the To-quahts, there were others of their own make, quite as handsome.

one and presented them, not according to ribands, or medals, or other decorations, for they have none, but according to their rank for honorable deeds, which he explained to me as he introduced them. What could be more gentlemanly than this? And he gave us a humble feast. It was the best he had; and whilst we ate, he ate nothing, but waited upon us as we were eating, and charged and lit the pipe for us to smoke when we had done. Humble and unpretending, but what could be more polite, more gentlemanly than this? Is such a man, who has had none but nature to teach him, a brute?

He had invited a dozen or more of his friends to see me, and to see my portraits of Indians, which were now opened, to their astonishment and amusement.

The wigwam of this man was an immense thing, one hundred feet or more in length, and twenty-five feet in width, with several apartments with intervening partitions of planks lodging the different branches of his numerous family.

As our time was to be very short, I set Caesar at work in a corner of the wigwam, amusing them with the portfolio, and the interpreter to explain, whilst I went to work upon a sketch of the chief and his wife and child, which I got tolerably well before night; and just at the time when I had got about through, an instant excitement arose, which I was at a loss to understand, and which I must say, for a few seconds, gave me a degree of *alarm,* accustomed as I have been to Indian modes. I heard the shouts first in the village, at a distance, and the next moment bursting forth from the whole multitude in the house and around it. All sprang upon their feet; some leaped in the air, and others clapped their hands and danced, and then I instantly saw, by the expression of their faces, that it was a jubilee rather than an alarm; that there was no bad news, for every face, even in its astonishment, teemed with joy, and vociferated and echoed in all parts (though in Indian), "A whale ashore! a whale ashore!" The interpreter ran to me, and echoed again, "A whale ashore!" News had just arrived that the northwest gale had landed a sperm-whale on the sands, near the entrance of "Hope Canal," at the head of Nootka Island.

Here was a "Godsend" for these poor people, and every throat was stretched with "A whale ashore! a whale ashore!" and all was "helter-skelter." The wigwams were all emptied, for "out-doors" was a larger and freer space for the circulation of the mutual expressions of joy that rang from every mouth. The dogs caught the excitement and howled, and knew as well as their masters that *something* had happened, but probably knew not *what*.

The chief came to me with the interpreter, and told me that news had just arrived that a whale was struggling on the sands at the head of the strait, and that every canoe of the village would be in a few minutes on the way to the spot to secure it.

He had told me in the morning that the northwest gale would drive many fine fish into the Sound, and in inlets and coves, where the water was calm, there would be fine spearing that night by torchlight; that salmon and halibut would be taken in great quantities, and it had been arranged that I should go and see the sport; but the sudden news of "a whale ashore" silenced every other excitement for the time, and engrossed everybody and everything that could be handled or moved.

Every canoe was starting off, filled with men, women, and children, and with harpoons and cords and spears, and everything that their wigwams contained that could be used in securing the monster on the sands. The wind was still blowing a gale outside, and yet their flying canoes were starting off and up the strait, through which, a distance of fifteen or twenty miles to the spot, they could creep along the shore and in quiet water.

"A whale ashore" is surely a gift from Heaven for these poor people, and they receive it and use it as such. They believe it is sent to them to be received and used by all alike, and, no matter how many tribes assemble on the occasion, all share alike, in their efforts to secure it, and all share equally of its flesh, its sinews, and its bones when it is dissected. A great proportion of its flesh is eaten; other parts produce oil for their lamps, sinews, bones, skin, and fifty other things useful for Indian existence.

Not only the canoes from this little village were on their way, but the coves and inlets of the sound were alive with canoes darting about, and wending their way to the whale wreck.

The chief sent the interpreter with us in a canoe to our vessel, and, night arriving, we lost sight of the Indians. The next morning the wind had so much abated that Captain Pasto put his schooner in motion, and sailing out of the sound, and outside of the island, we were on our course, and had Hope Canal, at the head of the island, before us, and almost exactly in our route.

Getting off the northern cape of the island, with glasses we had at once a view, at several miles' distance, of the monster lying high and dry on the beach, and the group of Indians, like ants around a sugar-bowl, moving in all directions about it. We were all curious alike, and prevailed on Captain Pasto to steer in towards the shore, and to give us his yawl for landing.

He ran us within two or three hundred yards of the shore, and, the yawl manned, Simms and Stevens and Caesar and myself got in, and Captain Pasto agreed to lie off and wait for us.

The beach looked smooth and sandy and the sea calm, but it being ebb tide and a current running off, we had a tremendous hard pull to reach the sands, and a tremendous sea-bath in landing. We got ashore, however, but drenched, and pulled our boat on to the sands.

Then the sight!—the spectacle! The monster lay embedded in the sand, yet a long distance from us, and we started towards it. On our way we met our mulatto boy interpreter and several Indians coming to meet us. We approached the monster on the sea side, and in the immense furrows which in its struggles it had grooved out in the sand, as the waves of the rising tide had forced it towards the land. The sight was imposing when we came near to it, but not until we came round it on the other side had I any idea of the scene we were to witness.

Some hundreds, if not thousands, of Indians, of all ages and sexes, and in all colors, were gathered around it, and others constantly arriving. Some were lying, some standing and sitting in groups, some were asleep, and others eating and drinking, and others were singing and dancing.

At our approach the women commenced crying, and a mournful murmur ran through the crowd;—eating and dancing and sleeping were all stopped. The women covered their mouths with their hands, and cried and howled in piteous tones, and the men were silent. I asked our fine little interpreter if the chief whom we had seen the day before was there, and he said that he had not yet arrived, but that he would be there in a little time. I asked him what the women were crying about, and he said they had seen us coming from the ship, and they knew that we were some of "King George's" men coming to claim the whale. I asked him if he thought he could interpret what I wanted to say, so that they could all hear and understand it, and he said yes.

"That's right," said Simms, "make a speech to them, Catlin."

Several immense baskets, which had been brought to carry blubber, &c., in, were lying near, and placing two or three of these one within the other, and bottom-side upwards, we lifted our little interpreter on to them, so that all could see and hear him.

I stood upon another by the side of him, but not quite so high, and began making significant signs, which they all understood, that what I should say I spoke from my heart.

I told them that I was sorry to learn that their women were crying because they thought we had come from our ship to claim the whale; and if that was what they were crying for, they need not cry any more or have any fear of us; that we are not "King George's" men, as they had thought, but that we were all friends of the Indians, and had come to see the whale, and to shake hands with them if they wished.

"Tell them," I said to Joseph, "that I consider the Great Spirit loves them, and has sent this large fish to them as an evidence of it; that it therefore belongs to them, and to nobody else."

This interpreted to them, there was a shout of applause from the whole crowd with uplifted hands.

"Tell them, Joseph, that we are only passing by on the ocean, never to see them again, and that we shall leave here in a few minutes, and wish them well."

Another uproar of applause, and Joseph got down. A great many of the chiefs came up and shook hands with us, and all troubles were ended.

The scene was now curious. No stones, no timbers, or anything of the sort were placed about the monster to secure it; but on the shore side some twenty or thirty harpoons had been thrown into its side during its struggles on the rising tide by the first who were on the spot, and with long cords, some reaching to the trunks of the trees on the shore and others fastened to stakes driven into the ground. These were watched, and at every lift of a wave moving the monster nearer the shore, they were tightened on the harpoons, and at low tide the carcass is left on dry land, a great distance from the water.

The whale, to Simms and Stevens, was the curiosity; and they took the measure—length and breadth of it; to me, the curiosity was the crowd of poor *humans* who were gathered about it, and of them I could take no other measure than by the naked eye; for though I had put a sketch-book in my paletot pocket, in the drenching which we got in landing, every leaf of it, like everything else upon us, was soaked.

The dissection of this monstrous creature, and its distribution amongst the thousands who would yet be a day or two in getting together, the interpreter informed us would not be commenced until all the claimants arrived, and I therefore lost one of the curious scenes of my life which I should have been glad to have witnessed.

Their mode of slaughtering such a beast and dividing it would have been curious in the extreme. A *per capitum* division is always the mode of the Indians in such cases—the poorest of the tribe and the youngest infant drawing the same as a chief.

I could have studied for hours, without pencil or sketch-book, amongst the curious group, and those studies I never could forget. The beach, for half a mile, was almost literally covered with something—with reclining groups of women and children—with baskets, and bags, and cribs, and pouches, and every sort of vehicle they possessed, for transporting their respective proportions of the prize; and the drying of blankets, red, blue, and green, and white, wet like ourselves in landing their canoes, made a carpet for the sands in the distance of the most extraordinary hues.

Not like the Sioux or the Crows or the Shyennes, covered and plumed and moccasined in full and handsome dresses, but poor and naked, excepting their breech-cloths and blankets, they were yet human—painted in a thousand forms and of all colors, and thus were subjects for a picture, and subjects for a sermon or a lecture.

Our drenched condition, and signals from Captain Pasto, terminated our visit here. A crowd of these poor people followed us to our boat, took it up bodily, and entered the water with it, and took us up in their arms one by one, and waded through the surf with us, and put us into it, and bade us a civil and affectionate farewell.

Sailing out of Nootka Sound, and again on our way to the visioned fields of gold and Indians, maps and charts were mustered out upon the table, correspondences relating to nuggets of fabulous sizes that had been seen amongst the Nayas Indians, and supposed localities in which they had been found, were brought out and referred to, and the second and last great effort to raise another "gold fever" on me was strenuously tried, but decidedly failed.

This, however, in no way impaired my influence in the consolidated strength of the expedition at that place, for the very field which was soon to become the scene of action for them, the actual *"El Dorado"* of America, was the very point to which my ambition led me, that coast being thickly inhabited by tribes of Indians of the most interesting character, and as yet but little known or appreciated.

Along the Pacific Coast of North America

Passing the picturesque shores of Vancouver, we were soon in Queen Charlotte's Sound, and gliding along in front of the ever varying mountain barriers of the mainland, covered alternately with rhododendrons and honeysuckles, or capped with moss-covered rocks, enclosed by deep and dark ravines shooting up their tall and pointed pines and cedars.

At the shore of the sea, huge blocks from the mountain tops stood in relief, like houses, and sometimes like immense ramparts and castles rising out of the water, and behind and around them quiet glades, overshadowed by outstretched arms of pines and hemlocks, and overhung by long-leafed laurel, under and through and around which brigades of the Nayas' painted canoes, with their cargoes of red shoulders and glistening paddles, were darting, and easily keeping us opposite company.

On our left, and towards the setting sun, and blue and purple in the distance, rose the shining summits of Queen Charlotte's Island; and near its base, a blotched mass of deep green (its pines and cedars), underlined by a streak of white, the sands of its shore, at ebb tide. No imagination could paint, and few artists' pencils ever have painted, scenes so grand and so picturesque as these.

We are gliding along from day to day, with our glasses beholding the "rocks that are doubtless full of gold," and my Indian subjects flying about in their light canoes, and the smoke of their villages on the shore, which, by our "agreements," we are bound to pass by, and leave for our homeward voyage. What temptations, and what glorious fields were beckoning us back!

These left behind, what then is before us? Liska is the chief town of the Alaeutian Islands; a little village of some sixty or eighty Russian and Indian houses and huts, where Captain Pasto goes once a year, gets skins, gets wool, and other products, for which he trades cotton and woollen cloths, hardware, cutlery, &c. The Russians here are half Indians, and the Indians are Americans, not Kamskatkans nor Mongol Tartars; not an expression or feature of either, as my portraits will show.

What next? The Captain's business done, we are on the sea, and a few days' sail brings us to the coast of Siberia, and the river Kamskatka, of twenty miles, transports us to the town of Nishna-Kamskatk, or Petropolovski. What a town! How droll! Russian houses built of pine poles and mud, adobes and mud! and huts of Koriak Indians, somewhat like the Mandan wigwams, earth-covered, but the doors in their tops—how strange—men, women, and dogs walk down a ladder to get into them!

There's Che-nish-ka Wabe (a mountain on fire), the volcano of Avatcha; its smoke stands up in a vast column, leaning to the right, and softening away in the distance in a long and straight cloud towards the western horizon. The mountain is blue in the distance, and yet we must look into its sulphurous crater. Mud, and then snow, and the most frowning and defiant rocks are in our way, but we go on. We get to the brink of the awful and boiling lake, when nature is completely exhausted.

Sulphur is glazed over everything we touch and everything we see. Excepting smoke, we see nought but rocks; we tread upon them, and lean against their slippery sides, and tremble at the awful sight that is before us; and rage and fret too, for all beyond, below, and all around us is smoke, smoke! and nothing else.

Hissing, like a thousand furnaces at work, is constant; a hollow and consumptive cough is frequent, and now and then a sneezing, ejecting jets of stones and gravel, coated with liquid blazing sulphur, whizzing past our heads, and rattling amongst the rocks around and over us. These significant monitors determine us to retrace our steps and get a view from the valley several miles below, for nothing of the Avatcha can be seen, at this season, from its fumy head and sides, above.

What a day of toil was spent to see a sight unseen! And yet, as we are sailing off upon the green waters of the bay, how splendid to gaze upon the snow-clad sides (yet blue in the distance), and the rising clouds from the crater of the Avatcha. Good-bye ye icy, muddy, willowy, cedared rocky coasts of Siberia, and ye *Koriaks* fine fellows, whose portraits I slipped into my portfolio.

"Back to Queen Charlotte's" said the Captain, and so said our "agreements."

"But stop—a codicil!" said our attorney, Simms. "Captain, we have agreed to see Petropetrovski, the Russian capital, and you must run us to it; and then we will sail for Queen Charlotte's and not before. And we four have agreed to give you thirty dollars each."

"I can't do it." said Captain Pasto. "You have all seen my papers, and you know if I leave my track I risk my insurance."

"Never mind the risk and the insurance," said Simms; "we will insure your vessel, and a better insurance you can't find on the face of the earth. Bring forward your agreements, all hands," said he; and in ten minutes the following "codicil" was appended:—

CODICIL, off the coast of Kamskatka, 1853.
Further agreed, to run the *Sally Anne* to Petropetrovski, and thence to Queen Charlotte's Sound; no risques; enough to eat; and nigger free.

(Signed) *J. Paulding.*
V. Simms.
J. Stevens.
Geo. Catlin.
Capt. Pasto, of the *Sally Anne.*

The thirty dollars each were put down, and the vessel headed for Petropetrovski. "You do things quick," said Captain Pasto to (Squire) Simms, as we called him. "Yes, sir, when I know I'm right, I go ahead. I've been a Missouri attorney for ten years—I take but little time to do up such things as this. I have sat three times as Judge Lynch, and signed death-warrants in half the time. Brevity is the life and strength of all business, and when I know I'm right, I lose no time."

Each one pocketed his agreement again, and the Captain went to the deck, evidently under a strong conviction of the necessity of following to the letter the meaning and intention of the document he had put in his pocket.

Petropetrovski had very little interest for any of us: the Captain had no business there, and the prospect of "gold" was a dead one. I saw, however, during the four days that we remained there, a group of Esquimaux Indians, and a number of Athapascas, who come in there occasionally. These were interesting to me, and I got my sketches of them.

My gold-hunting companions were getting impatient; and all hands, the Captain included, were sighing for wind, as we were sailing down the coast and aiming for Queen Charlotte's.

There was now another overhauling of papers between my fellow-voyagers, who, it seems, had before but partially informed me on the subject of their grand design, and the excitements which had turned their attention to it.

"Catlin," said Stevens (as they had got me to the table), "you must know all about our plans before we go any farther." A number of letters were read to me, and amongst them one from a brother of Stevens in New Orleans, who had drawn from a sailor, some years before, something like the following extraordinary narrative:—

"After a fatal shipwreck in Queen Charlotte's Sound, in 1825, he and one other sailor succeeded in reaching the land, on the mainland

131

shore, and in a state of starvation got into an Indian village, where the natives wore large round blocks of wood in their lips, and were very kind and friendly to them.

"That they remained there two years, when one of them died, and the other one, who gave the narrative, got permission to go with a party of Indians, in their canoes, to Nootka Sound, where he got on board of a vessel sailing for Panama."

The surprising and only supposed available part of the narrative was the astounding description of lumps and masses of pure gold which he had seen in the possession of the Nayas Indians; and amongst these, belonging to the chief, "a solid block, the full size of a man's head, and as much as one man could lift!"

What a cause for an epidemic or a contagion! Who would not catch the gold fever—unless he had had a touch of it before—at a recital like this?

No precise locality for this wonderful discovery was given; nothing more definite than that it belonged to one of the great chiefs, and was seen amongst the Nayas Indians, on the mainland side of Queen Charlotte's Sound, which has an extent of several hundreds of miles on the coast and some hundreds of miles in the rear.

The "gold fever," however, has the wonderful power of shortening distances and of solving the most embarrassing difficulties. "Such wonderful nuggets as this," I was informed, "must be known throughout the tribe, and the way, therefore, could easily be found to it; and the bed from whence it came must be known also to the Indians. That's what we want, Catlin, more than the big nuggets; but we'll get at them both, you may rely upon it."

The cool and perfect state of health I was in as to "gold" seemed to check a little the fever that was raging around me, but not to allay it, for I said, "Gentlemen, I am yours for any expedition we can agree upon into the interior of this interesting country; there are many things in it which I have heard of, and which I want. But, hold," said I, "do you know that the whole of this country and its populations have been for these fifty years in the possession and under the control of the Hudson's Bay Company, who are gold-hunters as well as yourselves? They have their trading houses amongst these people, and has it occurred to you that such a wonderful nugget would probably have found its way into their hands before this, if it actually existed amongst the Nayas Indians? I do not suggest this to discourage you, but I will go ashore with you and use all my endeavors to assist you in discovering these wonderful treasures."

The third day of sailing brought us into the sound, and nearing the coast, the smoke of an Indian village was soon in view; and getting near to it, the roofs of houses, which at once informed us that we were in front and in full view of one of the Hudson's Bay Company's factories. All hands suggested, and I agreed, that we had better proceed farther down the coast, and land at some of the villages which we had passed on our northward passage.

My comrades seemed evidently surprised at the information I had given them as to the Hudson's Bay Company and their influence in that country, and began to show symptoms of fear lest they should excite an enemy more fatal to their enterprise than the Indians themselves. They evidently were approaching a country that they had known little about, and which, they had believed, with all its treasures, lay open and free to all comers.

I explained to them as near as I could the vast influence the Company had over the whole of that country, from the Rocky Mountains to the Pacific Ocean—the great number of trading houses they had, that one or more of their *employés* would probably be found in every Indian village, and that the present existence amongst the Indians of such a block of gold as had been described was a matter of impossibility, or that rich mines of gold known to the Indians could have escaped their acquisitive investigations.

My advice and suggestions, which were less patiently listened to at first, were now being more thankfully received, as I reiterated with them my intention to use my best efforts and all my influence, under any circumstances, to promote their views, whilst any chance of success remained.

We were running on, and sundown and twilight approaching, we ran into a deep cove, sheltered by a high and precipitous rock escarpment, and the *Sally Anne* cast anchor, and lay till morning. At sunrise, and before coming on deck, I heard distinctly Caesar's loud voice and broad laugh, as he was ejaculating English, Spanish, and the *Lingua-geral,* all in rapid succession, convincing me that we had visitors on board. I got on deck (the gold-hunters yet fast asleep), and found our forward deck half-covered with a party of Indians, and double the number resting on their paddles, in their painted canoes, lying around us. Fresh salmon and dried, in great abundance, and oysters and whortleberries, were brought on board for barter, and the captain and mate were busily engaged in laying in supplies, while Caesar, a head taller than all the group, and the sun shining on his glistening cheek-bones and forehead, stood, with his rifle in his arms, a model, vainly endeavoring by his *Lingua-geral* and Spanish to get some clue to conversation with the curious group around him; but all in vain, and for the first time I had seen him put to his trumps completely.

All eyes were upon him, and the Indians were as much surprised and perplexed at his sudden advent and novel appearance as he was perplexed with the total unintelligibility of their language. It required but a *coup d'oeil* to see that shining, glistening, black Caesar was to be the lion, the paragon of the enterprise. The Indians on deck all shook hands with him, and, in total default of his Spanish and *Geral,* he had got into a partial conversation with them by signs manual, of which he was master, and which (a curious fact) are much the same amongst all the tribes, both in North and South America; and by the time I got on deck he was becoming a tolerable interpreter for me.

"Well, dear me, Massa Catlin," said Caesar, "dem dar bery curious people. I b'lieve dey bery good. I guess you go ashore, Massa?"

"Yes, Caesar, we are going to land here for a while, after the other gentlemen get up."

We were lying about four hundred yards from the shore at this time, and though no signs of a village could be seen, their light and bounding canoes were constantly putting out from the nooks and crevices in the rocks overhung with cedar and impenetrable masses of red, and white, and purple rhododendrons, and gathering in a gay and dancing fleet around us.

Though I had heard of the beauty of their canoes and their dexterous mode of handling them, I had formed but an ignorant notion of them. The sluggish logs and tubs that Caesar and I had been knocked about in on the Amazon and the Xingu gave us no clue to the light, the gay, the painted gondolas now dancing on the ocean's waves about us. Excavated from the trunks of the immense cedars of the country, they were fashioned with grace and lightness, and painted in all colors, and so were the naked shoulders that were seen within them.

Like a flock of goats playing up and down upon a group of hillocks, upon the rising and sinking waves they were sporting and vaunting in all directions, and seemed, at times, actually rearing, as if to leap upon the deck. Their paddles were all painted with similar designs as those upon their boats, and their robes, when worn, showed characters the same, and all seemed like some system of hieroglyphic signs yet to be understood. . . .

In the midst of the group now assembled on the deck, our attorney, Simms, emerged from the cabin below, exclaiming—

"Why, Catlin, we are prisoners!"

"On, no; we are in the midst of one of the most friendly receptions, and it is a great pity that you and Paulding and Stevens should lose any part of it. We are in the midst of the Nayas Indians, and their largest village is just around the point ahead of us."

"Halloa, below there, fellows!" exclaimed Simms, putting his head as far down the hatchway as he could. "You are losing everything!"

Half-awake, and misunderstanding the two last words, and hearing the voices of Indians on deck, and catching a glimpse of the group through the sky-lights, they advanced most bravely, and at a jump were on the deck, with their rifles up and their revolvers ready! Simms sprang at one, and I at the other, and, just in time, saved the carnage that was at the instant of commencing.

The Indians, unarmed, flew to the bow of the vessel, and a number of them overboard. And well they might, from the frightful aspect of the two gladiators, but half-dressed, and rising, like demons, from below, at the signal call, for their extermination.

I spread my hands forward and over the Indians, and made signs for them to come back, whilst Simms and myself were cooling down the two fire-brands; when Caesar threw himself between the two groups, and, a figure like the Colossus of Rhodes, he stood, explaining by signs to one party, and by tolerably good English to the other, that "it was only a little mistake, and dat we were all bery good friends."

This little sensation over, others of the Indians began climbing on board from their canoes, and, last of all, some half a dozen of their women, whose eyes were riveted on Caesar; and he began to loom up, as he used to do amongst the Muras, the Connibos, and the Chetibos and other tribes of the Amazon.

He was naturally a tremendous gallant, and, stimulated by the gaze of these fair beauties, he was frequently in the clouds.

The singular appearance of one of them, whom he had observed, brought him to me at this instant.

"Well, Massa Catlin, I bery sorry for dat poor gal dar, she got mighty soa lip!"

"Yes, Caesar, it's a great pity: for she seems, from her dress and manners, to be a very nice girl; I should say, the belle of the village."

Breakfast was ready below, and Caesar and the hands of the vessel amused the group on deck whilst we were taking our coffee and discussing the movements of the day, to be made on the land.

Caesar had learned that their village was just around the point, and at the request of the mate, the Indians were returning to their village, where they were informed we should follow them when our breakfast was over.

About nine o'clock we four, with Captain Pasto (with only revolvers, our rifles being left on board), and Caesar, carrying my portfolio on his back, and his Minié rifle in his hand, got into the yawl and went ashore, and were conducted to the village, which was at the head of a little cove, half a mile or so from the shore.

The Indians, informed of our visit, had all gathered into their huts, and the chief, a very dignified man, was seated in his wigwam and ready, with his pipe lit, to receive us. We were seated on mats spread upon the ground, and whilst the pipe was being passed round, the first ceremony on all such occasions, the Indian dogs (half-wolves), of which there were some hundreds, got upon our tracks, and completely invested the chief's wigwam, and set up the most hideous and doleful chorus of yells and howls and barks. The sentinel whom the chief had placed at the door of his wigwam, to prevent all access except by his permission, drew his bow upon one of the foremost of the gang and shot it through the heart, when the throng was silenced and dispersed by the Indian women, who set upon them with their paddles.

Our position was rather awkward, having no other interpretation than the imperfect knowledge of signs already named, of Caesar and myself, brought from South America and the valley of the Missouri. However, we effected a general understanding, and learned from the chief that he had sent to another village not far off, and would have an excellent interpreter in a little time.

I told my companions I thought they had better not say a word of their object in visiting the country until the interpreter arrived, when it could be clearly explained without being misunderstood, and in the meantime I would not lose a moment's time in making a sensation, and of exciting a friendly interest.

"Good," said Simms, "I know what it is, Catlin, go ahead! Show him your pictures."

I had beckoned Caesar, who was at that moment unstrapping the portfolio from his back, and advancing towards me. I opened it before the chief, and sat by the side of him explaining the portraits, as I turned them over. He was a very deliberate and dignified man, and exhibited no surprise whatever, but at the same time evidently took a deep interest in them.

I showed him several chiefs of the Amazon, and also several of the Sioux, Osages, and Pawnees, and the last one turned up, a portrait, full length, of Caesar Bolla. He could not hold his muscles still any longer, but burst out in the most uncontrollable and vociferous laugh, and turning around to Caesar, who was sitting at the farther side of the lodge, extended his hand, which Caesar, advancing, shook, and, at the chief's request, took a seat by the side of him.

The book of portraits was creating such an excitement, that three or four sub-chiefs came in and took their seats. And the wigwam being in two sections, and divided by a door made by a hanging bearskin, which was put aside, two women and a young man entered, and also took their seats on the ground, to get a peep at the portraits; one of these was the wife of the chief, and the other his daughter, an unmarried girl.

Caesar had his attention at this time fixed upon one of the men who had taken his seat, with the block of wood in his under-lip, and the chief's daughter was decorated in the same way.

"Caesar," said I, "here are more sore lips."

"Well, now, I do decla, Massa Catlin, *dea* me, I think it is ketchin!"

I turned the portfolio through again, to the amusement and astonishment of all, and when Caesar Bolla was turned up, there was a roar of laughter again, all eyes were upon him, and turning his face one side and a little down, he whispered to me, "Well now, Massa Catlin, I neber felt so shame in all my life, afoa." And when he had mustered courage to raise his head and cast his eyes around, I said, "Caesar, your portrait has cured the sore lips" (the two wearing blocks of wood in their lips having slipped them out in order to enable them to laugh).

About the instant that Caesar had observed that the blocks were out and the broad laugh was over, they were slipped in again, when he exclaimed, "Well, Massa Catlin, affer dat, I neber know wat I will see nex."

Though this curious and unaccountable custom was known to me, my companions had been as ignorant of it as Caesar was, and evidently were regarding it with equal astonishment. I said to them and to Caesar,

"Of the 'sore lips' take no more notice until the interpreter comes, and then we will learn all about it."

My attention was then fixed on a beautiful mantle worn by the chief's daughter, made, as I learned, of mountain sheep's wool and wild dogs' hair, wonderfully knitted with spun-yarn of beautiful colors, and so assembled as to exhibit the most eccentric and intricate figures, and bordered with a fringe of eighteen inches in length, the work of three women for one year, I was told, and its price, five horses.

The bowl of the pipe which the chief had been passing round was full fourteen inches in length, of pot stone, jet black, and highly polished, the whole, a group of figures, human and animal, interlocked and carved in the most ingenious manner.

Of these pot-stone pipes I saw many, and obtained several, and the eccentric designs on them, on their robes, their canoes, their paddles, their leggings, and even the paintings on their faces and limbs, are peculiarly tribal, and their own, differing from anything seen in the other tribes of the continent.

The same extraordinary characters are written on their spoons, their bowls, their vases, their war-clubs; on their pottery, of which they make great quantities, and on everything else that they manufacture, and seeming to be a system of hieroglyphics not yet explained, and which, for the archaeologist and ethnologist, may yet be a subject of peculiar interest.

Instead of the stupid superstitious fears and objections which generally stood in the way of my painting their portraits in the valley of the Amazon and other parts of South America, this intelligent and rational man at once said, when I asked him—

"Yes; if you find any of us worthy of so great an honor, and handsome enough, we will all be ready to be painted."

"Good!" said I (by intelligible signs). "I love such a man. Caesar, bring my painting-box and easel from the vessel, and I will begin this noble fellow's portrait this afternoon."

"Catlin!" said Simms, "you are getting altogether ahead of us."

"Never mind," said I, "I am on the right track—the right vein. I know these people better than you do; they must be pleased first, amused, complimented; and the compliment I am now paying to the chief will make him the friend of all. I will secure his good will first for the whole party, and when the interpreter comes tomorrow, you may put in your claims in the best manner you can devise."

The afternoon came, and my paint-box and the chief were before me, and with him his lovely daughter. He told me he loved her, and always made it a rule to have her by him, and he thought I had better place them both in the same picture. I told him I loved him for that; it was natural and noble.

Vanity is the same all the world over, both in savage and civilized societies. Good looks in portraiture and fashions, whatever they are—crinoline of the lip or crinoline of the waist (and one is just as beautiful and reasonable as the other), or rings in the nose or rings in the ears, they are all the same.

Night came, and my picture was taken on board.

"Catlin," said my companions, "you are leaving us all in the background."

"Never mind," said I again, "I am introducing you where you never could have got a foothold for an hour. We will have a council tomorrow in the chief's lodge, and, his interpreter present, your plans will progress as well as mine."

During the night the wind veered about, and being very nearly driven on to the rocks, the Captain set sail, and crossing the Sound, got shelter under the lee of Queen Charlotte's Island. The wind abating the next day, we were able in the afternoon to return to our anchorage in front of the Indian village.

The Indians were all on the shore and received us with shouts, and many in their canoes gathered round us whilst we were coming to anchor; and amongst them came on board the interpreter who had been sent for by the chief. He was a young man, a Frenchman, by the name of Frénié, an *employé* in the fur company, and met us with much civility.

From him we soon got an account of the numerous tribes of Indians along the coast, and on Queen Charlotte's Island, over which also the fur company's business extended. The interpreter had learned from the chief that I had painted his portrait, and it being brought on deck, he was excessively delighted with it, holding it up over the gunwale and showing it to the Indians paddling about in their canoes.

Caesar was on the spot with my cartoon portraits, and ready to make a further sensation. "Yes, Caesar," said I, "bring it forward." We had a look at the portraits, and the interpreter then asked my name. When I wrote it for him with my pencil, he said my name had been familiar to him for the ten years past, and that there was not a man in the Hudson's Bay Company nor an Indian between the Rocky Mountains and the Pacific coast who had not heard my name and of the collection of Indian paintings I was making, though he believed I never was in that part of the country before.

He told us that the chief expected myself and my companions to eat and to smoke with him in his wigwam that afternoon, and that at night the doctors were going to give us a medicine dance. Simms agreed with me that "all was going right," and that it would be best not to start the inquiries about gold until these festivities were over.

We were soon ashore, all excepting Captain Pasto and his crew, he having hinted to me that there might be a plot in all this to get all ashore, and then take possession of his vessel. I was quite agreed to this, as the festivities would now be tendered to us alone who could appreciate them.

As we approached the village, a great throng came out to meet us, and I observed the mass (and particularly the women) were sidling up to Caesar, who was marching at his fullest height, with the portfolio of portraits strapped on his back.

The concourse of people, seeming to me too large for so small a village, led me to make the suggestion to the interpreter, who replied that "news of our arrival and the masquerade dance to be given that evening had brought a great number from Jaurna's village, and that others were coming."

"Soa lips" now began to thicken around Caesar, who had got the portfolio off from his back, and was carrying it under his left arm, whilst the other was constantly employed in answering the questions put by signs. He was evidently the lion, and as soon as I could, I got him and his portfolio into the chief's lodge, to be subject to the chief's orders.

My companions found enough for their amusement amongst the throng whilst I was sketching two other portraits, and at sundown we sat down to a feast of venison in the chief's wigwam. This and "a smoke" kept us till some time after dark, when a dozen or more flaming torches, with yelping and barking and singing, approached his wigwam, and in front of it commenced the masquerade dance.

Bizarre is but a lame word for the startling eccentricity and drollery that were then before us. Caesar was not in the midst of it, but by the side of it, and overlooking it. I had serious apprehensions that I should lose him, from the hysterical bursts and explosions of laughter that fell in bolts and half-strangled hiccups from his broad mouth.

Some fifteen or twenty, all men, were engaged in this singular affair, all masked and otherwise dressed in the most strange and curious taste; and many of the lookers-on, in the front ranks, both men and women, were masked and dressed in a similar manner.

The leader of the dance, a *medicine man,* the drollest of the droll, was the *"King of the Bustards,"* another was *"King of the Loons,"* another was the *"Doctor of the Rabbits,"* one was *"the Maker of the Thunder,"* one was *"the White Crow,"* one was *"the Bear that travels in the night,"* and another *"the Cariboo's Ghost,"* &c. &c., until the names of the animal and feathered tribes were chiefly exhausted.

The masks which the dancers wore (and of which I procured several) were works of extraordinary ingenuity. Carved in a solid block of wood, excavated in such a manner as closely to fit the face, and held to the dancer's face by a transverse strap of leather, from corner to corner of the mouth of the mask, inside, so that when the mask was on, and close to the face, the strap of the leather was taken between the teeth, counterfeiting thereby, not only the face, but the voice—a perfection in masking yet to be learned in the masquerades of civilized frolickings.

Besides the ingenuity exhibited in the forms and expressions of these masks, they were all painted of various colors and with the most eccentric designs. These masks (with the exception of that worn by the leader of the dance) were all made to imitate the mode of the people, of wearing a block of wood in the under-lip.

The custom of masking and of masquerade dancing is by no means peculiar to the Nayas Indians, for in many of the tribes, both in South and North America, I have witnessed similar amusements. . . .

The ornament of the lip is a mode belonging chiefly to the women, though there are some eccentric men who also practice it. And of the women, it is but a portion of them who perforate the lip, and even by them it is only on particular occasions that they wear the blocks, to be seen, as they term it, in full dress. When eating and sleeping the blocks are removed, and also when much use of their tongues is required; for, with the block in the mouth there are many words not pronounced. . . .

The perforation for the block in the lip is made at a very early age, and is kept open through life, and is scarcely perceptible when the block is out.

For inserting the block, the thumb of the left hand is forced upwards through the aperture, and by the side of it the thumb of the right hand, and the block is delivered into its place by the fingers, from above, as the thumbs are withdrawn.

The whole of the next day after the masquerade I was painting, and Caesar was showing and descanting on the portfolio; and my three companions, with the interpreter, were discussing gold nuggets and gold placers; and as near as I could ever learn it, the total of their discoveries led to this: that there had been about two years before, a party of gold-hunters from California in that country, having heard marvellous accounts of gold nuggets in the possession of the Indians, and that they had been ordered out of the country by the Hudson's Bay Company, and were obliged to leave in a great hurry; and that there had, no doubt, been some nuggets in the hands of some of the Indians, but that they had been found at a great distance off, near the mountains on the banks of a great river (supposed to be Frazer's River, where the rich mines are now being worked).

The Frazer River mines at that time were just becoming known; and my companions very judiciously decided that their best way would be to return to Victoria, and take the track of the flood of Frazer River miners at that time ascending the Frazer's River.

This resolution suited the captain of our little craft exactly, as time was precious to him, and his vessel more or less at risk whilst lying along the coast. Victoria, which was then but a town of some forty or fifty houses, was our next aim, and stopping a day or two in several villages of *Hydas* and *Bella Bellas,* on the coast, we were safe at anchor in Smith's Inlet, opposite to the northern cape of Vancouver's Island. Its shores were alive with the smokes of Indian villages, and there was no need of leaving the vessel to see Indians. We were at all hours of the day surrounded by their bounding and galloping pirogues, and often had more than the Captain was disposed to accommodate on deck, mostly a miserable, almost naked, and squalid-looking multitude, bringing fish and oysters to barter for rum, or whatever else they could get. Amongst these were *Skidegates, Stickeens, Bella Bellas, Hydas,* and several other tribes inhabiting the coast and islands in the vicinity. Some were flat-heads, and others were not.

It mattered little to me what the shapes of their heads were, and for a couple of days I was gathering them into my portfolio, whilst Caesar kept all comers, and of all languages, amused with the portraits, which he was lecturing on alternately in English, in Spanish, and *Lingua-geral,* from which they learned just as much as they would have learned from the squalling of a parroquet or cockatoo.

It seemed a perfect mystery to my impatient companions "how I could sit out two whole days without my dinner, painting these ill-looking Indians." They killed time, below the deck with the Captain, at cards; and during the third night sails were up to pass the straits and run to Victoria, which our chart showed us was but a short run.

Morning came, and where were we? not in the harbor of Victoria, nor near it, but in front of Nootka Island, where we had been before, off the west coast of Vancouver, and its tall pines and rocky peaks but just discernible! And for what? nobody could tell unless the Captain's reasons were correct, that the shape and character of the winds made it hazardous to run the strait and the sound, and that an open sea and fair sailing which he was making was apt to be the quickest and the safest.

A forty-eight hours' run brought us round the southern cape of the island, and into the Strait of Juan de Fuca, and hugging the shore, and heading towards Victoria. And hugging a little too close, at low tide, the keel of the *Sally Anne* was rubbing on the sands, and losing her headway, and hitching inwards a little at every wave, as the tide was rising. She was hitched up, and hitched up, until, at high tide, she was lying, and was left, broadside upon the sands in a little sandy cove, between huge and frowning rocks.

We remained on board until another flood time, which only lifted us higher up and left us again, a few rods farther on to the island, and, of course, a few rods nearer to Victoria. All chances of getting his little craft nearer to Victoria harbor being now apparently ended, with due sympathy for the poor captain, which we all felt, as we were taking leave, we each agreed to leave him a *bonus* of thirty dollars, and each signed his "agreement" to take us to Victoria, *"executed."* We got some Flathead Indians on the shore to carry our luggage, and at their guidance we trudged through the forest to Victoria.

In Victoria all was confusion, complete pell-mell; houses were filled, steamers and vessels were full, and men and women were sleeping in carts and waggons in the streets; and others were not sleeping at all, but with bonfires built upon the bank, or under the pines, were dancing away the nights in wild and frantic whirls.

Frazer River had just *débuted* as the *El Dorado* of the world, and it seemed as if California had emptied itself, "neck and heels"—its men, its mules, and its steamers—into the sound of Vancouver.

Reports were hourly arriving from the mines, and all was on—on! and "bad luck to the hindmost." The "Celestials" were there, with two oblique sabre cuts and two gimlet holes for eyes; New Yorkers and

George Catlin

Londoners were there, and all the nations of the earth seemed to be assembling. The Omnipotent hand had spread nuggets and sands of gold in such profusion over the newly discovered fields that it required but the hand of industrious man to pick and scrape it up, and load his pockets with it.

The midst of this grand mêlée was the place exactly for my three impatient companions, and the mere hurried "Good-bye, and God bless you, Cat." was about all that I could get from them as they disappeared.

The poor Indians living in the vicinity of Victoria, on Vancouver's Island, and all belonging to the Flathead family, seemed alarmed, and withdrew their encampments into the forest.

In the midst of such an epidemic, after having had the fever myself, one can easily imagine my position anything but agreeable, and in a few days, by a returning San Francisco steamer, Caesar and I got a passage to Astoria, and from thence, by another craft to Portland, the head of navigation on the Columbia River.

This thrifty little beginning of a town has the prospect of wealth and greatness before it.[2]

The "Dalles" (and we soon made it) was the next and the last destination foreshadowed in that direction thirty miles above and on the same river. This famous place, from time immemorial the living, the life, and support of tens of thousands of surrounding Indians, from the endless quantities of salmon taken in it, is a bold and furious rapid, for several miles dashing and foaming through compressed channels in the rocks, in the eddies of which the fatigued fish, in their laborious ascent, stop to rest, and are pierced by the harpoon arrows of the overleaning and overlooking Indian, and lifted out.

The fresh fish for current food and the dried fish for their winter consumption, which had been from time immemorial a good and certain living for the surrounding tribes, like everything else of value belonging to the poor Indian, has attracted the cupidity of the "better class," and is now being "turned into money," whilst the ancient and real owners of it may be said to be starving to death; dying in sight of what they have lost, and in a country where there is actually nothing else to eat.

[2] Whilst halting a few days in this little seaport town, I learned by accident that Captain Pasto had got his schooner afloat, and had put out to sea.

CHAPTER 10

The Flathead Indians

(CHAPTER IV FROM *Last Rambles*)

JUST AT THIS TIME another epidemic was raging, and not less prolific in its victims than the scourge of the country I had just escaped from; the crusade from the States across the Rocky Mountains to Oregon, by waggons, by ox-carts, and by wheel-barrows, spotting the prairies and mountains with recent graves, and strewing the wayside with carcasses of oxen and horses, and broken waggons and abandoned household furniture.

The greater portion of this disastrous and almost fanatic pilgrimage crossed the mountains at what is known as the "south pass," that is, south of the terrible and impassible piles of twice-upheaved rocks, where the Salmon River Mountain traverses the Rocky Mountain range, and over, or through, the mountains, and descended through the valley of the Shoshonee (or Snake)River to the Columbia.

Learning by some of the most recent of these arrivals that the Paunch (Grosventres), a band of the Crow Indians, had crossed the mountains north of the Salmon River Mountain, and were encamped in the Salmon River Valley near its sources, I made the instant and desperate resolve to reach them, if impossibility were not in the way.

I asked Caesar how he would like to take a trip on horseback and see the Rocky Mountains.

"Well, dat ar just wat suit me now, zactly. You guess you go?"

"Yes, if I can get a horse and a couple of good mules. This I can't do here, Caesar, but at Fort Walla Walla, farther up the river, I think it can be done."

Flatheads we were now in the midst of, and for the time I had my work to do. The *Klatsops,* the *Chinooks,* the *Clickatats,* the *Walla Wallas,* and the *Nez Percés* and *Spokans,* constituting the principal

145

bands of the Flathead family, I was there in the midst of, and had enough to do. Some of these flatten the head, and others do not, yet all speak the Flathead language, or dialects of it.

The Flathead tribe, so called from their singular practice of flattening the head, is one of the most numerous (if not the most numerous) west of the Rocky Mountains, occupying the whole country about the lower Columbia, including the island of Vancouver. It is altogether a canoe race, living in a country where there is little else than fish to live upon. The tribe is divided into something like thirty bands, speaking nearly the same language, and generally spoken of (but erroneously) as so many different tribes, the names of the principal of which I have already mentioned.

The strange and unaccountable custom of flattening the head in this tribe is confined mostly to the women, and amongst them it is by no means general, and ornamentation, singular as it may seem, appears to be the sole object of it. In the [illustrations] I have given copies of two of my portraits of women showing the artificial shapes produced by that strange custom; and portraits of a Flathead chief, curiously wrapped in his blanket, and his wife, with her infant in its crib (or cradle) on her back, which is undergoing the processes of flattening. The infant, at its birth, is placed in its cradle, dug out of a solid log of wood, and fastened down with bandages, so that it cannot move, and the frontal process is pressed down by an elastic lever, which is tightened daily by strings fastened to the side of the cradle. The bones of that part of the head, at that period, being cartilaginous, are easily pressed into that unnatural form, and after two or three months of this pressure the required shape is obtained, which lasts through life. By pressing the frontal region back, the head is pressed out on the sides to an unnatural extent, as seen in the illustration.

If this were a natural deformity, stultility would undoubtedly be the result; but as it is an artificial deformation, no such result is produced, or need it be looked for, as it is only a change in the form and position of the mental organs, without interfering with their natural functions. The evidence of this is, that those with their heads flattened are found to be quite as intelligent as the others in the tribe; and it would be a monstrous supposition to believe that the fathers of families and chiefs would subject their infants to a process that was to stultify them.

Near Fort Walla Walla, for the first time in my life, I procured a tolerable horse, a stout mule for Caesar, and a pack-mule, at a fair and honest price; and in company with three young men who had recently arrived from the States, and were going back to meet and aid the sick and disabled of their party that had been left behind, we started, with our faces towards the mountains.

After five days' march together, their course being to the right and through the Snake River Valley, we were obliged to part company, and Caesar and I, with an Indian guide, took to the left, hugging as near as we could the ragged and frightful, and all but impassible, southern bank of the Salmon River, until, at length, after many days of deep repentance, we entered the more calm and beautiful meadows and prairies of the Salmon River Valley.

Our ride (or rather walk, for we had to walk and climb most of the way, leading our horses) was one which I deeply regretted from day to day, but which I never have regretted since it was finished. The eighth day opened to our view one of the most verdant and beautiful valleys in the world; and on the tenth a distant smoke was observed, and under it the skin tents, which I at once recognized as of a Crow village.

I was again amongst my old friends the Crows! men whose beautiful forms and native, gentlemanly grace had not been deformed by squatting in canoes, nor eyes bridled by scowling on the glistening sun reflected on the water, no heads squeezed into wedges, nor lips stretched around blocks of wood.

As soon as we were dismounted, and in the midst of the crowd around us, I was struck more forcibly than ever with the monstrous and pitiable deformities of man, which the peculiar necessities of life often drive him to, as seen amongst the squatted, paddling tribes of the Amazon, Vancouver, and the Columbia coast and river.

It was a pleasure that I cannot describe to find myself again amongst mankind as Nature made them, the Crows, whom I had long since thought I had seen for the last time.

The Crows (as they are called by their neighbors), *Belantsea,* of whom I gave some account [elsewhere], are probably the most unbroken, unchanged part of the original stock of North American Man. Their numbers, at the time when I was amongst them, in 1832, were about 10,000, living on the head waters of the Yellow Stone River and in the Rocky Mountains.

From their traditions, which are very distinct, they formerly occupied the whole range of the Rocky Mountains and the beautiful valleys on each side, from the sources of the Saskatchewan in the north, and as far south (their traditions say) as the mountains continue: that would be to the Straits of Panama.

They say that their people were a great nation before the Flood, and that a few who reached the summits of the mountains were saved when all the tribes of the valleys were destroyed by the waters.

That they were the most ancient American stock, and the unique, original American type, I believe; and that they were the original Toltecs and Aztecs, who, history and traditions tell us, poured down from the mountains of the northwest, founding the cities of Mexico, Palenque, and Uxmal.

My portraits of Crows, made in my first series of voyages, in 1832, and exhibited in London, from their striking resemblance to those on the sculptured stones of Mexico and Yucatán, excited suggestions to that effect from many of my friends; the first of these, and the most enthusiastic, my untiring and faithful friend Captain Shippard, an indefatigable reader amongst the ancient archives of the British Museum; and my friend the Baron de Humboldt, who told me also that the subject was one of profound interest to science, and well worthy of my further study.

These reiterated suggestions, added to my own intelligence, have kept alive, for many years, my anxiety on that subject, and undoubtedly were the uncombatable arguments which determined me, when hearing, at The Dalles, of a band of Crows encamped in the Salmon River Valley, west of the Rocky Mountains, to "make shift" (*coûte qui coûte*), and, with Caesar, to throw myself amongst them.

I have said that "we were there," and whatever I found amongst them in customs and contour and traditions, as well as amongst other tribes that I visited in more southern latitudes, between them and the Straits of Panama, tending to establish the belief above advanced, that they were the Toltecs and Aztecs of Mexico and Yucatán . . . .

The Crow village that we were in, consisting of some forty or fifty skin tents, had crossed the mountains on to the head waters of Salmon River, to take and dry salmon, there being no salmon on the east side of the Rocky Mountains.

The chief of the band, a sub-chief, called the *"Yellow Moccasin,"* was a very intelligent man, and gave me a clear and, no doubt, true account of the recent history of the tribe, as he had received it from his father and grandfather. According to this, the Crows were originally confined to the mountains and their valleys, from which their enemies of the plains could never dislodge them; but that since horses have made their appearance in the plains, a great portion of their people have descended into the prairies, where they have been cut to pieces by the Sioux, the Blackfeet, and other tribes, and their former great strength destroyed.

I was received with great kindness by these people, and told by the chief that I should be welcome, and that his young men should watch and guard my horses. The incidents here, enough in themselves for a small book, must be passed over, for there are yet many adventures ahead of us.

One thing, however, cannot be passed by. Whilst seated in the chief's lodge, where there were some six or eight men besides the chief, and endeavoring, as the necessary preliminary in all first interviews with Indians, to make the object of my visit distinctly known, I opened the portfolio of cartoon portraits, which all were examining with great interest and astonishment, when on turning up the fifth or sixth portrait, one of the party gave a sudden piercing yelp, and sprang upon his feet and commenced dancing in the most violent jumps and starts, and vociferating, *"Bi-eets-e-cure! Bi-eets-e-cure!"* (the name of the young man), whose portrait I had painted at the mouth of the Yellow Stone twenty years before, and was now holding up.

The portrait was recognized by all, when on their feet, and darting out of the wigwam, were three or four of the party, and through the village to where the women were drying fish, on the bank of the river, and back, they re-entered the chief's wigwam, and with them, out of breath, and walking as if he were coming to the gallows, entered *Bi-eets-e-cure* (the very sweet man).

I instantly recognized him, and rising up, he took about half a minute to look me full in the eyes, without moving a muscle or winking, when he exclaimed, *"How! how!"* (yes, yes), and shook me heartily by the hand. I took up his portrait, and showing it to him, got the interpreter to say to him that I had "kept his face clean"!

The reader can more easily and more correctly imagine the pleasurable excitement, and the curious remarks amongst the party at this singular occurrence, than I can explain them; for, not knowing their language, I was ignorant of much that passed myself.

"One thing I'm *sua,* Massa Catlin," suddenly exclaimed Caesar, who had not before opened his mouth, "I quite *sua* dat ar man knows you, Massa!"

All eyes were now turned for a moment upon Caesar, who was sitting a little back, and evidently looked upon by most of the party as some great chief, until the interpreter explained that he was my servant.

During this interlude, and which required some little exchange of feeling and recollections between the *"very sweet man"* and myself, I had shut the portfolio, to begin again where we left off; and proceeding again with the portraits, after showing them several of their enemies, the Sioux and Blackfeet, *Ba-da-ah-chon-du* (the Jumper), one of the chiefs of the Crows, whose portrait also was painted at Yellow Stone twenty years before, turned up! All recognized him, and *Bi-eets-e-cure* told them that he saw me when I was painting that picture twenty years before.

Through the interpreter, I told them that more than 100,000 white people had seen the chief's face, and, as they could see, there was not a scratch upon it! The chief then rose upon his feet, and making signs for me to rise, embraced me in his arms, and each of the party saluted me in the same affectionate manner. . . .

In conversation which I had with *Bi-eets-e-cure,* he informed me that the chief *Ba-da-ah-chon-du,* whose portrait we had just seen, was dead—that he died soon after I painted his portrait, and many of his friends and relations believed that the painting of the portrait was the cause of his death. "But," said he, "I told them they were very foolish—that I had no fears when mine was painted, and here I am alive, after so many years!"

I told them that no man of good sense could see any way in which the painting could do them an injury, and that amongst the white people we all had our portraits made, and it did us no harm. They all gave their assent in a "How, how, how!" and the next day I slipped off the "skin," as they called it, of two or three of them; and, amongst them, and the first, that of the young chief whose hospitality I was enjoying.

I painted him at his toilette, as he was letting down his long hair and oiling it with bear's grease, which his wife was pouring into his hand from a skin bottle. She, poor woman, from a custom of the country, not to compete with her husband in a feature so ornamental, was obliged to keep *her* hair cropped close to the head. . . .

The day before I left, a report was brought, by one of the Hudson's Bay Company's men, that a party of Blackfeet—their deadly enemies—was preparing to march upon them from the north. All, of course, was excitement and confusion; and they were preparing to move into a defile in the mountains, where they could protect themselves if attacked; whatever was the result of this movement I never heard.

With a faithful guide, who knew the route, recommended by the chief, we started to cross the Salmon River Mountain into the Snake River Valley—a pass difficult to traverse, and requiring the most desperate resolution. Ravine after ravine, amidst the most frowning and defiant rocks of all sizes, which had tumbled down from the snow-capped summits on either side of us. Our guide entered us well into them, and, sleeping with us one night, instructed us how to proceed, and left us to our fate, returning to his village.

We had an ample supply of dried salmon for our five or six days' march, which was to bring us to Fort Hall, one of the Company's fur factories, near the source of the Snake River. We might have returned to The Dalles by the same route by which we had come and escaped the terrible task we were now performing, but for two reasons—the first, that in all the travels of my life I have had a repugnance to return by the same route; and the second, that I had an unconquerable desire to cross this range of palaeozoic rocks, and to examine the strange confusion produced by a mountain lifted by a rising mountain.

This mountain range, running from west to east, traversing the Rocky Mountains, and becoming the "Black Hills" on the eastern side, is known to geologists to have been a mountain under the sea before the continent of America arose, and to have been relifted up at the intersection by the Rocky Mountains rising underneath at a later date. How sublime! A stupendous mountain, with its hidden treasures from the bottom of the sea, lifted up to the heavens and crumbling to pieces, is tumbling into the valley and ravines below! And what a field for the geologist to get at the deepest production of the earth's hidden material!

Gneiss and granite, from their deepest beds in the earth, raised in stupendous mountain piles under the sea, and, risen with a continent, have again been shoved up by deeper beds of granite underneath, until their sub-aqueous, cavern-formed lime-stones of all colors—of snow-white, of green, and blue, and grey, and their associated felspathic rocks and massive blocks of felspar—are turned out upon their tops and tumbled down their sides.

What a field for geologists, and why are they not there?

Amongst these immense and never ending blocks I was reading an instructive book and making notes, which Caesar could not understand; he had enough to do to take care of the horses, whilst I was sometimes for hours out of his sight and hearing; and coming back, and waking him and the mules from their sleep, all I would hear was, "Well, Massa Catlin, you bery strange man, dat's all I got to say." He was getting sick on dried salmon and no excitement; and our poor animals were all but starving to death, there being sometimes, for miles together, not one solitary blade of grass for them to crop. What a time to study geology!

We had a sort of a path—a track—to follow, which we could keep to only with the greatest difficulty. The tracks of horses shod convinced me that the men of the trading houses were in the habit of passing from one trading post to another by it, and it was our only confidence that we should sooner or later discover the valley of the Snake River.

This we did on the fifth day; and even our poor and jaded animals neighed and brayed when we saw, through a ravine, the blue of the valley, and the *"Trois Buttes"*—three beautiful and stupendous natural pyramids—through blue in the distance, standing in the center of it.

Getting out, and upon the flank of the mountain, green grass was in abundance and shady trees; and I spent several hours in revising and rewriting my hasty notes on the rocks and the minerals we had passed, whilst our poor animals were luxuriating and Caesar was sleeping.

At a great distance, and before us, where a forest of shrubbery seemed evident, a smoke was seen rising, which I decided was Fort Hall, to which we were aiming, and minuting its bearing by my pocket-compass, we launched off into the (not grass, but sand-covered) valley towards it.

We started at noon, and hoped to reach it before night. The Trois Buttes, three conical hills of granite and of great height, standing in a group and at many miles' distance, were on our right. We travelled slow, and night overtook us, and we encamped, not in sand, but in cinders and pulverized pumice, and without vegetation for our horses.

The valley, though beautiful to look into when seen at a distance, like too many things in this world, is anything but beautiful when we get into it. The surface is generally without grass and without timber, or even bushes, excepting here and there bunches of artemisia, and is everywhere covered with volcanic ashes and pumice, which are wafted by the winds; and all roads and all tracks of living beings before us are obliterated before we see them.

No living animal or fowl is seen to afford us food, not even a rabbit or a prairie hen; and the tail of our last dried salmon for us, and nothing for our poor horses, put us to sleep upon this barren and desolate waste.

Our course was continued in the morning, and about noon we came upon the bank of a small stream covered with luxuriant grass; and here we were *obliged* to stop, for our poor animals could have gone no farther; and who could have had the heart to push them beyond it? But *we* had nothing to eat, and our only chance to get anything was to lie down and quietly wait till our animals were satisfied, and able to carry us, and then move on, which we did; and a little before sundown we approached the patch of timber we had seen, and soon after (not Fort Hall, but) the encampment of some twenty or twenty-five emigrants from the States, who had crossed the Rocky Mountains at the South Pass, and were on their way to Oregon.

When we rode up to their tents, or waggons and carts (for these were mostly used for tents), they seemed as much surprised as ourselves; and if not the first sentence that I pronounced, certainly the *second* was, "Have you got anything to eat?" "Well, neighbor," said one of them, a middle-aged man, who stepped forward as spokesman, "we are pretty hard up; our flour has long since gin out; but we have a plenty of hard biscuits, and some good salt pork." "Don't say any more, my dear sir," said I, "that's enough; we are just starving to death."

"*Oh, Dear* ME," said his tidy and red-cheeked wife, as she jumped down fron one of the waggons and came up to my stirrup, her face beaming with sympathy. "Dear *sir,* if you had come a little sooner! We had a nice pot of boiled beans and pork today, and I don't know— Sally! my *dear,* look into the iron pot and see if any of them beans is left!"

Sally, without running to look, came to her mother, ejaculating, with a sort of a hiccup, "Oh *yes,* mother; I *know* there is a *heap* left; we didn't eat a *half* on 'em; and there's a *large lot* o' pork, too!"

Here my young readers must again *imagine* (to save space) how comfortable Caesar and I were made when there was a pot of boiled pork and beans all ready, and a plenty of hard biscuits, and good grazing for our horses; and in the midst of twenty-five intelligent persons, old and young, male and female, with all their traps and accoutrements, from the state of New Hampshire, on their way to a new and unseen home in Oregon.

What Caesar and I first did was to discuss the pork and beans, and how we did it need not be described; and other matters discussed in the course of the evening must be brief, if noticed at all in this place.

Thirty-six days before, this party had started from Fort Leavenworth on the Missouri River, in eight waggons and two carts, drawn by oxen and using no horses. Their waggons, which supported hoops covered with sail-cloth, were all made new, and of great strength, expressly for the purpose. Their oxen were shod like horses, to preserve their feet, and grain was transported for their food, to be used in places where the grass should give out.

In rising from the prairies on to the arid plains of the mountain regions, the wood of their waggon-wheels shrunk, and the tires were loosened; and without smithing utensils, their misfortunes became irreparable, and all but fatal to their existence. Wheels that went to pieces were left by the wayside; wheels were withed and mended as well as ingenuity could devise, and changed from axle to axle until waggons were left, and at length oxen after oxen, as they died, or fell, or gave out from fatigue which they could no longer endure. And when we met them, but three of their waggons remained, and less than half of their oxen were living.

Substantial food they had transported enough of; and their little children, as well as the rest of the party, were in good health; and all, yet in unbroken spirits, approaching, with a prospect, their new homes.

They had met that day a half-caste interpreter from Fort Hall, to which they had been steering, from whom they learned that the trading post was yet twenty miles in advance, which showed me how far Caesar and I had mistaken our course in entering the valley.

These people told me that, since they entered Sweet River Valley in the mountains, they had passed over 150 carcasses of oxen lying by the wayside; some partly devoured by wolves and bears, and others not in the least decayed, though they had been dead for weeks and, perhaps, months. Such was the unaccountable and almost incredible pilgrimage, in those days, from the States to the "promised land" on the Columbian coast.

This party, where we found them, had left the travelled road for several miles to get grass for their cattle, and they assured me that for fifty miles which they had last passed there was not a blade of grass left for poor oxen or horses to live upon; and, by the interpreter they had met, they were informed that such had been the crowd of emigrants over the mountains, that for the distance of ten miles around Fort Hall every particle of grass had been exhausted, and the people in the fort, as well as their horses, were in a state of almost absolute starvation, and had notified all emigrants and travellers to keep at a distance from them, where they and their animals might possibly find something to subsist upon.

This little caravan started the next morning on their route, in good spirits, leaving Fort Hall on their right, and steering for Fort Boissey, another trading house 140 miles farther west, towards their destined home.

Caesar and I "saddled up," and, to their great delight, started in company with them, our destination being the same. We were soon on the emigrants' road, and both they and we in absolute apprehensions of losing our animals conveying us, the poor creatures getting but here and there a bite of short grass that had been twenty times bitten by other animals before them.

The stench exhaling from the carcasses of oxen and horses that we passed on the wayside became sickening and almost unendurable. I did not count, but I believe that in the two days we passed more than fifty; and, in one of these instances, two of these poor creatures lay dead in the yoke together! Such was the lamentable fate of these poor and faithful beasts, after dragging man and his effects over the vast prairies and arid mountains, a distance of 1,400 miles, and not even getting their food for it.

On the second day, the interpreter of whom I have spoken overtook us, galloping on a very fine horse—a half-caste Snake (or Shoshonee) Indian—a rakish looking young man, speaking French, English, and several Indian languages; dressed out in all the flaming colors that broadcloths and ribbons could give him, and carrying in his hand a first-rate rifle.

I at once suspected, and soon learned from him, that his business was that of galloping about amongst the lost, the straggling, the suffering parties that were traversing the country at that time, guiding them and interpreting for them, and depending upon their generosity for compensation.

Learning from him that one day's ride would bring us to the great or "smoky" falls of the Snake River, the vicinity of which he told me was his native place, and with the whole localities of which he was familiar, I made an arrangement with him to conduct me there the next day, which he did, we having procured several days' provisions of the little and, as yet, stout-hearted colony, and taken leave of them, at all events, for a few days.

They travelled so slow that we could easily calculate on spending a day or two about the falls, and overtake them before they reached the settlements. Our ride to the falls took us the most of two days, instead of "one," over a sandy and barren waste; but, with a guide who knew the way and the modes of the country, we felt secure, and rode it with tolerable ease.

The great or "smoking" falls of the Snake River may well be classed amongst the greatest natural curiosities of the world. Not that they resemble in character or magnitude the *chûte* of Niagara; but, from a character peculiarly their own, of an awful grandeur, which strikes the beholder in quite a different way.

For a hundred or two miles around, in different directions, the country is chiefly as barren a waste as the deserts of Arabia. The earth is everywhere almost entirely destitute of vegetation, and even of birds and insects, and covered with a light and moving sand or dust, composed of pulverized pumice and volcanic ashes.

In the midst of this vast plain of desolation we discovered, at many miles distance—not a pyramid of spray rising, forming and piling away a mass of clouds in the heavens, as we see above the fall of Niagara—but a chain, of several miles in length, of jets of spray, rising apparently out of the level ground, not unlike the smoke of the camp fires of an army of men; and, approaching it, we scarcely realize its origin until we are quite upon the brink, and the awful abyss, with all its grandeur, is beneath us; and, even then, it is but here and there that we can approach near enough on the sand-covered brink, with no tree or rock to cling to, to catch more than a partial view of the scene before us.

Instead of looking upwards, as we usually do, to see a waterfall, or of seeing it leaping off from the rock on which we are standing, all is here below us at the bottom of an awful chasm, and the very surface of each successive fall is several hundred feet below us.

The term "Great Fall," which has been known for more than half a century, is applied to a succession of leaps which the river makes within the space of three or four miles, dashing and foaming from side to side, in a zig-zag channel cut in the solid rock, varying from six hundred to eight hundred feet in width, with precipitous—and much of the way, perpendicular—walls of basaltic rocks on either side, from 150 to 200 feet in height, and with here and there an avalanche or graded way, where, with great fatigue, and with somewhat of danger, we can descend to the bottom of the chasm, and, at the water's edge, behold with wonder and enchantment the spirit of these wild scenes.

Owing to the zig-zag shape of the channel, the views from these points are exceedingly limited; but the frantic rage (or play, for it seems to partake of both) of the leaping, bounding, and foaming torrent, dashing alternately from wall to wall, with the overhanging rocks on either side, furnish for the artist's pencil scenes of spirit and wildness which I never have been able to see anywhere else, and which no imagination could create.

Comparatively, but a small portion of the cataract can be viewed from below, owing to the few chances there are of descending to the river's bed; and where we descend we are obliged to retrace our steps, as we can neither follow the shore nor cross the stream.

From the top of the wall, with great fatigue, and with the guidance of our good cicerone, I was enabled to see the whole extent of this wonderful scene. Owing to the depth of the chasm, when looking down from the top of the wall, the water seemed to be running nearly on a level, though its tremendous leaps and bounds, as well as the corresponding decline of the brink of the opposite wall, gave us something like an estimate of descent in the various *chûtes*.

The trappean bed through which this wonderful gorge is cut slopes to the west, and as the heights of the walls on either side are generally about the same, the gradual descent of the summit surface, for the distance of four miles, would indicate a near estimate of the descent of the river in that distance; and judging as well as I could from these premises, without the use of instruments, I was led to believe that the whole descent in four miles was something like three or four hundred feet.

I have seen some statements, recently made public, of travelers who reported the great perpendicular fall of Snake River to be 198 feet—"thirty-five feet higher than the fall of Niagara, and the volume of water quite equal to that of Niagara River." This statement is certainly quite Quixotic, and demands contradiction, if it were only for the benefit of school-boys' education.

The Snake River has its extreme source for about 150 miles above these falls, and has no large tributaries above the falls to swell it; therefore the statement that this volume of water is equal to that of the Niagara is necessarily incorrect. There is one point of view from which, looking up the stream, four or five successive leaps are seen in the distance, so ranged one above the other as to appear at the first glance to be one entire fall of great height; but from other points these are seen to be separated by intervening distances of a quarter or half a mile.

In all the cataracts which compose what is called the great or "smoking" fall on the Snake River, however terrific and picturesque they are, there is not amongst them, I should think, a perpendicular leap of more than forty feet. And the Columbia River at The Dalles, four hundred miles below, after uniting the Snake and Salmon rivers with the north fork of the Columbia, contains, from the nearest estimate I could make, but about one-fifth of the volume of water that passes over the fall of Niagara, and the Snake River, at the great (or smoking) falls, probably not more than one-twelfth or one-fifteenth part.

Few travellers who visit the fall of Niagara are aware of its real magnitude; no object on earth more completely deceives the human eye. In 1830 I spent six months at the falls, making a survey and estimates for a model; and even then I was in ignorance of its real magnitude until I went to Black Rock Ferry, twenty-five miles above, where I ascertained by measurement the width of the river to be seven-eighths of a mile, and its average depth eighteen feet, and its surface movement four and a half miles per hour; which, as the river at that place glides over the smooth surface of a level rock, would give a mean movement of four miles per hour. Such a mass of water, moving at the rate of a man under a fast walk, is easily contemplated; and with pen, ink, and paper, one can soon bring into cubic feet and avoirdupois weight the quantity of water per minute, per hour (and per annum, if figures can define it), which pours through the rapids at Niagara, and leaps down a precipice of 163 feet.

Such is the might and such the magnitude of Niagara, which, amongst waterfalls (like this little book amongst Indian books), still will stand without a rival on the globe!

After having examined all the features of the great falls, and made my sketches, we laid our course for Fort Boissey, following the course of the river for many miles, which still ran through a deep and rocky *cañon,* and from the summits of its banks we had often views of its deep-bedded and foaming waters, still dashing amongst rocks and down precipices, with a continuous wall on either side, of several hundred feet in height.

Near a ford which we were to make we met an encampment of Shoshonee (or Snake) Indians, about thirty in number, and being all men, and without women, I supposed them to be a war party; but our guide said no—that they had no enemies near them to fight, and had been down to Fort Boissey to trade. He knew them all—was amongst his relatives, and introduced us without any difficulty.

The Flathead Indians

I had previously seen but a specimen or two of this tribe, and when meeting face to face this fine and elegant *troupe* of young men, I said to myself, "These are Crows!" The impression was instant and complete. I then said to our interpreter that these people resembled the Crows, whom I had just been amongst. "Well, they may," said he. "The Crows are our friends and relations, and we know them all." I said, "Then you are Toltecs." This I could not make him understand, as he had never heard of Mexico or Yucatán; but as the Snake Indians occupy a great portion of the mountains lying between the Crows and Mexico, it made a strong impression on my retina, as regards the origin of the Toltec and Aztec tribes, which history says poured down from the mountains of the northwest into Mexico and Yucatán.

These handsome young men had been playing a desperate game of ball at Fort Boissey, and having their ball-sticks and balls with them, were proud to show us what they could do with them. The ground was not good, but from the beautiful catches and throws which they made, I consider them quite a match for the Sioux or the Choctaws, and their rackets are formed much in the same way.

We spent a day very pleasantly with them, Caesar showing the pictures, and I painting three of the young men, their names—*Yau-nau-shaw-pix, Naw-en-saw-pix* (he who runs up hill), *On-da-nout* (smooth bark).

All objected to being painted until the portrait of the Crow chief, *Ba-da-ah-chon-du,* was shown them; they all recognized him, and the gallant little fellow, *Yau-nau-shaw-pix,* then sprang upon his feet, and throwing a beautiful Crow robe over his shoulders, exclaimed, "There! you may paint *me*—I am not afraid."

The rest then all agreed to be painted, but I selected the three named above, and got the rest to wait until I should come again.

We parted, but not without regret, from our friends the Snakes (not *Rattle*snakes), who went on their way to their village, near the base of the mountains, and commenced our winding and dangerous descent of some hundreds of feet, to the river-shore, where we were to make the ford. There was no other place for a great many miles where it was possible to descend to the bed of the river, or to ford it if we could get to it.

I had engaged our gay and dashing chevalier to lead us safely across the river, and to put us fairly in the track for the frontier settlements, instead of Fort Boissey, which I felt a confidence in reaching from that place, without a guide, there being a well-beaten road to follow.

159

Down at the bottom of the terrible gulf, the river, with its transparent waters, was smoothly, but rapidly gliding along before us. The next thing was to cross it, and the thing next to that, to reach the opposite shore above, a huge point of perpendicular rocks projecting into the stream, and below which our interpreter said there was no chance of getting out.

The river here was some eighty or a hundred yards in width, with a pebbly bottom; and from the various contortions of the surface of the water, evidently of unequal bottom and full of bars. Our guide explained to us, as well as he could, the circuitous route we were to take, after we should get into the stream, not to fall into the troughs and currents; and to show us the course, dashed in and led the way.

We stood and watched him closely, and seeing the water nowhere higher than his stirrups, our apprehensions were all at an end. He mounted about half-way up the opposite cliff, and dismounting from his horse, sat overlooking our movements. We had but one fear, and that was for our pack-mule, which was a little creature; and Caesar, a tremendous tall fellow, said, "Massa Catlin, I radder wade, and den I take 'Nelly' moa safe."

"Well, Caesar," said I, "do so—give me the portfolio (which I slung on my own back), and I will lead your mule when I see you and Nelly safe over."

He handed me his pantaloons, and was on his way, his rifle in his left hand and his donkey in the other, whilst I was sitting on my horse and watching the results. When about the middle of the river, I observed they were at a halt; the mule was pulling one way and he the other. Instead of the lasso around its neck, he was leading it by a halter with a rawhide headstall, somewhat in the shape of a bridle. After mutual and stubborn pulling in this way for a minute or so, I saw Caesar, who had been standing up to his navel in the water, fall suddenly back, and quite under the surface of the water! The bridle had slipped from the animal's head, and they at once took different directions.

Caesar, it seems, falling backwards, was thrown from the shoal water into a deeper channel, where the current was stronger, and off from his feet, he was rapidly drifting away, his head and his hands now and then above the water!

I instantly threw my portfolio and my rifle to the ground, and dropping the rein of the mule I was holding, I plied my spurless heels with all the muscle that was in me to the sides of my slow and stubborn

"Rozenante"—and thought, "Oh (not my 'kingdom,' but), my 'collection!' for a horse! for *'Charley,'* for my *'Ancient Charley!'* " But I believe my convulsive kicks and blows frightened my poor beast into untried leaps and bounds, which soon passed me over the bar of shoal water into swimming depth, where Caesar, ahead of me, and not able to swim, was paddling with his hands, and keeping his head, most of the time, above the water.

He saw me coming, and I hailed him—"Hold on, my brave fellow—you are safe."

My horse was all below the water but its head and tail, and I was down to my armpits. There was but *one* way—and as I got near to him I said—"Now mind!—as I pass by you, don't touch me, but seize my horse by the tail, and hold on!"

I passed him, and looking back over my right shoulder and seeing nothing of him, I instantly exclaimed, "Oh, mercy! he's lost!"—when added to that, without a period or a comma—

"Dat ar bery good; now I guess I go ashoa!" And looking over my left shoulder, with an astonishment that nearly threw me from my saddle, I saw he had both hands clenched to the tail of his own riding mule, which, it seems, had plunged in when I threw down its bridle, and without my observing it, had swam by my side, and a little back of me, to the rescue of poor Caesar, whom it was now pulling to the shore! I reined my horse towards the shore, and Caesar, holding on, was gliding along by the side of me—

"Well, Massa Catlin, dis ar beat all; I no feas now!"

Our horses' feet were now getting hold on the bottom, and at that moment came down the shore at full gallop, and dashing through the water, our faithful guide, who, thoughtless of any accident, had placed himself too far from us sooner to lend a helping hand.

We were all upon the beach, and safe, and our little pack-mule, with all our baggage soaked, had swam to the same shore from which it started, but half a mile below, and was standing in a nook of rocks, from which it did not know how to escape.

Our demi-"Snake" dashed into the river to recover it, and I hailed him—pointing to my rifle and portfolio, left on the beach. He soon had them strapped on his back, and the donkey in his hand; and, with little difficulty and without fear or danger, was soon with us.

"Now," said I, "Caesar, we are all saved, and there is but one thing that I see missing, that is the old Minié."

Caesar, whatever might have been his education, or want of education, was a very moral and a religious man—and in all my travels with
him, under the hundreds of instantaneous excitements and vexations
which we had met together, I never heard him use a profane or an in-
decent word; but his sudden exclamations were, "Oh, de goodness me!
My soul alive!" &c.; and on this occasion, such as was his attachment
to the Minié rifle, "Well, as I am a libbin being, I guess, Massa Catlin,
dat ar gun is neber seen no moa! I no recollection; but when I slip in
de deep water, I guess de minny has slip from my hands widout my
know it; I bery sorry."

The fact luckily was, that the eyes of our guide had been upon it
when it slipped from Caesar's hand, and, marking the place where it
sank, he was now wading his horse to the spot, and with his eagle eye
was scanning the bottom through the clear water, and, after wading
and then swimming awhile, he gave a piercing yell and a wave of his
hand, signifying that he had discovered it. He instantly rose, with his
feet upon his horse's back, and making a plunge headforemost, brought
it up; and then, not swimming for his horse, made his horse swim
to him, for he had a long lasso of rawhide of ten yards in length, fastened
round its neck, and its other end in his hand.

"Well, now, dat ar de mose wondeful man I eber saw yet! I neber
see de like afoa!"

There is no sunshine in the deep and gloomy *cañon* of this part of
the river; and ascending the avalanching cliff, and fairly on its top and
in the sun, our soaking packs were spread out to dry. We all took a
lunch and a sleep, and our animals found a little grass to regale upon.

Our guide gave us instructions for the ride that Caesar and I were
to make alone; and, putting into his bullet-pouch what he acknowledged
as a liberal compensation for his services, he galloped off, intending to
overtake his party of Snake warriors during the day.

In our course, after riding a mile or two, I halted, and said to Caesar,
"Have you got your rifle dry and in order?"

"Yes, Massa; and loaded."

"Then," said I, pointing to a bunch of wild sage at a little distance,
"go and fetch that rabbit; it is a very large one, and has set down behind
these weeds. Be careful, and don't touch anything but its head."

"Yes, Massa; you hold de mule."

This rabbit, the first fresh meat we had had for a long time, came in admirably well with our salt pork, and was the first creature of the kind that we had seen since we left the coast of the Pacific.

Six or eight days of hard work, and fording the Snake River at two different places on our way—but why should I stop to narrate more particularly here?—brought us to the border settlements near Fort Walla Walla. I had then a horse and two mules to dispose of—an affair that, as well as buying, I have always approached with a displeasure; for, until now, in all my travels, when I have wanted to buy horses, I have been "a little too late; there were a plenty for sale a few days since, but the last of them have been bought up and taken away." And, when wishing to sell, "They would have brought you a good price a little back, sir; but so many have been brought in lately, that they are a mere drug now. You may be able to *give* them away, but I am not sure that you will even get a thankie for that."

However, in this instance, I was not long in looking up Thompson, the man of whom I bought the animals for my campaign to the Salmon River Valley. I said to him, "What will you give? They are all in tolerable trim, and as valuable as when I bought them." I expected him to name about half the price I had given him for them, and I was quite ready to have taken it.

"Well, I know the animals, and I don't care to give you the same that you gin me for them."

"Agreed," said I; and, having the money in his pocket, the affair was soon ended. I said, "Thompson, you are a very prompt dealer, and I like to deal with such men."

"Well," said he, "I'm glad you're satisfied, sir. You see, sir, there's just now sich a crowden into the diggins, that they've taken up the last crittur; and notwithstanding that, horses is about at a standstill, but mules has riz."

He got about double the price for his "critturs" an hour afterwards. They went to the "diggins," and Caesar and I steamed from Portland to California.

CHAPTER 11

California

(CHAPTER V FROM *Last Rambles*)

THE READER must not think that because we were again in California, we were at *home,* and our Indian peregrinations finished. In California we were on the wrong side of the mountains; and, as I hinted in a former chapter, that though a straggling Apachee was once in a while seen there, better specimens of that interesting tribe would probably be seen on our return.

The Apachee Indians, at this time probably the most powerful and most hostile tribe in America, hunt over and claim a vast extent of country within the Mexican lines, through the province of New Mexico, and extending northward nearly to the Great Salt Lake, and westward quite to the Pacific Ocean, embracing the silver mines of Sonora, and, until quite lately, the gold mines of California.

At this last point continued struggles, with much bloodshed, have resulted from the claims of white people to the gold mines on the Sacramento River, and in and east of the Sierra Nevada. These Indians, met by the California miners, are known by various names, and so are the Indians from San Francisco to St. Diego, and the peninsula of Lower California, though they are but bands of the great family of Apachees, speaking dialects of the Apachee language.

The aggregate of this great tribe, when counted all together, is something like 30,000; and the traveller who only meets a few of their border bands on whose rights he is trespassing, gets but a partial knowledge of their real numbers, or of their actual strength.

I learned from one of their chiefs, the "Spanish Spur," that they could muster 8,000 men well mounted, and equipped in the same manner as a war party of 300 which I saw him review. This gallant fellow had gained his laurels in his battles with the Mexican troops on the

Mexican frontier; and his name from a pair of huge spurs, which he often wore as trophies, taken from the heels of a Spanish officer whom he had killed in single combat.

The greater portion of this tribe are strickly migratory, changing the sites of their villages several times in the course of the year. And to reach the village of this chief's band, at present some thirty miles north of the Ghila, the *voyageur* should cross the Rocky Mountains from Santa Fé, taking the "Pony Express" route, or start, as Caesar and I did, from Santa Diego, on the Pacific coast, with a strong mule under him, and a light mule to carry his packs, and ride to La Paz, on the Rio Colorado, and thence to the great village of the *Ghila Apachees*—north bank of the Ghila, some sixty or eighty miles from La Paz, and thence cross the mountains to Santa Fé.

The Apachees, like the Snakes, are a part of the Great Crow or Toltec family. As with the Snakes, from a wandering specimen or two I was not struck; but looking about me in the center of the tribe, I was instantly impressed with the conviction of the relationship and unity of type which I was regularly tracing from the Belantsea (or Crow) to the mountains of Mexico.

Like the Crows, their tradition is, that "their tribe is the father of all the existing races—that seven persons only were saved from the Deluge by ascending a high mountain, and that these seven multiplied and filled again the valleys with populations; and that those who built their villages in the valleys were very foolish, for there came a great rain, which filled the valleys with water, and they were again swept away."

The Apachees in Mexico, being mostly in the vicinity of the Catholic missions, have made some progress in civilization, and are clad in ponchos, in leggings and tunics of cotton-stuffs or of bark, and broad-brimmed hats of grass, of Spanish manufacture. In the province of New Mexico, and the vicinity of the Ghila, and the mountains of the north-east, they are dressed in skins, when dressed at all, and in their costumes and weapons bear a strong resemblance to the Comanches.

Their manufacture of flint arrow and spear heads, as well as their bows of bone and sinew, are equal, if not superior, to the manufactures of any of the tribes existing; and their use of the bow from their horses' backs whilst running at full speed may vie with the archery of the Sioux or Shyennes, or any of the tribes east of the Rocky Mountains.

Like most of the tribes west of and in the Rocky Mountains, they manufacture the blades of their spears and points for their arrows of flints, and also of obsidian, which is scattered over those volcanic regions west of the mountains; and, like the other tribes, they guard as a profound secret the mode by which the flint and obsidian are broken into the shapes they require.

Their mode is very simple, and evidently the only mode by which those peculiar shapes and delicacy of fracture can possibly be produced; for civilized artisans have tried in various parts of the world, and with the best of tools, without success in copying them.

Every tribe has its *factory,* in which these arrow-heads are made, and in these only certain adepts are able or allowed to make them, for the use of the tribe. Erratic boulders of flint are collected (and sometimes brought an immense distance), and broken with a sort of sledge-hammer made of a rounded pebble of horn-stone, set in a twisted withe, holding the stone, and forming a handle.

The flint, at the indiscriminate blows of the sledge, is broken into a hundred pieces, and such flakes selected as, from the angles of their fracture and thickness, will answer as the basis of an arrow-head; and in the hands of the artisan they are shaped into the beautiful forms and proportions which they desire, and which are to be seen in most of our museums.

The master-workman, seated on the ground, lays one of these flakes on the palm of his left hand, holding it firmly down with two or more fingers of the same hand, and with his right hand, between the thumb and two forefingers, places his chisel (or punch) on the point that is to be broken off; and a co-operator (a striker) sitting in front of him, with a mallet of very hard wood, strikes the chisel (or punch) on the upper end, flaking the flint off on the under side, below each projecting point that is struck. The flint is then turned and chipped in the same manner from the opposite side; and so turned and chipped until the required shape and dimensions are obtained, all the fractures being made on the palm of the hand.

In selecting a flake for the arrow-head, a nice judgment must be used, or the attempt will fail: a flake with two opposite parallel, or nearly parallel, planes is found, and of the thickness required for the center of the arrow point. The first chipping reaches near to the center of these planes, but without quite breaking it away, and each chipping is shorter and shorter, until the shape and the edge of the arrow-head are formed.

The yielding elasticity of the palm of the hand enables the chip to come off without breaking the body of the flint, which would be the case if it were broken on a hard substance. These people have no metallic instruments to work with, and the instrument (punch) which they use I was told was a piece of bone; but on examining it, I found it to be a substance much harder, made of the tooth (incisor) of the sperm-whale or sea-lion, which are often stranded on the coast of the Pacific. This punch is about six or seven inches in length and one inch in diameter, with one rounded side and two plane sides; therefore presenting one acute and two obtuse angles, to suit the points to be broken.

This operation is very curious, both the holder and the striker singing, and the strokes of the mallet given exactly in time with the music, and with a sharp and *rebounding* blow, in which, the Indians tell us, is the great *medicine* (or mystery) of the operation.

The bows also of this tribe, as well as the arrow-heads, are made with great skill, either of wood, and covered on the back with sinew or bone, said to be brought from the sea coast, and probably from the sperm-whale. These weapons, much like those of the Sioux and Comanches, for use on horseback, are short, for convenience of handling, and of great power, generally of two feet and a half in length, and their mode of using them in war and the chase is not surpassed by any Indians on the continent.

[Among the illustrations] are copies of three of my portraits made in their little village—(a) The chief, *"Spanish Spur,"* wrapped in a beautiful buffalo-robe, with his battles painted on it; (b) *Nah-quot-se-o* ("The Surrounder"); (c) Nic-war-ra ("The Horsecatcher"), two distinguished warriors, in war costume and war paint, armed, and ready for battle.

We remained several days in this village, and found abundance of curious customs and things for our amusement; and on the day before we left we had the luck to witness an excitement of curious interest, and which might, with propriety, be called "Tir-national."

Much like the Sioux and Comanches, this tribe are all mounted, and generally on good and fleet horses, and from their horses' backs, while at full speed, with their simple bows and arrows, they slay their animals for food, and contend with their enemies in mortal combat. With their short bows, which have been described, as they have but a few yards to throw their arrows (the rapidity of their horses overcoming space), their excellency in archery depends upon the rapidity with which they can get their arrows upon the string and off, and the accuracy with which they can throw them whilst their horses are at full speed. Their practice at this is frequent and very exciting, and certainly more picturesque than rifle-shooting of volunteers in the educated world.

For this day's sport, which is repeated many times in the year, a ground is chosen on the prairie, level and good for running, and in a semi-circle are made ten successive circular targets in the ground by cutting away the turf, and making a sort of "bulls-eye" in the center, covered with pipe-clay, which is white. Prizes are shot for, and judges are appointed to award them. Each warrior, mounted, in his war costume and war paint, and shoulders naked, and shield upon his back, takes ten arrows in his left hand with his bow, as if going into battle, and all galloping their horses round in a circle of a mile or so, under full whip, to get them at the highest speed, thus pass in succession the ten targets, and give their arrows as they pass.

The rapidity with which their arrows are placed upon the string and sent is a mystery to the bystander, and must be seen to be believed. No repeating arms ever yet constructed are so rapid, nor any arm, at that little distance, more fatal. Each arrow, as it flies, goes with a yelp, and each bow is bent with a "wuhgh!" which seems to strain its utmost sinew, and every muscle of the archer.

This round and its scoring done, a little rest, and the same strife repeated. And after the tenth round, when each warrior's arrows have been claimed by his private mark in their feather, and the scoring done, the stakes and honors (not medals) are awarded, and a feast is given to the contending archers. I have seen "tirs-national" and "tirs-*international*," but amongst them all, nothing so picturesque and beautiful as this.

Taking leave of the great Apachee village, our little party (now consisting of two Santa Fé traders—acquainted with the route—two brothers Gleeson, of Texas, Caesar, and myself) laid its course for the "Santa Fé Pass," in the Rocky Mountains, unknown at that time as the "Pony Express" route, being, twelve years ago, but known to Kitt Carson and other guides in the habit of conducting parties through those dark and dreary solitudes.

The first mountain passed, in a beautiful valley we were in another Apachee village; and *another* mountain passed, we found another village of Apachees; and fifteen days of riding, of walking and leading, and prying and lifting sides of hills, on avalanches of snow and mud, and through ravines, and in the beds of roaring and dashing torrents, with overhanging rocks, and gloomy hemlocks and pines, we crept out of and began descending the eastern slopes of the Rocky Mountains, with the Spanish town of Santa Fé a great way ahead of us, and in the valley near it the Rio del Norte (if we should ever get to it), an easy and safe highway to the Gulf of Mexico.

Descending from the base of the mountains into the plains, and rising out of a deep ravine, which we had followed for some miles, we came instantly, and without a moment's warning, on to a group of human beings, lying mostly stretched upon the grass, in a sunny place, without fire, and apparently seeking the warmth of the sun. Nothing could surpass the expressions of astonishment and fear exhibited on their faces when they arose, and seeing the inutility of trying to escape, they were, with uplifted hands, imploring for mercy, as we were all mounted and armed, and white men, their enemies.

The little party, about twenty, were all women and children but two, who were old men and rheumatic, and were almost unable to walk. From our signs they soon saw that we did not wish to harm them; and riding up to them, we saw that they had not a weapon of any sort with them, and, from their haggard looks and signs, that they were in a state of starvation. We dismounted, and one of our Santa Fé companions, who understood something of the Apachee language, learned from them that they were the wives and children of a little village of Apachees that had been a few days before destroyed, and all their warriors killed, by a large army of white soldiers, after many terrible battles—that they had fled so far, and had nothing to live upon but roots from the ground, and no one to hunt for them—that the whole country to the north and the east was full of white soldiers, and that the whole Indian race were being killed off!

This was the first knowledge we had of a border war that it seems was then raging between the United States dragoons and volunteers and the Apachees, united Yutahs, their allies; and from which we drew the instant inference of the danger we were facing in moving farther in the direction of Santa Fé!

We had no alternative but to leave those poor and helpless and pitiable objects, with their little children, as we found them, dividing with them our provisions, which were then running low, and laying our plans to save ourselves, in the best way we could. I gave to one of the old men part of a box of lucifer matches I had, and showed him how to make fire with them, to warm their children by, for, from the snowy atmosphere from the mountains, the weather was very cold there. He thanked me as he took them, but said, "To make a smoke would be our certain destruction!" They all came up and shook hands with us, with the pitiful "Ya Ya," as we were mounting our horses; and, with tears in our eyes, I believe all felt as I exclaimed, "Would to God that we could save these poor creatures!"

Our trail leading to the northeast, right in the hostile ground, was now a dangerous one, and I said to our Santa Fé companions, "Is it possible that these are Apachee Indians, and that a nation of Apachees is living on the *east side* of the mountains?" "Most assuredly, sir," said the Santa Fé gentlemen—"the *Jiccarilla Band,* and half a dozen other bands; they are everywhere, and the greatest set of thieves and rogues in the world."

Our courses was towards Santa Fé, but we rode in trembling and doubt; and a couple of hours after we left the group of women and children, whilst passing through a narrow and rocky defile, two dashing and naked Indians on high-mettled horses plunged into our view and in our path, some forty or fifty rods ahead of us. They halted for a moment, and evidently were alarmed, seeing us all with our rifles in our hands. There was no escape, except by retreat, which they seemed unwilling to attempt. We all agreed to move on, without changing our course or halting; and they no doubt discovering from our costumes and our pack-mules that we were a party of travellers, and not soldiers, advanced slowly, lowering their rifles, and we did the same, and made the signs of friendship at the same time.

We met and shook hands, and the foaming state of their horses showed us at once that they were riding on an express, the object of which we suspected, and our Santa Fé companions soon drew the same from them, and, also, that the whole country to the northeast was in a state of the most bloody warfare, that the country was filled with soldiers, and that several hundreds of the Jiccarilla Apachees and Yutahs had already been killed, and their villages burned, and that they two, one an Apachee and the other a Yutah, were on an express to the great Apachee villages west of the mountains, to call for reinforcements. Their halt with us was very short, and they rode off, suggesting to us very distinctly that the course we were pursuing was in a very dangerous direction. On emerging from this mountain defile, we struck upon a strong trail leading to the southeast, which was known to lead to St. Diego, a small village on the bank of the Del Norte.

Here, from the intelligence obtained from the two unexpected interviews we had just had, a sort of council of war was held, in which it was
decided that the two Santa Fé traders and the elder Gleeson would continue on their route to Santa Fé, and run all the risks of meeting the
Apachee and Yutah war parties; and that Caesar and I, who had no
particular desire to see Santa Fé, should take the trail leading to St.
Diego, and with us the younger Gleeson, who, like ourselves, was destined for Matamoras, at the mouth of the Rio del Norte.[1]

Our tracks here diverged—the one leading to Santa Fé tending to
the northeast, and ours to the southeast. Ours was but an Indian trail,
and difficult to follow, and was still over mountains, through valleys,
and across river and swamps; and yet we kept it, not learning from any
landmark, or from any human being, whether one day or one week
would bring us to the bank of the Río Grande, and knowing only by
my faithful and never failing little pocket-compass that we were advancing in the right direction.

Impressions are daily and hourly made in rides through such vast
and dreary solitudes as these that are never effaced from memory; and
one, at the end of our first day's march, that was curious enough for
narration. On a little plateau of a few rods in breadth, covered with grass
and near the bank of a small stream, with a tremendous and dreary
forest of rocks and pines behind us, we had bivouacked at sundown,
and for the night.

Gleeson had taken the lassoes off the animals, and gone down a little
descent, nearer the stream, where the grass was more abundant and
fresher for the horses. Caesar had collected dried wood and made a
rousing fire, and was boiling the pot, whilst I, at the distance of ten or
fifteen rods from him, seated on the bank of the stream, and with back
towards him, was making a sketch of the picturesque landscape before
me. "My soul *alive!* wat you want dar?" suddenly exclaimed Caesar; and
turning round, I saw him on one hand and one knee, by his fire, swinging
around and over his head a flaming firebrand; and in the direction where
he was aiming it, and but a few rods from him, two grizzly bears of

---

[1] After reaching the frontier settlements I learned that a most relentless and
bloody war had been waged for several months past between the United States
forces and the Apachee and Yutah Indians; that Lieutenant St. Vrain and Colonel
Fontleroy, with large forces, had destroyed a great many of the Apachees; and
that our position had been one of great danger.

the largest kind, one seated and the other in advance, and galloping upon him!

The firebrand fell a few feet before it, when the beast sprang upon it with both paws, and seized it in its mouth! He dropped it, and wheeling about, and crying in the most piteous manner, retreated, wiping his nose and his paws upon the grass.

The female, with the curiosity (perhaps) natural to her sex, must have a smell of it too, and was advancing for the purpose. An instant snuff (and I think a *taste*) was enough for her too, and they both galloped off together, whining in the most doleful manner as they disappeared amongst the rocks.

Gleeson knew nothing of the affair until he heard our relation of it; and all of us, without our weapons in hand, were spared the necessity of asking mercy of these unmerciful beasts, only by the whirling of a firebrand which Caesar happened to have in his hand at the moment, instead of vainly attempting to run for his rifle!

Delivered thus from the jaws of those monstrous animals, which had gone off evidently with a distaste for us, we began collecting wood for the night, each of us carrying a firebrand in his hand as a precaution; and between two rousing fires, and our horses close picketed to our heads, and one of the three always on sentry, we slept tolerably well.

After several days from this, and continuing our course over hills, and valleys, and, in the latter part of the way, having lost the trail, we at length approached a conical hill of considerable height, and with the appearance of a low, level country beyond it, which we had reason to believe was at last the valley of the Rio Grande del Norte, and that we must necessarily be nearing the settlements on its borders.

It was agreed that Gleeson should turn it on the right, and that Caesar and I would flank it on the left; and that, as our horses were shod, and a sandy plain with thin grass was around it, we could not cross each other's tracks without recognizing them; and, in this way, with a certainty of joining company again somewhere beyond the mound, one or the other of us would probably stumble upon some trail leading to the settlements.

Caesar and I, after a few miles, came upon a well-beaten track of shod horses, showing us beyond doubt that we were nearing the settlement; and, in a little time, following it, we turned a small hillock and came upon a settler's hut—a well-built log-house—and its smoking chimney showed us that it was occupied. We rode up in front of it, and a nice and tidy middle-aged woman, with two little children, came to the door.

I addressed her in Spanish, inquiring how far we had yet to ride to reach the mission of St. Diego, or any other town on the Rio del Norte. She replied, in English, that she did not understand Spanish. I then asked her in English, when she promptly answered that we could not get to the river that night.

"Then, good woman," said I, "can we get lodging here tonight, and something to eat; for our provisions are entirely out?"

"Well, sir," said she, "I am very much ashamed; we have been here but a very short time, and we hain't got things agoin' very well yet; but you shall be welcome to the best we have got, if you can put up with it."

"Don't have any fears, madam," said I; "we are not very particular, and I know what allowance to make. We don't require beds; we have each a good buffalo robe, and all we will ask will be a part of the floor to spread them on where the planks are not too hard."

"Well, I'm sorry to say, sir, we hain't got our floor laid yet. We've nothin' but some birch bark for floors now, but I think you will find 'em dry."

"That's enough, madam; the principal thing we want is shelter."

We dismounted, and Caesar picketed the horses—for there was abundance of good grass—I then sat down in conversation with the good-natured woman.

"I can give you a steak," said she, "and pan-baked bread, and a cup of coffee, but we have no sweetening for it but molasses."

"Never mind," said I; "that's quite enough—we don't wish to fare better."

From a few minutes' conversation, I learned that she was a native of Ohio; that she was married in Texas, and, a year or two previous, had, with her husband, moved to Santa Fé; and, not satisfied with Santa Fé life, they had squatted on the fine little prairie of rich land on which they were living, which cost them nothing; and that they had no neighbors nearer than three miles.

Caesar and I had supped on the steak and coffee promised us, and we had enjoyed it very much; and night had approached. "But, Gleeson, where is he? He has not arrived—he has not struck our trail! Maybe a grizzly bear has chewed him up, or that some of those Navaho Indians have taken his scalp in order to get his horse. We have got to go back in the morning and look him up."

The morning seemed to come very quick; and, having taken a steak and our coffee the same as the evening before, Caesar led up our animals, and, as we were saddling them, Gleeson turned the little hillock and rode up.

His circuit the day before had been so much longer than ours, and having been impeded by a difficult stream to cross, he had struck our trail too late in the day to overtake us, and had slept in his saddle all night, without anything to eat. I presented him to our kind land-lady, and told him I believed he could get a steak for his breakfast. But the poor woman, who seemed embarrassed at this, replied that she was sorry she could not give him a steak—"For," said she, "I cooked the last I had for your breakfast. We can't get any meat here, gentlemen, except what my husband kills with his gun. All game is very scarce now, and he has had very bad luck lately; he was out all the day before yesterday and got nothing; and yesterday he went out again, and hasn't got back yet; and, to tell the plain truth, we have had no meat but that *painter* for the last two weeks."

"Painter!" said I, "What painter?"

"Well, *dear* me! now, I'm afraid I forgot to tell you that them steaks was *painter's* meat. I should have mentioned it; and if I forgot it, I hope you will excuse me."

Gleeson, who was standing by, and starving, relieved the poor woman in a measure from her embarrassment by exclaiming, "Why, my good woman, I am nearly starved to death—I could eat anything! Have you not got the *tail* of the panther left? I could make a breakfast on that, without any ceremony."

"Well, no, sir; I am sorry also to say that the animal was very fat, and we roasted the tail the first night when it was brought in."

I helped the kind woman as well as I could, by assuring her that the steaks which we had eaten were very good, and that I should be glad if I could get another like them for my supper. And sympathetic Caesar, who had been listening, put in, "Well, I guess, missus, no harm is done, anyhow."

Gleeson took a turn at the pan-baked bread and coffee, after which we took leave of the good and hospitable woman, by leaving with her what Caesar called "a silber dolla," though she positively refused to make any charge for what we had eaten.

We reached the Rio Grande del Norte, sold our jaded animals—in my accustomed way—for less than half the price we had paid for them, took a "dug-out"[2] and paddles, and began drifting towards Matamoras, then eight hundred miles ahead of us.

This, being in the spring of 1855, was five years before the Civil War in the United States, and seven years before the French invasion of Mexico—so that all was peace and good will on the banks of that noble and beautiful river, of which I may say something more near the end of this book, if there should be space enough for it. From Matamoros, a sailing vessel took Caesar and me to Sisal, in Yucatán; and, after a very short visit to Uxmal, and some points of interest on the coasts of Campeachy, I started for Liverpool....

[2] A pirogue.

Indian Names and Some Curious Incidents

(FROM CATLIN'S 1871 *Catalogue*)

THIS NOTE WILL explain the vexatious difficulties about Indian names in South America, and also communicate some curious incidents of a voyage worth being known.

From 1852 to 1857, I made three voyages from Paris to South and Central America. In my first voyage, I left Pará, mouth of Amazon, on the steamer *Marajo,* having been advised to visit the numerous Catholic missions on the Amazon and its confluents, as a means of making my Indian portraits and other sketches on the shores of that river.

I visited one of these, and was received and treated with kindness. I stayed nearly two weeks, and, owing to their superstitions, got *not one sitter.* The civilized Indians about these establishments did not suit me; the time and expense I could not afford; and with unfortunate deafness (making me a tedious guest among strangers), to listen to thousands of questions put to me in Spanish and *Lingua-geral* (neither of which did I at that time understand), though kindly meant, *worried me,* and having an English passport with an English name, I could not be known in that suspicious country as Geo. Catlin with a different name in my pocket. In this dilemma, I returned to Pará, and soon looked up Smyth, who had crossed the Acarai Mountains with me from British Guiana, and who had stopped in Pará, with nothing as yet to do, and with him I took steamer to Barra, to Tabatinga and Nauta. At the latter place I found a Portuguese, the owner of a cupola trading boat, with whom I made an arrangement to descend the Amazon with us to Obidos, a distance of one thousand miles, giving me every opportunity of stopping in front of various Indian villages and making my sketches. The cupola enabled us three to sleep comfortably, and was a good *atelier* in which to finish up my sketches as we moved along; and with the exhilarating prospect before me of seeing, face to face, and in their native habits and expressions, ten thousand Indians, and the magnificent shores of the Amazon, we started off.

The owner of the boat, a river trader, was familiar with the localities of most of the tribes of the upper Amazon, and though not speaking their languages, had a tolerable facility of conversation with them by sign manual.

With these advantages, I trusted to getting my sketches as we descended the river, anchoring our boat in front of their villages and encampments, as we might discover them.

In the first day of our voyage, we anchored in front of a small village, and the boatman, who knew the chief, invited him and his wife on board and I made a portrait of him.

It was taken ashore and created a great excitement among the crowd, and his wife agreed to be painted the next morning, and came with the chief for that purpose. I asked the chief for his name, to be put on the back of the portrait, but a medicine man who came on board with them raised violent objections to it, alleging that if the chief gave his name to be put on the back of the picture, *he would be a man without a name,* and that some harm would certainly accrue to him. "This man," said he to the chief, "has got your skin, from the top of your head to the bottom of your feet, and in a little time he will have glass eyes in it. How will you feel then? How will you sleep? A few years since, several such things were made at the Barra, and everyone who was painted, or some of their relatives, died soon after."

At this the wife of the chief became frightened, and refused to be painted; and when she was told that I was going to take the chief's portrait with me, she commenced crying and howling in a most piteous manner, and the affrighted crowd dispersed on the shore. A bright-colored cotton shawl, however, quieted the poor woman, and as we were about to start off, the medicine man bawled out to us sarcastically, as he turned his back upon us, the chief's name. No doubt from his manner and as the boatman said, a fictitious one.

We moved on and soon were in front of an encampment of some fifty or sixty, a fishing party of the same tribe. We anchored at the shore and brought the whole party to the water's edge, but, for no consideration that we could offer, would anyone allow his portrait to be painted, and we moved along again.

From the events of these two days, I foresaw the difficulties ahead of me, and was *nearly discouraged*. The shores of this mighty river, lined with tens of thousands of human beings unchanged by civilization, and in their simple, native habits and in their own homes, the most interesting display of savage life that could appear to me during my existence, and for which I was a voluntary and unknown exile to this distant land, and my project to be lost, or to be achieved by a maneuver.

A council was held, and it was resolved that my sketches must be made (if made at all) without their knowledge and without exciting their suspicions.

Our boat was afterward anchored in front of their villages and encampments, some four or five yards from the shore, bringing the excited groups with their toes to the water's edge, when I took my pick of them, at full length, as my portfolio was screened from their view by the bulwark of the boat or by the transparent sides of the cupola; whilst Smyth, conspicuous in his scarlet capot, riveted their attention by discharging cylinder after cylinder of my revolver rifle, the first ever seen on that river; and if *the seance* was not long enough for my object, the boatman held them amused with his fiddle, which often set them to dancing and at other amusements, or displayed on the bulwark of his boat a variety of bright-colored cotton shawls and other attractive objects, with which, as a trader, he was supplied, and struck up a trade for fish, fruit, and turtles' eggs, with which we were in this way abundantly supplied.

Our halts were more often in front of their encampments and fishing parties than before their villages, for *there* my plans were not impeded or learned by the inquisitive Gaucho population, who live in or contiguous to most of the Indian villages.

By this means, during the sixty-nine days which took us to Obidos, I obtained what I never could have obtained in any other way. I saw and made my sketches amongst thirty different tribes, containing many thousands of those simple people, in their canoes, at their fishing occupations, and in groups at the river's shore; and our little boat, being subject to my own control, enabled me to run into the coves and lagoons inaccessible to steamers, and to see and sketch the unknown grandeur of these solitudes—the gloomy but decorated abodes of reptiles and alligators.

By the mode explained (and by that mode alone) I was sure of *obtaining their portraits,* and sure of *bringing them away,* and as sure of losing their unimportant names, after having painted my pictures; for to have demanded their names would have excited their suspicions and superstitions, and defeated my object. And if asked for and given, no correct translation could have been obtained through our signs manual.

My portraits and sketches of scenery in South America have nearly all been made in boats or canoes, alike on the Amazon, the Uruguay, and the Yucayali, or in the open air of the *pampas* or *llanos,* as seen in my numerous paintings, without interpretations, that would authorize me to hold myself responsible for the correctness of any names thus procured.

These timid and superstitious people would not give their real names to strangers passing them in a boat, and would be very great fools if they did.

I had too much character and type constantly before me to think much of Indian names, and of those which my men picked up on the shore, correctly or incorrectly given, and which I had registered, I have struck out many; and for the correctness of the rest (not to mislead anyone), I am unwilling to vouch, being under the conviction that more or less of them are wrong.

In my travels in North America, also, in my remotest wanderings, when I have had no faith in their names given, as all Indians, away from home, on war parties or hunting excursions, refuse to give their real names to strangers whom they meet; and if they have an interpreter with them, he is instructed, at the peril of his life, to keep their individual identity unknown.

In that hemisphere, also, where the Indians are more intelligent, less superstitious, and more warlike, and their names more celebrated and more important, when I have painted them in their villages or trading establishments, I have generally obtained, with accuracy, their names, with translations, . . . and even there, the most famous of them take new names for every great achievement.

Itinerary

(FROM CATLIN's 1871 *Catalogue*)

. . . In 1852 I sailed to Havannah, to Venezuela, went to the Orinoko and Demerara; ascended the Essequibo, crossed the Tumucamache (or Crystal Mountains, to the head waters of the Trombutus, which I descended in a pirogue, to the Amazon, at Obidos . . . and from that to Pará, having seen the Carribbees, Gooagives, Arowaks, Wayaways, Macouchies, Tarumas, and Zurumatis.

From Pará (near twenty years ago), I took steamer to the Barra, to Tabatinga, and Nauta; from Nauta I descended the Amazon to Obidos, one thousand miles, in a cupola boat, as described in Appendix A of this catalogue, helping to row my own boat, and seeing thirty of the one hundred tribes of Indians said to inhabit the shores of that river.

I afterwards ascended the Amazon again, and went on a gold-hunting expedition to Acarai Mountains . . . . Returning to the Amazon, I took an ascending steamer to Nauta, and ascended the Yucayali to the Connibos, four hundred miles, and made a tour on horseback across the "Pampas del Sacramento" to the base of the eastern sierra of the Andes, making many sketches of the beautiful *pampas* and mountains. And seeing on the Yucayali and the *pampas,* the Remos, Pacapacuris, the Connibos, the Chetibos, and Sepibos; descended the Yucayali in a pirogue to Nauta, crossed the mountains by the mail route to Lima, steamed to Panama, to San Diego, and San Francisco, and took a sailing vessel to the mouth of Columbia, to Nootka Sound, Queen Charlotte's Inlet and Island, to Liska, in the Alaeutian Islands, to Kamskatka, to Sitka, back to Queen Charlotte's, and to Victoria, seeing Indians—Klah-o-quats, Hydas, Nayas, Chippewyans, Stone, Dogrib, Athapascas, Esquimaux, Alaeutians, and the Koriaks about Petropolovski, in Kamskatka.

From Victoria I went to Dalles, on the Columbia, to Walla Walla, and on horseback to the Salmon River Valley, crossed the Salmon River Mountains into the Snake River Valley at Fort Hall, made a visit to the Great (or "Smoky") Falls of the Snake River, made many sketches, and returned to Walla Walla, to Portland, and thence by steamer to San Francisco and St. Diego; having seen Indians—Paunch (a band of Crows), Walla Wallas, Snakes, and Flatheads in many bands.

From St. Diego, on horseback, crossing the Colorado of the West at La Paz, and the Rocky Mountains to St. Diego on the Rio Grande del Norte, and from that point, in a "dug-out," steering with my own paddle, descended that river to El Paso, and to Matamoros, eight hundred miles, seeing Indians, Cochimtees, Mohaves, Yumas, Yumayas, and several bands of the Apachees.

In 1855, from Matamoros, I sailed for Sisal, in Yucatán—visited the ruins of Uxmal, painted Indians, Mayas; sailed from Sisal to Havre, went to Paris, and to Berlin to see my old friend the Baron de Humboldt, then in his eighty-seventh year, who presented me to the king and queen at "San Souci," and gave me a letter of introduction of Baron Bonpland in Santana, in Uruguay, to which place I was prepared to start in a few days.

I took steamer at Havre in the fall of that year to Rio de Janeiro and Buenos Ayres, from Buenos Ayres by steamer up the Paraguay to the mouth of the Paraná, ascended from Paraná on a trading boat seven hundred miles, and crossed the "Entre Rios" Mountains to Conception, on the headwaters of the Uruguay, and descended that river, seven hundred miles in a pirogue, to the mouth of the Rio Negro, steering with my own paddle, and thence to Buenos Ayres, seeing Indians, Chaymas, Chacos, Payaguas, Botocudos, and Tobos, and, in a ride to the Rio Salado and the "Grande Saline," saw the Aucas and Puelches.

From Buenos Ayres, in 1856, by a sailing packet, I coasted the whole length of Patagonia, and passed through the Strait of Magellan, seeing Indians, an encampment of Patagons and Fuegians; sailed to Panama; by rail went to Chagres, and thence to Carraccas, in Venezuela, a second time, and to Santa Martha and the lake and mountains of Maricaybo, to witness the effects of the cataclysm of the Antilles, where the Andes chain was broken, and of which some account (as well as some of my last rambles of three years, to see *rocks,* not *Indians*) will be seen in my little book, "Lifted and Subsided Rocks of America."

Views of the Crystal Mountains

Rhododendron Mountain. A mountain covered with rhododendrons, and its base surrounded with orange and fig trees. "Crystal Mountains." (Cart. No. 515.)

[1]

View in the Tumucamache (or Crystal) Mountains, Northern Brazil. (Cart. No. 504.)

View in the Crystal Mountains. Brazil. (Cart. No. 516.)

[3]

The "Beetle Crevice," in the Tumucamache (or Crystal) Mountains, Northern Brazil. (Cart. No. 508.)

Views along the Amazon River

View of the Shore of the Amazon above the mouth of the Rio Jupura.
(Boat sketch). (Cart. No. 543.)

[5]

An Amazon Forest, looking ashore from the steamer. (Cart. No. 513.)

Spearing by Torchlight, on the Amazon. (Cart. No. 596.)

[7]

Entrance to a Lagoon, shore of the Amazon. (Cart. No. 554.)

[8]

An Alligator's Nest. Lagoon of the Amazon. (Cart. No. 553.)

A Lagoon, of the Upper Amazon. The Alligator's Home. (Cart. No. 549.)

South American Indians

A secondary chief (center), leading his little son; O-ho-kó-ra-u-ta
(right), a medicine man and orator of the tribe; a young warrior (left),
armed with his lance. A small remnant of a numerous tribe, on the coast
of Venezuela, decimated by dissipation and smallpox. (Cart. No. 451.)

"The Handsome Dance" ("Mach-e-o-a"). Indians, Gooagives, of Venezuela. Three young girls, selected by the chief, their bodies nude, but
covered with pipe clay (having the appearance of statues), gave this
very pretty dance to please the author. Their toes, which were not separated or lifted from the ground, rested on tiger skins, and their motions
were exceedingly graceful, and in time with the beating of the drum.
(Cart. No. 483.)

[12]

A Miriti Forest, mouth of Orinoko. Caribbe Indians. (Cart. No. 548.)

Caribbe Village, in Dutch Guiana. (Cart. No. 502.)

Turtle Hunt by Torchlight, on the Trombutas. The Indians having turned their victims on their backs, the women are approaching with torches, to do the butchering. (Cart. No. 495.)

[15]

A Fight with Peccaries. Rio Trombutas. The author and a Caribbe Indian coming to the rescue of Smyth, who is regularly "treed," and his powder expended. (Cart. No. 496.)

[16]

Dighst-ó-ho (The Singer), a chief (right), wearing a robe made of a tiger's skin; Wahpt (The Great Runner), H'kee-ne (The Little Eater), [two unidentified]—four young warriors in their ordinary apparel. A numerous tribe, living on the coasts of Venezuela and British Guiana. 1852. (Cart. No. 448.)

Oxt-wá-kon (second from left), a secondary chief, armed with his bow and arrows; Fyne-fyne (next, right), a Macouchi woman, wife of the chief; Oo-je-én-na (left), a celebrated warrior, armed and equipped for war. A small but friendly tribe of British Guiana. 1852. (Cart. No. 456.)

Shore of the Essequibo. The author and his party encamping in the green forest of British Guiana. (Cart. No. 499.)

Tunxt-ó-me (On the Hill), a secondary chief (center), curiously dressed
and painted; Min-nee (right), wife of the chief; O-to-no-tóm-me (left),
a young warrior, dressed and equipped for war. A small tribe, on the
upper Essequibo, British Guiana. 1852. (Cart. No. 450.)

Arowak Village. British Guiana. (Cart. No. 505.)

A celebrated medicine man (right), and claiming to be a great orator;
a warrior (center), said to be very distinguished, carrying his shield
and war club; U-hón-da (left), a young man, said to be chief of a band.
A small and friendly tribe of British Guiana. 1852. (Cart. No. 452.)

[22]

Yo-ma-tós-tos (center), a war chief of the tribe; Súm-tee (right) and
His-se-tún-ne (left), two young warriors armed and equipped for war.
A small tribe of Guiana and Brazil, inhabiting the Acarai Mountains.
1852. (Cart. No. 449.)

[23]

A Forest above a Forest. View taken on the Rio Trombutas, above the great rapids. (Cart. No. 503.)

[24]

Shore of the Trombutas, above the great rapids. (Cart. No. 509.)

[25]

Interior of an Amazon Forest. Zurumati Indians transporting to market
the skins of wild cattle and turtle butter. (Cart. No. 512.)

[26]

Ignis Fatuus. Rio Trombutas. Zurumati Indians approaching it. (Cart. No. 497.)

[27]

"Pont de Palmiers," and Tiger Shooting. Rio Trombutas. Northern
Brazil. (Cart. No. 492.)

O-be-lohts-dy-ke-dy-ke (The Wise Man Who Teaches), a celebrated
sorcerer, speaking to the Sun, whilst his portrait is being painted. 1852.
(Cart. No. 453.)

[29]

Wohkst-ú-be (left), a young chief, handsomely equipped and armed with his bow and war club; O'bs-teft (center) and U-na-dís-ko-lots, two young men, equipped for war and the chase. A small tribe, entirely primitive, about the sources of the Trombutas, in northern Brazil. 1852. (Cart. No. 454.)

Four Zurumati children, selected by the chief, to be painted. 1852.
(Cart. No. 455.)

A celebrated man (center), said to be chief of his tribe, his ears curiously slit and elongated and ornamented; an Iquito woman (left), wife of the chief; a good-looking man (right), a fair specimen of the tribe, and said also to be a chief. A very small tribe, reduced by smallpox and dissipation, and mostly residing in one small village, on the bank of the Amazon, near Nauta. 1853. (Cart. No. 461.)

[32]

Mauhees Encampment, looking ashore from the steamer, below Rio Negro, lower Amazon. (Cart. No. 546.)

Spearing by Torchlight, Xingu Indians. (Cart. No. 534.)

[34]

Dregs-ín-dich (center), a fine man, handsomely dressed, and armed with his lance, represented to be a chief; a Xingu woman (right), wife of the above chief; a warrior (left), carrying his shield and lance. A small tribe, on the Rio Xingu, lower Amazon. 1853. (Cart. No. 463.)

[35]

An Omagua Village, southern shore of the upper Amazon, the author getting the portrait of the chief and wife, from his boat. (Boat sketch). (Cart. No. 539.)

[36]

A man (center), said to be celebrated and chief of the tribe, armed with his bow and arrows; this man (right), with his ears elongated and curiously ornamented with quills and feathers, was also represented to be a chief; a medicine man (left), his ears slit and elongated, and he wears at times a huge boulder of flint attached to his under lip. A small fishing tribe, south bank of the Amazon, near Nauta. 1853. (Cart. No. 462.)

[37]

An Orejona Small Village. The author painting the chief and his two wives. (Boat sketches). Upper Amazon. (Cart. No. 538.)

Head chief of the tribe, his ears ornamented with rings, and his upper lip and breasts are decorated with quills, etc.; two Orejona women, wives of the chief; an Orejona boy (left), son of the chief, wearing weights in his ears to elongate them. A small fishing tribe, living north of the Amazon, near to Nauta. (Cart. No. 467.)

[39]

A man of Herculean strength, said to be the chief, holding his young
wife for her portrait to be made, *not willing to have his own painted;*
young wife of the chief; a group amused at the eccentric affair. (Cart.
No. 468.)

[40]

Luxuriant Forest on the bank of the Amazon, above Obidos. (Cart. No. 500.)

[41]

An Indian Village. Shore of the Amazon, above Obidos. (Cart. No. 510).

Tapuya Encampment. The author ashore, and the Indians giving the war dance, north shore of the Amazon, above Obidos. (Cart. No. 545.)

[43]

A Ya-hu-a Village. The author getting his portraits and sketches whilst the boatman is trading for fish and turtles' eggs, south shore of the upper Amazon. (Boat sketch). (Cart. No. 542.)

[44]

A Mayoruna Village, north shore of the upper Amazon, the author gets
his sketches from the cupola of his boat. (Cart. No. 541.)

[45]

Encampment of Cocomas, looking ashore from the steamer, north bank
of upper Amazon. (Cart. No. 544.)

[46]

Young Indians (Marahuas) fishing on the shore of the Amazon with harpoon arrows. (Cart. No. 489.)

[47]

An aged chief (right), seated on a canoe, his ears elongated and ornamented, and his face and body decorated with blue beads; a young man
(center), his body ornamented with quills, etc.; a Marahua woman and
child (left), wife of the chief. A small fishing tribe, north bank of the
Amazon, above Tabatinga. (Cart. No. 466.)

[48]

Two young men (left), thought to be brothers, holding their paddles;
two young, unmarried women, clad in the ordinary mode of the tribe.
A small tribe, shores of Amazon, above Tabatinga. 1853. (Cart. No. 464.)

A Mura Encampment, shore of the upper Amazon, the author sketching the chief and wife from his boat. (A boat sketch). (Cart. No. 540.)

[50]

A chief (center), resting on his lance, his ears slit and elongated, and his body and limbs and face most curiously ornamented; a Mura woman (left), wife of the chief; a young warrior (right), armed with his shield and lance [bow and quiver?], and his ears and face most curiously ornamented with feathers and rings. A small tribe, both sides of the upper Amazon, above the Barra. (Cart. No. 465.)

Mouth of Rio Purus, upper Amazon. (Cart. No. 584.)

[52]

A Sepibo Village. Rio Yucayali, west bank. (Cart. No. 575.)

[53]

A fine man (center), said to be a chief, his ears elongated and ornamented with plumes and skins of paroquets; a Sepibo woman (right),
wife of the chief; a famous warrior (left), holding his little son. A small
tribe, on the bank of the Yucayali, below the Chetibos: Canoe Indians,
mostly destroyed by smallpox. 1853. (Cart. No. 460.)

[54]

Cla-hú-ma (center), said to be a secondary chief, his ears are curiously elongated and his headdress a cotton shawl; Vin-vín-ne (right), a Chetibo woman, wife of the chief, curiously ornamented with the fragments of a cotton shawl presented to her by the author; a Chetibo boy (left), son of the chief. A tribe of 4,000 (Canoe Indians), residing on the east bank of the Yucayali, below the Connibos. 1853. (Cart. No. 459.)

[55]

The Great Ant-Eater, visiting the author's camp on the Rio Yucayali. (Cart. No. 481.)

A Long Seance on the Pampa del Sacramento, in Peru. The author making a sketch. (Cart. No. 482.)

[57]

View on the Pampa del Sacramento. The author halting to make a sketch, near the eastern Sierra of the Andes. (Cart. No. 498.)

[58]

Halting to Make a Sketch. Border of the Pampa del Sacramento. (Cart. No. 594.)

[59]

Band of Wild Horses, on the Pampa del Sacramento. (Cart. No. 556.)

[60]

Connibos, starting for wild horses, with lassos, Pampa del Sacramento.
(Cart. No. 557.)

"Grand Lavoir," Pampa del Sacramento. The wild horses come to these pools in vast herds, and, exhausted from thirst, many kill each other in terrible conflicts, and others die from over-drinking, and their bones whiten the plains for miles around. (Cart. No. 558.)

Throwing the Bolas, for wild horses, Connibo Indians. (Cart. No. 537.)

Driving the Pampas for Wild Cattle, Connibo Indians. (Cart. No. 536.)

[64]

Reconnoitering a Herd of Wild Cattle, on the Pampa del Sacramento, Connibo Indians. (Cart. No. 532.)

Wild Cattle Grazing on the Pampa del Sacramento. (Cart. No. 533.)

Shooting Condors. The author and his men, in the eastern Sierra of the Andes. (Cart. No. 517.)

[67]

A Connibo Wigwam. Border of Pampa del Sacramento. (Cart. No. 591.)

A Connibo Village, on the border of the Pampa del Sacramento. (Cart.
No. 555.)

[69]

A very handsome man, said to be the chief, and much celebrated; his ears are elongated and ornamented with brass rings, and his necklace of the shells of nuts; two Connibo women, wives of the chief. A tribe of 5,000 inhabiting the western banks of the Rio Yucayali and the vast Pampas del Sacramento. 1853. (Cart. No. 457.)

[70]

Tu-wis-kaw, a young bridegroom, Connibo, giving his bride, not a "drive," but a daily *ride,* on the Pampa del Sacramento. 1853. (Cart. No. 458.)

[71]

Return from a Turtle Hunt. Connibo Indians. (Cart. No. 519.)

A Small Village of Remos Indians, border of Pampa del Sacramento.
(Cart. No. 566.)

[73]

Pacapacurus Village. Border of Pampa del Sacramento. (Cart. No. 592.)

[74]

Warn-wárn-tsoo (right), a secondary chief, armed with his shield and bow; a warrior (center), carrying his bow and quiver; a warrior (left), wearing the skin of a tiger. A small remnant of a numerous tribe, on the banks of the Rio Paraguay. (Cart. No. 469.)

Spearing by Moonlight, Chaco Indians, Rio Paraguay. (Cart. No. 535.)

Men-e-sáy-so (center), a chief, armed with his bow and quiver; a Chaco
woman (right), wife of the chief; a warrior (left), carrying his shield,
bow, and quiver. Small remnant of a numerous tribe of Horse Indians,
living on the right-hand shore of the Rio Paraguay. (Cart. No. 470.)

A Small Village. Payaguas Indians, lower Uruguay. (Cart. No. 565.)

A very fine man (center), said to be the chief of the tribe: his ears elongated, and he wears a necklace of shells and beads; two Payaguas women (left and right), wives of the chief, wearing oval blocks of wood in the under lip, like the Nayas Indians in North America. At present a small Canoe tribe, living opposite to the Chacos, and always at war with them. (Cart. No. 471.)

Shore of the Uruguay. Making a sketch, below Conception. (Cart. No. 560.)

Painting the Lengua Chief, shore of the Uruguay. (Cart. No. 559.)

Lengua Indians ascending the Rapids of Rio Uruguay. (Cart. No. 562.)

A Small Lengua Village. The author painting the chief and wife from his canoe. Rio Uruguay. (Cart. No. 563.)

A Small Lengua Village. Uruguay. (Cart. No. 564.)

[84]

A chief, armed with his bow and arrows, his ears ornamented with large
brass rings and beads; two Lengua women, wives of the chief, wearing
oval block of wood in their under lips. A small tribe living on the banks
of the Rio Uruguay. (Cart. No. 472.)

A medicine man (right), clothed entirely with rattlesnake skins, his ears and his under lip ornamented with oval blocks of wood; two young warriors (left and center), armed, and ornamented with pendants of various kinds. A small tribe on the banks of the Uruguay. (Cart. No. 473.)

This man (center) was represented as chief of the tribe, his ears ornamented with oval blocks of wood and lips decorated with quills and
beads; a Botocudo woman (behind chief), wife of the chief, wearing
the oval block of wood in her under lip; a Botocudo warrior (right),
with the block of wood in his under lip; a medicine man (left), his ears
slit and his under lip ornamented with oval blocks of wood. The scattered remnants of a powerful tribe, on and east of, the Rio Paraná, in
Uruguay. (Cart. No. 474.)

A chief (center), armed with a gun, his lower lip ornamented with the oval block of wood; a young man (right), his ears ornamented with the oval blocks of wood; a Botocudo woman (left), wife of the chief. (Cart. No. 475.)

A Tobos Small Village, Uruguay. (Cart. No. 551.)

[89]

Painting of Tobos chief, Rio Negro, Uruguay, (Cart. No. 550.)

Three young men, names not known, their ears ornamented with blocks of wood and rings. A very small tribe on the banks of Rio Negro, of Uruguay. (Cart. No. 479.)

[91]

Bon-don-ne (That Is He), a secondary chief (right), armed with his
shield and war club; Yép and Yo-har-ne (left), two young warriors,
said to be distinguished. A small tribe, south of Buenos Ayres, reduced
by smallpox and dissipation. (Cart. No. 477.)

Throwing the Bolas. Auca Indians killing wild horses for their hair and skins. (Cart. No. 485.)

[193]

Ostrich Chase. Buenos Ayres. 1856. The author, armed with a carabine revolver of Colt, is followed by Portuguese and Auca Indians, who chase with the bolas. (Cart. No. 488.)

[94]

Reconnoitering Flamingoes, by the author, in the Grand Saline of Buenos Ayres. 1856. (Cart. No. 486.)

[95]

Shooting Flamingoes. Grand Saline. (Cart. No. 487.)

Three Auca children. A small tribe south of Buenos Ayres. (Cart. No. 476.)

Yal-kok-tsá-me (The Big Gun), (second from left), (cannon) chief of a band, his history unknown; Paw-in-o-renk (The Flying Cloud) (right), young brother of the chief; Coche (The Blue Sky), a young girl (left), daughter of the chief, painted in Pickett harbor, Straits of Magellan, in 1856. A numerous and warlike tribe, in Patagonia. (Cart. No. 478.)

Goy-o-Gé-tenc (The Good Spoon), a warrior and fisherman (second from left), armed with his paddle; Sham-e-noo (The Dog), a warrior and fisherman (third from left); a Fuegian woman (right), wife of the above warrior; Gol-gee (Tobacco), a young man (left), holding his paddle. Painted in Pickett harbor, Straits of Magellan, in 1856. A small tribe, living in and south of the Straits of Magellan. (Cart. No. 480.)

North American Indians

Whélts-bel-le (The Snow Walker), a secondary chief (center), living near Liska; Séals-cher-re (left), a celebrated warrior and hunter, armed and equipped for war; a young warrior (right). A small tribe, on the Alaeutian Islands. (Cart. No. 110.)

Gua-be-méd-gwin-ne (center), a celebrated warrior and hunter; Nín-jee (The Unknown), a warrior (left), equipped for war; Há-te-qua (The Eagle's Mother), a Chippewyan woman (right). A numerous and war-like tribe, living north of the K'nisteneux, in British possessions. 1855. (Cart. No. 108.)

Gux-tchá-when (second from left), a secondary chief, wearing a collar of grizzly bears' claws; two young men (left and right of chief), names not known; child of chief (far right). A small tribe, living in British and Russian possessions. (Cart. No. 106.)

Ve-hóots-áh-a (The Sleepy Eyes), a chief of a band (center), his head-dress of bear's skin, and his necklace of grizzly bears' claws; Kol-o-wós-ka (right), a warrior, armed and equipped for war; Ohkst (left), an Athapasca woman, wife of the chief. A small tribe inhabiting British and Russian Territories. 1855. (Cart. No. 105.)

Haunts-crash (center), O-síl-le (The Swimming Stone) (right), and Blats-quiver (left), three young men, in a group. A small tribe, band of the Flatheads, at the mouth of the Columbia River. 1855. (Cart. No. 97.)

"A Whale Ashore," on the western coast of Vancouver, and being harpooned and dissected by the Klahoquat Indians. 1855. (Cart. No. 330.)

Loon-dógst (center), one of the chiefs of the tribe, a celebrated and dignified man; Chín-nee (right), a Klahoquaht woman, wife of the chief;
a son of the chief (left), his head flattened. A small tribe, a band of the
Flatheads, on the west coast of Vancouver's Island. 1855. (Cart. No. 98.)

Wun-nes-tó-ye-when (center), a chief, armed with his shield and bow; a Copper woman (right), wife of the chief. A small tribe in British Territory. (Cart. No. 103.)

[107]

Stu-bén-sal-la (The Good Natured Man) (right) and Líps-líps-ketch,
two young men, equipped for fishing. A small tribe on the Pacific Coast,
between Vancouver and Queen Charlotte's. 1855. (Cart. No. 96.)

[108]

An Indian Ladder. Coast of the Pacific. Nayas Indians. (Cart. No. 396.)

Nayas Village, on the Pacific Coast, at sunset. Queen Charlotte's Island
is seen in the distance. (Cart. No. 393.)

Nayas Village, on the Pacific Coast at sunset. The Indians bathing in the ocean. (Cart. No. 276.)

[111]

Nayas Village, Pacific Coast—night scene. (Cart. No. 407.)

Masquerade by Torchlight, by the Nayas Indians, Queen Charlotte's
Inlet, on the Pacific Coast. 1855. (Cart. No. 249.)

[113]

Excavating a Canoe, by Nayas Indians. British Columbia. 1855. (Cart. No. 332.)

[114]

Launching a Canoe, by Nayas Indians. British Columbia. 1855. (Cart. No. 333.)

[115]

Salmon Spearing by Torchlight, by Nayas Indians. Pacific Coast. (Cart. No. 409.)

Tsa-hau-míxen (right), said to be a secondary chief; Kíb-be (The Night
Bird), a Nayas woman (left), the young wife of the chief, wearing in
her under lip an oval block of wood, two and a half inches in length.
1855. (Cart. No. 94.)

Eeh-zep-ta-sáy-a (right), an aged man, said to be a chief; Wý-en-wý-en-ne (center), grandchild of the chief, with the block of wood in her under lip; a Nayas boy (left). 1855. (Cart. No. 95.)

Wuhxt (center), the chief of a band, with his ears elongated and ornamented with large blocks of wood; a Nayas woman (right), wife of
the chief; a young man (left), holding a handsome paddle; his under
lip supports an oval block of wood. A numerous tribe on Queen Charlotte's Island and on the mainland facing it. (Cart. No. 93.)

Sée-de-guts (center), a warrior, his shield on his arm [*sic*], and bow in
hand; a Stone woman (right), wife of the warrior; a young boy (left).
A small tribe in British Territory. (Cart. No. 102.)

Ya-táx-ta-coo (center), a celebrated warrior; Yún-ne-yún-ne (right), a young boy, with his salmon bow and harpoon arrows; Lás-tee (left), a Flathead woman, with her infant undergoing the process of flattening the head. 1855. (Cart. No. 90.)

The chief of a band (second from left), at the Dalles; two Flathead women (right), wives of the chief, selling salmon; a young boy (left), son of the chief. (Cart. No. 91.)

Hoogst-áh-a (right), chief of a band, wrapped in his blanket; Lée-le (left foreground), a Flathead woman, wife of the chief, with her infant in its crib (or cradle) undergoing the process of flattening the head; a Flathead boy (left background), taking salmon with his harpoon arrows. A numerous tribe, inhabiting the lower Columbia and Vancouver's Island. (Cart. No. 89.)

[123]

Thule-chér-re (center), a handsome young man, holding his paddle;
a warrior (left), with his bow and arrows [*sic*]; a Klatsop woman
(right), wife of one of the warriors. A small tribe, forming one of the
bands of the Flatheads. (Cart. No. 99.)

U-ná-sits (He Who Complains) (center), a warrior who had taken five scalps; Oón-na, a young man (left), wearing a tunic made of the skin of a grizzly bear; Sée-cha (right), wife of the warrior. A small band of the Flathead tribe, on the coast of the Pacific, British Columbia. 1855. (Cart. No. 107.)

Hee-óhks-te-kin (The Rabbit Skin Leggings) and H'co-a-h'co-a-h'coates-min (No Horns on His Head) (left), two young warriors, in Blackfoot dresses, given to them by Sublette, a fur-trader; Hee-dóghts-e-ats (right), a boy of fourteen years. A band of the great Flathead tribe, though they do not flatten the head. 1855. (Cart. No. 92).

Sims-tów-el (center), said to be a chief, in a handsome dress, carrying his shield and bow; Jím-jím-tén-ne (right), a celebrated warrior, with shield and lance; a celebrated warrior (left), with his little boy. A small tribe in British Territory. (Cart. No. 104.)

[127]

One of the chiefs (center), secondary, a distinguished man; a warrior
(left), armed with his bow and arrows; a Wallawalla woman (right),
wife of the chief. A small band of the Flathead tribe, north of Columbia
River. (Cart. No. 100.)

Yau-nau-shau-pix (center), a celebrated warrior, wearing a handsome
Crow robe, taken from a Crow chief killed in battle; Nau-en-sau-pic
and On-da-wout (on either side of the chief), two young warriors, celebrated for their exploits. The Shoshonee is a tribe of 12,000, west of the
Rocky Mountains. 1855. (Cart. No. 87.)

Shoshónee (Snake)

Oon-jes-sie, Tis-sim-un-ye, and Wat-e-goes-bil, three handsome warriors,
armed and equipped for war. 1855. (Cart. No. 88.)

Halting to Make a Portrait. Snake Indians, Snake River Valley. 1855.
(Cart. No. 383.)

Stats-óo-ven (The Great Archer) (center), chief of a band, in a handsome robe, and smoking a long pipe; Bee-ó-nas-ás-sa (The Bear Killer) (right), a celebrated hunter; a warrior (left), seated on the ground, and wearing a handsome Crow robe. 1855. (Cart. No. 41.)

Salmon River Mountains, west of the Rocky Mountains. 1855. (Cart. No. 284.)

[133]

A Crow Village, and Salmon River Mountains, west of the Rocky Mountains. 1855. (Cart. No. 397.)

A Small Crow Village, bank of Salmon River, west of Rocky Mountains. (Cart. No. 398.)

A Crow Village, of skin tents, on Salmon River, west of the Rocky
Mountains. (Cart. No. 279.)

[136]

A secondary chief (left), in a robe ornamented with a figure of the sun; Steen-vér-re (He Who Reasons), a warrior in a costume richly ornamented with porcupine quill embroidery; a Crow woman (right), wife of the warrior. 1855. (Cart. No. 29.)

[137]

Apáchee

An Apachee Village, on Lake Ahrocum, at sunset. 1855. (Cart. No. 278.)

War Dance of the Apachees; a war party preparing to march against
the Navahos. 1855. (Cart. No. 275.)

Archery of the Apachees. In crossing the mountains from St. Diego to Santa Fé, in 1855, the author witnessed this exciting scene. Excellency in archery with mounted Indians consists in the rapidity with which the arrows can be put upon the string and got off, and the accuracy of aim, whilst their horses are at full speed—for in this way their enemies and their game are killed. (Cart. No. 178.)

Making Flint Arrow-heads (Apachees). The boulders of flint are broken by a sort of hammer of hornstone, fixed in a withe. The flakes, which will serve as the basis for arrow-heads, are passed to two other operators who work them into the forms required by chopping on the palm of the hand, whilst a choir of young females chant in time with their own song and the blows of their hammers. (Cart. No. 207.)

Chin-hool-hool-a (center), a celebrated Apachee of the Ghila, wearing a handsome robe, with his battles painted on it; Chash-ka (left), a warrior, armed with his lance; Til-dee (right), an Apachee woman. The Apachees are a numerous and warlike tribe, numbering 30,000, and reside on the Rio Ghila, and in New Mexico, east of the Rocky Mountains. 1855. (Cart. No. 86.)

Be-las-o-quá-na (second from left), called the "Spanish Spur"—chief
of a band, celebrated for his battles with the Mexicans; Nic-wár-ra (The
Horse Catcher), Nah-quát-se-o, and Hú-tah (left and right), three warriors armed and equipped for war. 1855. (Cart. No. 84.)

[143]

Quoth-e-qúa-ra (second from right), chief of a band, armed with bow and quiver; Mine-sín-ne (second from left), a celebrated warrior, carrying his shield, quiver, and lance; two [*sic*] warriors, names not known. (Cart. No. 85.)

[144]

"Paint me," said Eltono, a famous Apachee warrior (having thrown his entire costume and weapons into the hands of his three wives, and presented himself in his war paint), "my dress can always be seen." (Cart. No. 287.)

[145]

Sthán-to (center), said to be chief of a band, his headdress formed of
a cotton shawl, and his robe a red blanket; Cha-níth-co (left), a distinguished warrior, resting on his bow, and his splendid hair falling over
his back; Mél-mél (right), a Cochímtee woman, wife of the chief. A
small tribe of Mexico, south of the Ghila. 1855. (Cart. No. 112.)

Dunt-se-ó-ho (center), one of the chiefs of the tribe, handsomely dressed; The Strong Runner (left), a celebrated warrior, in war costume; Mingst (right), a Mohave woman, wife of the warrior. A small tribe of Mexico, south of the Rio Ghila. (Cart. No. 113.)

[147]

A secondary chief (center), armed with his war club; Jéems-fér-re (right), a young warrior, with shield and lance; a young girl (left), daughter of the chief. A very small tribe, semi-civilized, south of the Ghila. 1855. (Cart. No. 114.)

A celebrated warrior (center), armed and equipped for war; a warrior in war costume (right); a celebrated orator and medicine man (left). A small tribe of Mexico, north and south of the Rio Ghila. Cart. No. 115.

[149]

Ma-há-ta-níse (left), a medicine man and orator; Chóoxt (center foreground), a hunter, armed with his bow and arrows; a Maya woman
(right foreground), wife of the hunter. Remains of the once numerous
tribe of Mayas of Yucatán. These Indians are supposed by some writers
to have been the builders of stupendous edifices now in ruins in Yucatán.
1855. (Cart. No. 116.)

Mole-hule-be-áu-be (The Rising Sun) (center); Pet-ti-áu-be (The Black Day) (left); an Esquimaux woman (right). A numerous tribe, coast of Labrador. 1855. (Cart. No. 109).

[151]

Books and Articles

Anon. "The Museum of Mankind," *The Art Journal,* New Series, Vol. IV (1852), 98.

Anon. "Rochester Collects the American Nineteenth Century," *The Art Digest,* February 15, 1943, 72.

Balch, E. S. "The Art of George Catlin," *Proceedings of the American Philosophical Society,* Vol. LVII (1918), 144–54.

Bushnell, David I., Jr. *Drawings by George Gibbs in the Far Northwest, 1849–1851. (Smithsonian Miscellaneous Collections,* Vol. 97, No. 8.) Washington, D. C., 1938.

Catlin, George. *Letters and Notes on the Manners, Customs, and Conditions of the North American Indians.* London, 1841.

——. *Adventures of the Ojibbeway and Ioway Indians in England, France, and Belgium: Being notes of eight years travel and residence in Europe with His North American Indian Collection.* London, 1852.

——. *Life Amongst the Indians: A Book for Youth.* London, 1861.

——. *The Breath of Life, or Mal-Respiration.* New York, 1864.

——. *Last Rambles Amongst the Indians of the Rocky Mountains and the Andes.* London, 1868.

——. *The Lifted and Subsided Rocks of America.* London, 1870.

De Voto, Bernard A. *Across the Wide Missouri.* Boston, 1947.

Donaldson, T. "The George Catlin Indian Gallery in the U. S. National Museum (Smithsonian Institution) with Memoire and Statistics," *Annual Report of the Board of Regents of the Smithsonian Institution to July, 1885,* Part II (Washington, 1886), 265–939.

Evans, Marion Annette. "Indian Loving Catlin," *Proceedings and Collections of the Wyoming* [Penna.] *Historical and Geological Society,* Vol. XXI (1930), 68–82.

Ewers, John C. *Early White Influence upon Plains Indian Painting: George Catlin and Carl Bodmer among the Mandan, 1832–34. (Smithsonian Miscellaneous Collections,* Vol. 134, No. 7.) Washington, D. C., 1957.

——. *The George Catlin Collection of Paintings in the U. S. National Museum.* Ext. from *The Smithsonian Report* for 1955.

————. *George Catlin, Painter of Indians and the West.* Ext. from *The Smithsonian Report* for 1955.

Haberly, Loyd. *Pursuit of the Horizon: A Life of George Catlin, Painter and Recorder of the American Indian.* New York, 1948.

Miner, William Harvey. "Bibliography of Catlin's Works," *Proceedings and Collections of the Wyoming* [Penna.] *Historical and Geological Society,* Vol. XXI (1930), 83–97.

Norman-Wilcox, G. "The Almanac: Catlin's Lithographs Showing Colt Firearms," *Antiques,* Vol. XXVII (1940), 35.

Exhibitions

Catlin, George. *Catalogue, Descriptive and Instructive, Catlin's Indian Cartoons, Portraits, Types, and Customs. 600 Paintings in Oil, with 20,000 Full length Figures, Illustrating their various Games, Religious Ceremonies, and other Customs and 27 Paintings of Lasalle's Discoveries.* New York, Baker and Godwin, 1871.

Catlin, George (1796–1872). American Indians. Paintings from the Collection of the American Museum of Natural History. Exhibition October 16–31 at Kennedy Galleries Inc., New York, 1956.

Studies and Sketches from Life of the Primitive Indian Tribes of North and South America in Oil by George Catlin. N.d. (Copy in the New York Historical Society.)

INDEX

345

of which *George Catlin: Episodes from "Life Among the Indians" and "Last Rambles"* is the fifty-fifth volume, was inaugurated in 1932 by the University of Oklahoma Press, and has as its purpose the reconstruction of American Indian civilization by presenting aboriginal, historical, and contemporary Indian life. The following list is complete as of the date of publication of this volume:

1. Alfred Barnaby Thomas. *Forgotten Frontiers:* A Study of the Spanish Indian Policy of Don Juan Bautista de Anza, Governor of New Mexico, 1777–1787. Out of print.
2. Grant Foreman. *Indian Removal:* The Emigration of the Five Civilized Tribes of Indians.
3. John Joseph Mathews. *Wah'Kon-Tah:* The Osage and the White Man's Road. Out of print.
4. Grant Foreman, *Advancing the Frontier, 1830–1860*. Out of print.
5. John Homer Seger. *Early Days Among the Cheyenne and Arapahoe Indians*. Edited by Stanley Vestal.
6. Angie Debo. *The Rise and Fall of the Choctaw Republic*. Out of print.
7. Stanley Vestal (ed.). *New Sources of Indian History, 1850–1891*. Out of print.
8. Grant Foreman. *The Five Civilized Tribes*. Out of print.
9. Alfred Barnaby Thomas. *After Coronado:* Spanish Exploration Northeast of New Mexico, 1696–1727. Out of print.
10. Frank B. Speck. *Naskapi:* The Savage Hunters of the Labrador Peninsula. Out of print.
11. Elaine Goodale Eastman. *Pratt: The Red Man's Moses*. Out of print.
12. Althea Bass. *Cherokee Messenger:* A Life of Samuel Austin Worcester. Out of print.
13. Thomas Wildcat Alford. *Civilization*. As told to Florence Drake. Out of print.
14. Grant Foreman. *Indians and Pioneers:* The Story of the American Southwest Before 1830. Out of print.
15. George E. Hyde. *Red Cloud's Folk:* A History of the Oglala Sioux Indians.
16. Grant Foreman. *Sequoyah.*

17. Morris L. Wardell. *A Political History of the Cherokee Nation, 1838–1907*. Out of print.

18. John Walton Caughey. *McGillivray of the Creeks*.

19. Edward Everett Dale and Gaston Litton. *Cherokee Cavaliers:* Forty Years of Cherokee History as Told in the Correspondence of the Ridge-Watie-Boudinot Family. Out of print.

20. Ralph Henry Gabriel. *Elias Boudinot, Cherokee, and His America*.

21. Karl N. Llewellyn and E. Adamson Hoebel. *The Cheyenne Way:* Conflict and Case Law in Primitive Jurisprudence.

22. Angie Debo. *The Road to Disappearance*.

23. Oliver La Farge and others. *The Changing Indian*. Out of print.

24. Carolyn Thomas Foreman. *Indians Abroad*. Out of print.

25. John Adair. *The Navajo and Pueblo Silversmiths*.

26. Alice Marriott. *The Ten Grandmothers*.

27. Alice Marriott. *María:* The Potter of San Ildefonso.

28. Edward Everett Dale. *The Indians of the Southwest:* A Century of Development Under the United States. Out of print.

29. Adrián Recinos. *Popol Vuh:* The Sacred Book of the Ancient Quiché Maya. English version by Delia Goetz and Sylvanus G. Morley from the translation of Adrián Recinos.

30. Walter Collins O'Kane. *Sun in the Sky*.

31. Stanley A. Stubbs. *Bird's-Eye View of the Pueblos*.

32. Katharine C. Turner. *Red Men Calling on the Great White Father*.

33. Muriel H. Wright. *A Guide to the Indian Tribes of Oklahoma*.

34. Ernest Wallace and E. Adamson Hoebel. *The Comanches:* Lords of the South Plains.

35. Walter Collins O'Kane. *The Hopis:* Portrait of a Desert People.

36. Joseph Epes Brown. *The Sacred Pipe:* Black Elk's Account of the Seven Rites of the Oglala Sioux.

37. Adrián Recinos and Delia Goetz. *The Annals of the Cakchiquels*. Translated from the Cakchiquel Maya, with *Title of the Lords of Totonicapán,* translated from the Quiché text into Spanish by Dionisio José Chonay, English version by Delia Goetz.

38. R. S. Cotterill. *The Southern Indians:* The Story of the Civilized Tribes Before Removal.

39. J. Eric S. Thompson. *The Rise and Fall of Maya Civilization*.

40. Robert Emmitt. *The Last War Trail:* The Utes and the Settlement of Colorado.

41. Frank Gilbert Roe. *The Indian and the Horse*.

42. Francis Haines. *The Nez Percés:* Tribesmen of the Columbia Plateau. Out of print.
43. Ruth M. Underhill. *The Navajos.*
44. George Bird Grinnell. *The Fighting Cheyennes.*
45. George E. Hyde. *A Sioux Chronicle.*
46. Stanley Vestal. *Sitting Bull: Champion of the Sioux, A Biography.*
47. Edwin C. McReynolds. *The Seminoles.*
48. William T. Hagan. *The Sac and Fox Indians.*
49. John C. Ewers. *The Blackfeet:* Raiders on the Northwestern Plains.
50. Alfonso Caso. *The Aztecs:* People of the Sun. Translated by Lowell Dunham.
51. C. L. Sonnichsen. *The Mescalero Apaches.*
52. Keith A. Murray. *The Modocs and Their War.*
53. Victor W. von Hagen (ed.). *The Incas of Pedro de Cieza de León.* Translated by Harriet de Onis.
54. George E. Hyde. *Indians of the High Plains:* From the Prehistoric Period to the Coming of Europeans.
55. *George Catlin. Episodes from "Life Among the Indians" and "Last Rambles."* Edited by Marvin C. Ross.

The type in which this book is set is Granjon, designed by George W. Jones in 1924. Though based on Garamond, it has been considerably modified and combines the elegance of Garamond with the smooth readability of Caslon.

The 151 illustrations following the text were printed by offset lithography in a green-toned black ink. The green cloth was chosen for its suggestion of the South American jungles, where many of the paintings in this book were made.